lonely

ANDALUCÍA

Anna Kaminski, Isabella Noble, Fiona Flores Watson

Meet our writers

Fiona Flores Watson
@ @seville_writer

Fiona Flores Watson is an English writer based in Seville. Originally from Essex, she edited magazines in London for 10 years before spending a year travelling and working in South America, ending up in Quito, where she taught English, learned Spanish, DJed in a bar and volunteered in an explorers' club. Now she works as a freelance writer, translator and guide in her adopted southern Spanish city, contributing to the *Telegraph*, *Times*, *Guardian* and *Independent*, among others.

Isabella Noble
@ @isabellamnoble

British-Australian on paper and brought up in Málaga, bilingual travel journalist Isabella has been exploring Andalucía for decades; she now splits her time between Andalucía, Barcelona and London. Her favourite experience is getting lost on the beaches of Cádiz's Costa de la Luz (p102).

Anna Kaminski

A freelance travel writer and guidebook author for 15 years, Anna Kaminski has contributed to over 30 Lonely Planet guidebooks, conducting research across six continents in destinations as diverse as Jamaica, Lithuania, Papua New Guinea and Arctic Canada (though the Spanish-speaking world remains her first love). Born in the Soviet Union, and having briefly lived in Kingston, Oaxaca and Bangkok, she found that her wanderlust has only increased with age. A keen hiker, she currently calls Andalusia's mountainous Axarquía region home.

VIÑA POMAL
RIOJA

GAMBAS 18
LANGOSTINO .. 18
ALMEJAS .. 12
CHOCOS 10
PRESA Ib .. 12
SOLOMILLO Ib .. 11
Boquerones 6

Tapas bar, Seville

Contents

Courtyard, Córdoba ((p166)

BEACH
LIFE

▬▬ Andalucía's 1000-plus kilometres of coastline yields a cornucopia of fabulous inlets, coves, spits and islands. Soak it all up from the water-sports hotspots on the Costa de la Luz to the popular crowd-pleasing Costa del Sol, family favourites on the Costa Tropical, and the remote rock formations of the Cabo de Gata. In July and August accommodation prices shoot up as beaches are crammed; May/June to September/October are beautifully warm and less frenetic.

→ THE EARLY BIRD

In high season (July and August), the sands are swamped with beach-goers, so it's worth the early rise for your parking and beach spot.

Left La Flecha del Rompido. **Right** Marbella beach. **bBlow** Beach at Cabo de Gata.

CHIRINGUITOS

The fish will be ocean-fresh at *chiringuitos* (beach bars/restaurants), but always check the prices, as sometimes it is charged by weight, which can be confusing.

Best Beach Experiences

▶ Jump on a boat across the Río Pedras to the stunning sandy spit Flecha del Rompido. (p86)

▶ Dive into crystalline waters of the Acantilados de Maro-Cerro Gordo's coves. (p211)

▶ Go naturist at the Calas de Barronal, four isolated beaches in the Cabo de Gata. (p232)

▶ Climb up the 30m-high sand dune at Bolonia on the Costa de la Luz. (p102)

▶ Soak up the sun at Playa de Cabopino in Marbella, with calm waters and great facilities. (p141)

↑ SNACK TIME

It may seem obvious, but if you're walking to a remote beach, take snacks and plenty of water, as it's likely that there won't be a beach bar.

CELEBRATING
LIFE

Eat, drink and be merry – expect loud music, excited crowds, firework displays, magnificent horses, barrelloads of sherry, and huge plates of prawns and *jamón ibérico*. Fiestas are a central part of life in Andalucía, from the smallest village to the most cosmopolitan city, especially in spring. Semana Santa (Holy Week) may represent religious fervour with a theatrical flourish, but is no less vibrant.

→ SEMANA SANTA

Try to get a good vantage spot to watch the Semana Santa processions – a balcony is perfect. Find out the routes and book a place accordingly.

Left Feria de Abril (p58), Seville. **Right** Semana Santa, Seville. **Below** Carnaval de Cádiz (p98)..

► Learn more about Semana Santa on p46

GETTING FERIA-READY

Brush up on your Spanish and take a Sevillanas dance class before going to a *feria*. A little preparation will pay rich rewards.

↑ LOCAL CELEBRATIONS

Every town, city and village has its own celebrations – check dates on the local *ayuntamiento* website of the place where you'll be staying.

Best Cultural Experiences

► Don a flamenco frock for the Feria de Abril in Málaga. (p130)

► Watch the processions of hooded penitents and life-size statues in Seville's Holy Week processions. (p48)

► Visit florally-festooned courtyards in La Fiesta de los Patios Córdobeses. (p166)

► Follow the pilgrims to the wild-west village of El Rocío in Huelva. (p77)

► Catch the sharp wit of *chirigota*. (p98)

GASTRONOMIC
GLORY

Food is a religion in Andalucía – revered and treasured for its variety, quality and local specialities, as well as its historic and multicultural influences. Markets are heaving with fresh produce, from award-winning cheeses to tomatoes in all shapes, sizes and colours, and fish you've never even heard of. Venture into new taste territory, whether on a farm or in a tapas bar.

→ FESTIVE PASTRIES

Discover the pastries made especially for events like Christmas, Easter and All Saint's Day. Previously made with lard (pig fat), most are now vegetarian-friendly, with sugar-and gluten-free versions too.

Left Mercado de Atarazanas (p150), Málaga. **Right** Fried sweets. **Below** Vegetarian meal, Cádiz.

FOOD FESTIVALS

Andalucía's calendar is bursting with local food festivals, from gazpacho and sea urchins to cherries and chestnuts, plus the traditional *matanza* (pig slaughter).

↑ DINING OUT

Eating out in Andalucía for vegans, vegetarians and those with food intolerances has become much easier, with special dishes and menus (though few places have a separate gluten-free kitchen).

Best Food Experiences

▶ Taste extra virgin olive oil at a farm in Jaén, where nearly half of Spain's olive oil is produced. (p176)

▶ Visit the *almadraba*, the sustainable tuna-fishing method on the Cádiz coast, before sampling the fish in Zahara de los Atunes. (p105)

▶ Learn about marmalade's star ingredient, the bitter oranges of Seville. (p64)

▶ Walk through Huelva's oak forests with purebred Iberian pigs, before savouring acorn-fed *jamón ibérico*. (p82)

▶ Tuck into *espetos*, skewers of coal-roasted freshly-caught sardines on a Málaga beach. (p140)

A RICH
HISTORY

▬▬▬ A melting pot and meeting point of cultures for millennia, Andalucía is heaven for history buffs – and guaranteed to enchant everyone, including little ones. Start with the unmissable Golden Triangle of Seville, Córdoba and Granada with their Unesco World Heritage monuments, yielding Moorish and Jewish treasures, but venture further to discover ancient dolmens, hilltop mosques, Roman mosaics, clifftop fortresses and Renaissance palaces.

Left La Mezquita, Córdoba. **Right** Alhambra, Granada. **Below** Plaza de Toros, Ronda (p137).

→ BOOK AHEAD

Book well ahead for the most popular monuments like the Alhambra – if you turn up without a ticket on the day, it's nigh-on impossible to get in.

SPECIAL VISITS

Some monuments have times when you can visit for free, and offer night-time visits or extra add-ons like private apartments. Check websites carefully for all the options.

↑ GUIDED TOURS

Consider a guided tour – local guides can offer in-depth knowledge and great anecdotes. Otherwise, read up beforehand, and watch out for QR codes to access information.

Best History Experiences

▶ Marvel at the mosque-inside-a-cathedral, La Mezquita of Córdoba, a glorious reminder of the mighty 10th-century Caliphate. (p157)

▶ Explore the magical palaces, patios and gardens of the Alhambra, the Moorish gem that crowns Granada. (p202)

▶ Climb up the Giralda minaret-turned-belltower of the Catedral de Sevilla. (p62)

▶ Take in thecityscape and sea views view from the Alcazaba, Almería's mighty Moorish fortress. (p230)

▶ Discover the medieval synagogues of Úbeda. (p184)

↘ **FLORA & FAUNA**

Parque Nacional de Doñana has more than 350 species of birds.

Parque Nacional Sierras de Cazorla, Segura y Las Villas covers 2099km².

Three species of dolphins and four of whales live in the Strait of Gibraltar.

Andalucía has 240 protected natural areas, representing 30% of the total region.

Best Nature Experiences

▶ Spot Iberian lynx and Spanish imperial eagles in Parque Nacional de Doñana. (p76)

▶ Make a splash in the Cascadas de Huéznar waterfall in the Sierra Norte. (p46)

▶ Meet whales and dolphins in the Strait of Gibraltar. (p116)

▶ Climb inside the crystal Geoda de Pulpí in Almería. (p236)

JUAN CARLOS MUNOZ/SHUTTERSTOCK ©

NATURAL
ENCOUNTERS

▬▬▬ With over 27,000 sq km of protected natural areas and monuments, you'll find endless opportunities to explore untamed Andalucía – remote vulture-filled canyons, densely forested valleys or prehistoric cave systems. While national parks must be visited on an organised tour, many stunning spaces are accessible independently, on foot, bike or horseback for the lowest environmental impact.

BEN WELSH/GETTY IMAGES ©

↘ TESTING YOUR LIMITS

Tarifa (pictured) has 300 days of wind per year.

Sierra Nevada ski resort is open from late November/early December to April.

Highest peak: Mulhacen (3479m).

The Sanlúcar de Guadiana cross-river zip-wire is 720m long and you reach speeds of 70 to 80km/h.

Best Adventure Experiences

▶ Fly over the sea on a foil wing in El Portil. (p87)

▶ Hit the slopes at Europe's southern-most ski resort, Sierra Nevada. (p212)

▶ Zipwire over the river from Sanlúcar de Guadiana into Portugal. (p87)

▶ Jump the waves on a windsurfer or kitesurfer in Tarifa. (p102)

▶ See Seville from Río Guadalquivir on a stand-up paddle-board. (p54)

ADRENALINE ADVENTURES

▬▬ Thanks to the region's long and varied coastline, the water-sports offerings are world-class, with wind-powered sports being especially strong – international competitions are regularly hosted in Tarifa, while SUP (stand-up paddleboarding), ideal for all abilities, is increasingly popular on rivers, lakes and in the sea. Thanks to mountain peaks of more than 3000m, exciting high-altitude activities can be enjoyed year-round.

VINE
TIME

Andalucía has been producing wine for thousands of years and new techniques – or renewed use of old ones and regeneration of local varieties – is seeing a new generation of winemakers come onto the scene. Traditional areas like the Sherry Triangle, Málaga and Montilla-Moriles are being complemented by the Sierra Norte, Guadix, Contraviesa–Alpujarras and Condado de Huelva.

Best Wine Experiences

▶ Taste sherries, from bone-dry to syrupy-sweet, at a **bodega** in Jerez, El Puerto or Sanlúcar. (p94)

▶ Venture to Córdoba's Montilla-Moriles region, where most fortified wines are made with the Pedro Ximenez grape. (p95)

▶ Savour sweet muscatel wines from Málaga's Axarquía region. (p133)

▶ Take a detour to the Contraviesa–Alpujarras wine area. (p221)

★ HOME DELIVERY

If you don't want to carry bottles of wine in your luggage, wineries will ship to your home address, though beware of non-EU countries' import taxes.

★ TAPAS PAIRINGS

Most wineries will offer tapas to pair with wines when tasting, so let them know in advance about any dietary issues.

Above Sherry, Bodegas Tradicíon (p95). **Left** Red wine, El Puerto de Santa María (p94).

LEFT: YADIC LEVY/LONELY PLANET ©. BOTTOM: BLANCHI COSTELA/GETTY IMAGES ©

TWO FEET OR
TWO WHEELS

██████ From coastal routes to converted railway lines, Andalucía is criss-crossed with a whole network of hiking and cycling routes. Small hilltop villages are linked by drystone-walled paths, offering easy scenic walks for all ages and abilities, and plenty of spots to stop and rest, refuel and take in the view before carrying on. In mountainous national parks, more demanding day-long excursions into the wilderness offer challenging terrain and rich rewards.

ECUADORPOSTALES/SHUTTERSTOCK ©

★ NAVIGATING TRAILS

Take a local route map and a fully charged mobile phone (with external battery). Alternatively, if you'd rather enjoy the scenery without navigating, hire a guide or go with a group.

★ ELECTRIC BIKES

Want the fresh air and views, without puffing up steep hills? Electric bike hire is widely available – just ask about your battery's kilometre range.

Best Trail Experiences

▶ Follow a former train track through woods, over rivers and up steady inclines in the Sierra Norte. (p46)

▶ Set off into the hills and pine forests of Grazalema, on foot or bike, especially in spring when flowers carpet the hillsides. (p110)

▶ Discover the Almería coast from Las Negras to Agua Amarga, passing a ruined castle and hippy community. (p235)

▶ Walk along old mule trails between villages in the Alpujarra mountain range. (p208)

▶ Splash through turquoise pools on a Río Higuerón hike. (p143)

Above Parque Nacional Sierra Nevada (p208).

July & August

Demand for accommodation peaks during July and August. Book tours and overnight adventures in advance at lonelyplanet.com/activities/andalucia/activities.

↓ Noche de San Juan

At **Noche de San Juan** (23 June), bonfires are lit on beaches; leap over the flames three times for good luck.

↗ Pride Month

Join the festivities with concerts, drag shows and a big parade on the last Saturday in Seville. Torremolinos celebrates in early June.

Corpus Christi

This Catholic feast day is celebrated two months after Easter. It's a holiday in Seville and Granada, with dancing and processions.

JUNE

Average daytime max: 28°C
Days of rainfall: 3 (Málaga)

JULY

Andalucía in
SUMMER

⬂ Festival Internacional de Música y Danza

Three weeks of classical and contemporary concerts and dance performances in Granada; held June/July.

📍 Granada

▶ granadafestival.org

Noche del Vino

Fandango music and dancing, treading of the grapes and imbibing *muscatel* are features of Noche del Vino in Cómpeta on 15 August.

📍 Cómpeta

⬉ Feria de Málaga

In mid-August, the week-long *feria* takes over the city centre during the day, and moves to the fairground at night.

ANDALUCÍA PLAN BY SEASON

AUGUST

Average daytime max: 30°C
Days of rainfall: 0 (Málaga)

Average daytime max: 31°C
Days of rainfall: 2 (Málaga)

If you can bear the heat, cities are quiet and crowd-free in August, but some museums and restaurants are closed.

📖 Packing notes

Cool, light clothes and sunhat for daytime plus a jacket or jumper for night.

Nature's Harvest

Fungi start appearing shortly after the rains start. Look out for *mosto* (young wine) festivals and other harvest celebrations.

↘ Fiestas de la Vendimia de Jerez

The cradle of sherry celebrates the Fiestas de la Vendimia de Jerez (wine harvest festival) in early September; expect tastings and bodega visits.

📍 Jerez, p94

↓ Bienal de Flamenco de Sevilla

Watch the best artistes of *cante* (song), *toque* (guitar) and *baile* (dance) perform over three weeks in September/October.

▶ labienal.com

10 de Octubre

Celebrating Columbus' arrival in the New World, 10 October is a national holiday in Spain.

SEPTEMBER

Average daytime max: 31°C
Days of rainfall: 9 (Córdoba)

OCTOBER

Andalucía in
AUTUMN

Romería de Torrijos Pilgrimage

Ox-drawn carts pull gypsy caravans to a nearby hacienda in the colourful Romería de Torrijos pilgrimage near Seville (second Sunday of October).

Chestnut Festival

Feast on roast chestnuts at the Fiesta de la Castaña in the Axarquïa mountain village of Alcaucín in early November.

📍 Alcaucín, Axarquïa

← All Saints' Day

Día de Todos los Santos (1 November) sees Spanish families visiting their loved ones' graves on 1 November.

NOVEMBER

Average daytime max: 26°C
Days of rainfall: 11 (Córdoba)

Average daytime max: 19°C
Days of rainfall: 10 (Córdoba)

← Southernmost Skiing

Europe's most southerly ski resort, Sierra Nevada (131 runs; highest point 3398m), opens from late November/ early December until April.

📍 Sierra Nevada

 Packing notes

Days are still warm but nights can be chilly; bring layers and a rain jacket.

Winter Warmers

Although the temperatures drop in January and February, (mostly) sunny weather and excellent prices attract savvy visitors unfazed by rain showers.

Navidad

At Navidad (Christmas), families gather for a meal on *Nochebuena* (Christmas Eve). *Nochevieja* (New Year's Eve) is celebrated by eating 12 grapes.

Nativity Scenes

In towns and villages (Arcos de la Frontera is notable), *belenes vivientes* (live nativity scenes) feature costumed townsfolk, plus animals.

↖ Verdiales

Flower-festooned flamenco-type fandango folk dances and singing at the Verdiales festival in Málaga province on 28 December.

📍 Málaga

DECEMBER

Average daytime max: 24°C
Days of rainfall: 13 (Granada)

JANUARY

Andalucía in
WINTER

↘ Three Kings Processions

On 5 January, children around Spain watch the Reyes Magos processions; the next morning, they open their camel-borne gifts.

ANDALUCÍA PLAN BY SEASON

↖ Dia de Andalucía

Commemorating the establishment of Andalucía as an autonomous community; 28 February celebrates the region's strong and proud identity.

Carnaval

Listen to the satirical singing groups at Carnaval (late February/early March) in Cádiz – and dress up to join in the party.
● Cádiz, p98

FEBRUARY

Average daytime max: 17°C
Days of rainfall: 11 (Granada)

Average daytime max: 18°C
Days of rainfall: 10 (Granada)

Packing notes

Bring a warm coat and scarf for going out at night. Snow on the highest peaks.

Lent

El Entierro de la Sardina sees the papier-mâché fish buried, or burned, soon after Carnaval, to signify the start of Lent.

↗ Holy Week

One of Andalucía's most important events, Holy Week consist of religious processions in Seville, Mála-ga, Granada and every town (mid-March to early April).

↙ Feria de Caballos

Jerez is known for its magnificent horses: the Feria de Caballos in late April/early May also celebrates sherry and flamenco.

📍 Jerez

Feria de Abril

At the week-long Feria de Abril in Seville, two weeks after Easter, *feriantes* ride horses, parade in carriages, eat, drink and dance.

📍 Seville

MARCH

Average daytime max: 22°C
Days of rainfall: 11 (Seville)

APRIL

Andalucía in
SPRING

El Rocio Pilgrimage

The pilgrimage sees a million people arrive in a small Huelva town at Whitsun (Pentecost) to venerate the Virgen del Rocio.

◉ Huelva, p77

↗ Cruces de Mayo

Most famous in Córdoba but also celebrated elsewhere, the Cruces de Mayo festival in early May features crosses decorated with flowers and shawls.

↖ Patios de Córdoba Festival

Visit plant-bedecked private courtyards around the city in the Unesco-recognised Patios de Córdoba festival, also held in May.

▶ patios.cordoba.es

MAY

Average daytime max: 24°C
Days of rainfall: 12 (Seville)

Average daytime max: 28°C
Days of rainfall: 11 (Seville)

↙ Feria de Manzanilla

If you like sherry, head to seaside town Sanlúcar de Barrameda for the Feria de Manzanilla (late May/early June).

🧳 Packing notes

Expect rising temperatures, so you'll need shorts, but a fleece too – and a *feria* touch!

SHERRY TRIANGLE & WHITE TOWNS OF CÁDIZ
Trip Builder

TAKE YOUR PICK OF MUST-SEES AND HIDDEN GEMS

Sherry wines are only made in this part of southern Spain – seeing the centuries-old *solera-criadera* ageing system and tasting salty *manzanilla* and nutty *amontillado* in situ *is not* to be missed. Then explore beautiful, unchanged hilltop villages like Grazalema, Olvera and little-known Bornos, with superb hiking through groves of almond and olive trees.

🗺 Trip Notes

Hub towns Jerez, Cádiz, Arcos de la Frontera

How long 10 days

Getting around The Sherry Triangle's three towns – Jerez, El Puerto de Santa María and Sanlúcar de Barrameda – are well connected, with frequent bus services, as well as trains between Jerez, El Puerto and Cádiz. Buses serve hill towns, though services are not frequent.

Tips If you're in town or nearby and there's a local spring fair on, be sure to go.

Sanlúcar de Barrameda
Tuck into a plate of king prawns or *tortillitas de camarones* married with an ice-cold glass of *manzanilla* sherry on Bajo Guia, gazing across the river to Parque Doñana.
🚌 *45mins from Jerez*

Golfo de Cádiz

Sanlúcar de Barrameda ●

Chipiona ●

Jerez de la Frontera
Tour sherry *bodegas* (the wine is named after the city), find out how it is made, and drop into a *tabanco*, where flamenco and tapas complete the perfect Andaluz trio.
🚌 *40mins from Cádiz*

Rota ●

Bahía de Cádiz

Cádiz

Atlantic Ocean

Cádiz
Dive into the city's superb gastronomic scene, from the Mercado Central de Abastos to small bars in characterful Barrio de la Viña. Wine-lovers shouldn't miss Magerit wine shop.
🚌 *40mins from Jerez*

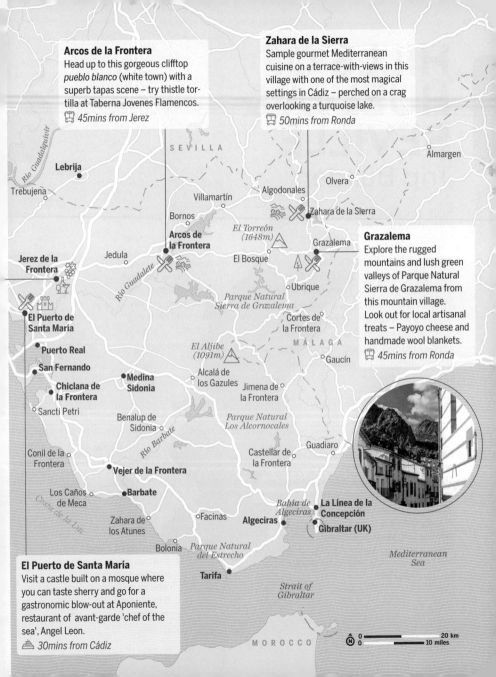

Arcos de la Frontera
Head up to this gorgeous clifftop *pueblo blanco* (white town) with a superb tapas scene – try thistle tortilla at Taberna Jovenes Flamencos.
🚌 *45mins from Jerez*

Zahara de la Sierra
Sample gourmet Mediterranean cuisine on a terrace-with-views in this village with one of the most magical settings in Cádiz – perched on a crag overlooking a turquoise lake.
🚌 *50mins from Ronda*

Grazalema
Explore the rugged mountains and lush green valleys of Parque Natural Sierra de Grazalema from this mountain village. Look out for local artisanal treats – Payoyo cheese and handmade wool blankets.
🚌 *45mins from Ronda*

El Puerto de Santa María
Visit a castle built on a mosque where you can taste sherry and go for a gastronomic blow-out at Aponiente, restaurant of avant-garde 'chef of the sea', Angel Leon.
⛴ *30mins from Cádiz*

SEVILLA

Almargen

Lebrija

Trebujena

Villamartín

Algodonales

Olvera

Bornos

Zahara de la Sierra

El Torreón (1648m) △

Arcos de la Frontera

Jedula

El Bosque

Grazalema

Jerez de la Frontera

Río Guadalete

Parque Natural Sierra de Grazalema

Ubrique

El Puerto de Santa María

Puerto Real

Cortes de la Frontera

MÁLAGA

San Fernando

El Aljibe (1091m) △

Gaucín

Chiclana de la Frontera

Medina Sidonia

Alcalá de los Gazules

Sancti Petri

Jimena de la Frontera

Benalup de Sidonia

Parque Natural Los Alcornocales

Conil de la Frontera

Río Barbate

Castellar de la Frontera

Guadiaro

Vejer de la Frontera

Los Caños de Meca

Barbate

Costa de la Luz

Zahara de los Atunes

Facinas

Bahía de Algeciras

La Línea de la Concepción

Algeciras

Gibraltar (UK)

Bolonia

Parque Natural del Estrecho

Mediterranean Sea

Tarifa

Strait of Gibraltar

Ⓝ 0 ———— 20 km
   0 ———— 10 miles

MOROCCO

HILLS OF HUELVA & SEVILLE
Trip Builder

TAKE YOUR PICK OF MUST-SEES AND HIDDEN GEMS

▬▬▬ Stay in hillside villages untouched by time nestled in the Sierra de Aracena y Picos de Aroche, visit an old mining town to see a Mars-like landscape, then head west to the more remote, little-visited Parque Natural Sierra Norte de Sevilla for great local wine and marvellous hikes.

🗺️ Trip Notes

Hub towns Aracena, Huelva, Seville

How long 1 week

Getting around Buses connect the Sierra de Aracena villages, but with few daily services. The *cercanías* C3 train line from Seville stops at Constantina/Cazalla station; there are buses too.

Tips Hikes between villages in the Sierra de Aracena and in the Sierra Norte are best done in spring, with fabulous wildflowers and mild temperatures. Constantina/Cazalla train station is not located in either town, but is well placed for hikes and bike rides.

Alájar
Hike from this picturesque, friendly village – choose from hilltop and riverside routes to Linares de la Sierra and the hamlet of Los Madroñales.

🚗 *25mins from Aracena*

Villanueva de la Fresno

Jerez de los Caballeros

Oliva de la Frontera

PORTUGAL

Jabugo
Follow the nutty aroma to the heart of the *jamón ibérico de bellota* industry – roam with the pigs in their oak-filled *dehesa* pastureland and see the salting and curing factories.

🚗 *30mins from Aracena*

Fregenal de la Sierra

Encinasola

Cumbres Mayores

Cortegana   Jabugo

Almonaster la Real   Alájar

Santa Bárbara de Casa

Cabezas Rubias

Calañas

Puebla de Guzmán   HUELVA

Río Odiel

Zalamea la Real

Valverde del Camino

Almonaster La Real
Step back in time in a medieval mosque on a grassy hillock; come for the *fandango* dancing at the Cruces de Mayo festival.

🚗 *40mins from Aracena*

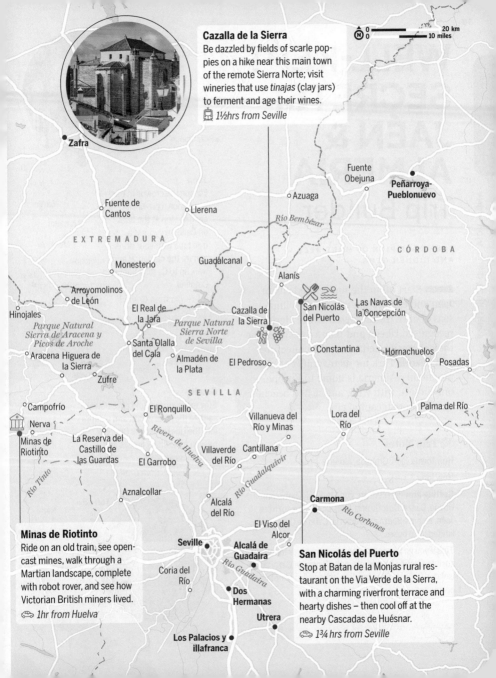

Cazalla de la Sierra

Be dazzled by fields of scarle poppies on a hike near this main town of the remote Sierra Norte; visit wineries that use *tinajas* (clay jars) to ferment and age their wines.

🚆 1½hrs from Seville

Zafra

0 — 20 km
0 — 10 miles

Fuente Obejuna

Peñarroya-Pueblonuevo

Azuaga

Río Bembézar

Fuente de Cantos
Llerena

EXTREMADURA

CÓRDOBA

Monesterio
Guadálcanal

Alanís

Arroyomolinos de León

El Real de la Jara

Cazalla de la Sierra

San Nicolás del Puerto

Las Navas de la Concepción

Hinojales

Parque Natural Sierra de Aracena y Picos de Aroche

Parque Natural Sierra Norte de Sevilla

Santa Olalla del Cala

Almadén de la Plata

El Pedroso

Constantina

Hornachuelos

Posadas

Aracena
Higuera de la Sierra

Zufre

SEVILLA

Campofrío

Nerva

El Ronquillo

Rivera de Huelva

Villanueva del Río y Minas

Lora del Río

Palma del Río

Minas de Riotinto

La Reserva del Castillo de las Guardas

El Garrobo

Villaverde del Río

Cantillana

Río Guadalquivir

Río Tinto

Aznalcollar

Alcalá del Río

Carmona

Río Corbones

Minas de Riotinto

Ride on an old train, see opencast mines, walk through a Martian landscape, complete with robot rover, and see how Victorian British miners lived.

🚗 1hr from Huelva

El Viso del Alcor

Seville

Alcalá de Guadaira

Coria del Río

Río Guadaira

Dos Hermanas

Utrera

Los Palacios y illafranca

San Nicolás del Puerto

Stop at Batan de la Monjas rural restaurant on the Via Verde de la Sierra, with a charming riverfront terrace and hearty dishes – then cool off at the nearby Cascadas de Huésnar.

🚗 1¾ hrs from Seville

WELL-KEPT SECRETS: JAÉN & ALMERÍA
Trip Builder

TAKE YOUR PICK OF MUST-SEES AND HIDDEN GEMS

▬▬▬ Start off in the underrated city of Jaén and explore the province's rolling seas of olive trees. Unesco World Heritage–recognised Úbeda and Baeza are famed for their exquisite Renaissance architecture, and Cazorla Park for its magnificent mountains. Almería is home to Europe's only desert, with wild, untouched beaches and a Moorish capital city.

🗺 Trip Notes

Hub towns Jaén, Granada, Almería

How long 2 weeks

Getting around There are good bus links between Úbeda, Baeza, Cazorla and Jaén, plus trains to/from Jaén, Linares-Baeza and Almería. Cabo de Gata has limited local buses.

Tips If you go by car, you can enjoy scenic detours, such as Castillo de la Iruela in the Sierra de Cazorla; the isolated Cabo de Gata beaches especially are not well connected.

○ Almadén

● Pozoblanco

Jaén
Escape the crowds in this least-known provincial capital, stop at the bars on Calle Arroyo, get a free tapa with your drink; admire the cathedral and walk up to Castillo Santa Catalina.
🚋 1¼ hrs from Granada

Bailén ○

● Andújar
Río Guadalquivir ○
Mengíbar

○ Porcuna

Jaén 🍴

Martos ●

● Montilla   ● Baena   ○ Alcaudete

Puente Genil ●

● Lucena   ● Priego de Córdoba

Alcalá ○ la Real

Guadix
Stay in a centuries-old cave house, sample the local wines, and venture into the Unesco Global Geopark, heaven for archaeologists and ornithologists alike.
🚋 1hr 15 mins from Granada

Río Genil

Santa Fé ●

○ Alhama de Granada

Torre del Mar ●   Nerja ●

● Almuñécar

Mediterranean Sea

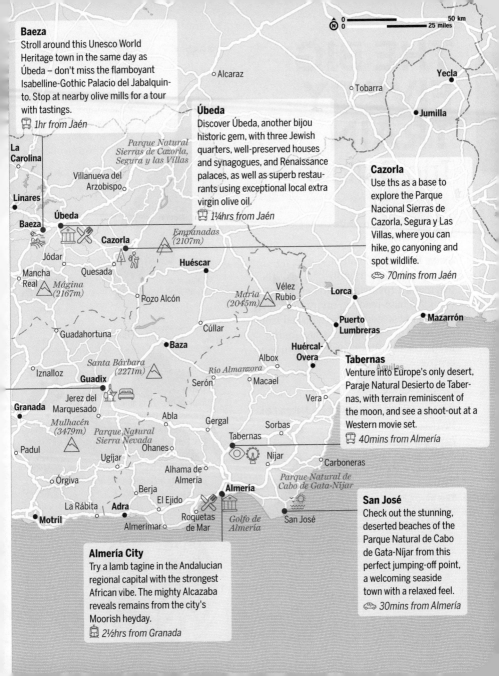

Baeza
Stroll around this Unesco World Heritage town in the same day as Úbeda – don't miss the flamboyant Isabelline-Gothic Palacio del Jabalquinto. Stop at nearby olive mills for a tour with tastings.
🚃 *1hr from Jaén*

Úbeda
Discover Úbeda, another bijou historic gem, with three Jewish quarters, well-preserved houses and synagogues, and Renaissance palaces, as well as superb restaurants using exceptional local extra virgin olive oil.
🚃 *1¼hrs from Jaén*

Cazorla
Use ths as a base to explore the Parque Nacional Sierras de Cazorla, Segura y Las Villas, where you can hike, go canyoning and spot wildlife.
🚗 *70mins from Jaén*

Tabernas
Venture into Europe's only desert, Paraje Natural Desierto de Tabernas, with terrain reminiscent of the moon, and see a shoot-out at a Western movie set.
🚃 *40mins from Almería*

San José
Check out the stunning, deserted beaches of the Parque Natural de Cabo de Gata-Níjar from this perfect jumping-off point, a welcoming seaside town with a relaxed feel.
🚗 *30mins from Almería*

Almería City
Try a lamb tagine in the Andalucian regional capital with the strongest African vibe. The mighty Alcazaba reveals remains from the city's Moorish heyday.
🚋 *2½hrs from Granada*

0 — 50 km
0 — 25 miles
Ⓝ

Alcaraz
Tobarra
Yecla
Jumilla
La Carolina
Parque Natural Sierras de Cazorla, Segura y las Villas
Villanueva del Arzobispo
Linares
Úbeda
Baeza
Empanadas (2107m)
Cazorla
Jódar
Huéscar
Mancha Real
Mágina (2167m)
Quesada
Pozo Alcón
María (2045m)
Vélez Rubio
Lorca
Mazarrón
Puerto Lumbreras
Cúllar
Guadahortuna
Baza
Albox
Huércal-Overa
Santa Bárbara (2271m)
Río Almanzora
Iznalloz
Guadix
Serón
Macael
Granada
Jerez del Marquesado
Mulhacén (3479m)
Abla
Vera
Parque Natural Sierra Nevada
Gergal
Sorbas
Padul
Ohanes
Tabernas
Uglíjar
Nijar
Carboneras
Órgiva
Alhama de Almería
Almería
Parque Natural de Cabo de Gata-Níjar
Berja
El Ejido
La Rábita
Adra
Roquetas de Mar
Golfo de Almería
San José
Motril
Almerimar

THE BIG FIVE BY TRAIN
Trip Builder

TAKE YOUR PICK OF MUST-SEES AND HIDDEN GEMS

▬▬▬ For the ultimate fuss-free, no-time-wasted, eco-friendly trip, visit the five major provincial capital cities by train. No map-reading, no traffic delays, no parking stress: just be whisked from cathedral to palace to mosque, taking in the cosmopolitan-yet-historic urban centres.

🗺 Trip Notes

Hub towns Seville, Córdoba, Granada, Málaga, Cádiz

How long 10 days

Getting around AVE (high-speed train) serves Seville, Córdoba, Granada and Málaga. Cádiz to Seville is by *media distancia* (medium-distance) train.

Tips You could easily visit Cádiz and Córdoba as day trips from Seville, and a new high-speed connection linking Málaga and Granada is handy for quick hops. It's worth booking these trips, and the monuments, in advance, especially on weekends or holidays.

Seville
Be awed by the majestic Réal Alcázar (Royal Palace) and the vast Gothic cathedral before sampling tapas with a modern twist and then taking in a flamenco show.
🚆 *45 mins from Córdoba*

Cádiz
Explore this small and ancient city, famous for its atmospheric *barrios*, feast on fabulous seafood and look out for the 126 watchtowers built to protect its boundaries.
🚆 *1½hrs from Seville*

Portalegre

Estremoz

Badajoz

Mérida

Zafra

PORTUGAL   EXTREMADURA

Moura

Parque Natural Sierra de Aracena y Picos de Aroche

Rosal de la Frontera

Aracena

Santa Olalla del Cala

Villanueva de los Castillejos

HUELVA

Valverde del Camino

Nerva

Seville

Ayamonte

Tavira

Huelva

Almonte

Golfo de Cádiz

Parque Nacional de Doñana

Matalascañas

Lebrija

Sanlúcar de Barrameda

CÁDIZ

Jerez de la Frontera

Cádiz

Vejer de la Frontera

Costa de la Luz

Barbate

Strait of Gibraltar

Atlantic Ocean

Tangier

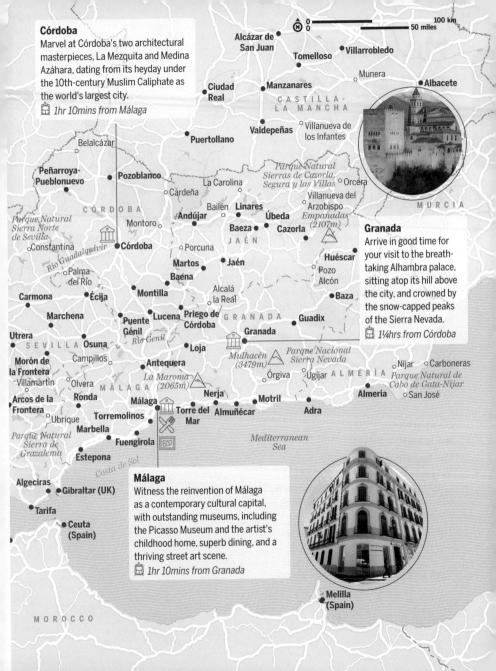

Córdoba

Marvel at Córdoba's two architectural masterpieces, La Mezquita and Medina Azáhara, dating from its heyday under the 10th-century Muslim Caliphate as the world's largest city.

🚆 1hr 10mins from Málaga

Granada

Arrive in good time for your visit to the breathtaking Alhambra palace, sitting atop its hill above the city, and crowned by the snow-capped peaks of the Sierra Nevada.

🚆 1¼hrs from Córdoba

Málaga

Witness the reinvention of Málaga as a contemporary cultural capital, with outstanding museums, including the Picasso Museum and the artist's childhood home, superb dining, and a thriving street art scene.

🚆 1hr 10mins from Granada

0 100 km
0 50 miles

Alcázar de San Juan
Tomelloso Villarrobledo
Munera
Albacete
Ciudad Real
CASTILLA-LA MANCHA
Manzanares
Valdepeñas Villanueva de los Infantes
Belalcázar
Puertollano
MURCIA
Peñarroya-Pueblonuevo Pozoblanco
La Carolina
Parque Natural Sierras de Cazorla, Segura y las Villas Orcera
Cardeña
Villanueva del Arzobispo
CÓRDOBA
Bailén Linares
Andújar Úbeda
Empañadas (2107m)
Montoro Baeza Cazorla
Parque Natural Sierra Norte de Sevilla
JAÉN
Constantina Córdoba Porcuna
Huéscar
Río Guadalquivir
Palma del Río Martos Jaén Pozo Alcón
Baena
Carmona Écija Montilla Alcalá la Real Baza
Marchena Lucena Priego de Córdoba GRANADA Guadix
Puente Genil Granada
Utrera Osuna Río Genil Loja
SEVILLA Mulhacén (3479m) Parque Nacional Sierra Nevada
Morón de la Frontera Campillos Antequera
Villamartín Olvera La Maroma (2065m) Órgiva Ugíjar ALMERÍA
Arcos de la Frontera Ronda MÁLAGA Nerja Motril Parque Natural de Cabo de Gata-Níjar
Ubrique Málaga Torre del Mar Almuñécar Adra Almería San José
Parque Natural Sierra de Grazalema Torremolinos
Marbella Fuengirola Mediterranean Sea
Estepona
Costa del Sol
Algeciras Gibraltar (UK)
Tarifa
Ceuta (Spain)
Melilla (Spain)
MOROCCO
Níjar Carboneras

MÁLAGA'S CELEBRATED COAST & VILLAGES
Trip Builder

TAKE YOUR PICK OF MUST-SEES AND HIDDEN GEMS

▬▬ Beyond the glamour of Marbella and the ever-popular Costa del Sol, heading off the tourist track will reap rich rewards. You'll find a raft of outdoor pursuits like climbing and hiking to suit all levels, the mountainous Axarquía bursting with pretty villages and lush valleys, and Ronda's new-generation wines.

🗺 Trip Notes

Hub towns Málaga, Ronda

How long 10 days

Getting around Málaga city is well connected to Ronda and Antequera by train; buses link the coastal towns, but more remote inland areas are best visited by car.

Tips Costa de Sol beaches and car parks get very busy in summer; arrive early and bring coins to pay the parking attendants.

Check out guidetomalaga.com to see what's on.

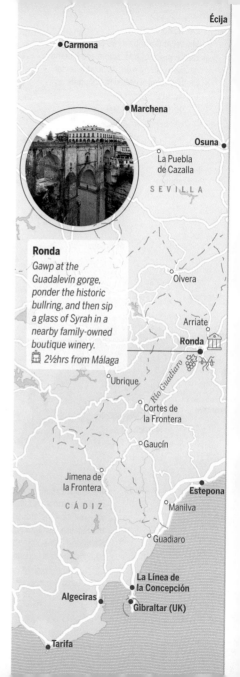

• Carmona

• Marchena

Osuna •

○ La Puebla de Cazalla

S E V I L L A

Ronda
Gawp at the Guadalevín gorge, ponder the historic bullring, and then sip a glass of Syrah in a nearby family-owned boutique winery.
🚃 *2½hrs from Málaga*

○ Olvera

Arriate

Ronda 🏛

○ Ubrique

Río Guadiaro

○ Cortes de la Frontera

○ Gaucín

○ Jimena de la Frontera

C Á D I Z

Estepona •

○ Manilva

○ Guadiaro

La Línea de la Concepción •

Algeciras ○

Gibraltar (UK)

• Tarifa

El Chorro

Challenge yourself with world-famous climbing, as well as via ferrata and canyoning, in the limestone gorge next to this village.

🚆 *40mins from Málaga*

Competa

Hike from this pretty Axarquía village to the summit of El Lucero mountain, spotting ibex and eventually the distant Sierra Nevada.

🚌 *1hr from Málaga*

Málaga

Grab a table at a buzzing fusion joint and bite into some tuna tataki with porra antequerana, then ponder local wines paired with innovative tapas.

Nerja

Jump on a stand-up paddleboard at this pleasant seaside town or scramble down to peaceful Cabo del Pino cove. Refuel on just-cooked paella at a chiringuito (beach restaurant).

🚌 *1½hrs from Málaga*

Marbella

Live it up at minimalist-chic Nobu hotel or the luxurious former summer residence of Napoleon III's wife, before soaking up the rays at Calahonda or Casablanca beach.

🚆 *45mins from Málaga*

0 | 20 km
0 | 10 miles

Alcalá la Real

Priego de Córdoba

CÓRDOBA

Montefrío

Algarinejo

Benamejí

Río Genil

Iznájar

Loja

Fuente de Piedra

Archidona

Ventas de Zafarraya

Alhama de Granada

GRANADA

Campillos

Río Guadalhorce

Antequera

Villanueva del Rosario

Parque Natural Sierras de Tejeda, Almijara y Alhama

Almargen

Teba

Valle de Abdalajís

Villanueva de la Concepción

Riogordo

Periana

La Maroma (2065m) △

Ardales

El Chorro

Casabermeja

Canillas de Aceituno

Cómpeta

Frigiliana

El Burgo

MÁLAGA

Vélez Málaga

Torrox

Nerja

Almuñécar

Torrecilla (1918m) △

Alozaina

Cártama

Río Guadalhorce

Málaga

Rincón de la Victoria

Benajarafe

Torrox Costa

Parque Natural Sierra de las Nieves

Coín

Alhaurín de la Torre

Torre del Mar

Istán

Alhaurín El Grande

Torremolinos

Benalmádena

Ojen

Mijas

Benahavís

Marbella

Fuengirola

San Pedro de Alcántara

Mijas Costa

Costa del Sol

Mediterranean Sea

7 Things to Know About
ANDALUCÍA

INSIDER TIPS TO HIT THE GROUND RUNNING

1 Fiesta Time

It's easy to get caught short by a holiday in Andalucía, with shops, offices and monuments unexpectedly closed, whether local (town), regional (Andalucía) or national (Spain). So do your homework, checking websites for information about where you'll be staying and visiting. In any case, you'll get a glimpse of authentic Andalucía, whether it's a *feria* with the townsfolk dressed up and dancing, or a seasonal food-themed event.

▶ Check out the Feria de Abril on p58 or the Feria de Málaga on p130

2 Fitting in at Fiestas

If you're going to a local fiesta but lack the full garb – a fitted flamenca dress, for example – find accessories, such as earrings, a flower for your hair, or even a shawl that matches your outfit. It's easy to do, costs little, and makes you feel like you fit more into the event – plus the effort is always appreciated. Men should wear a button-down shirt. Try to dance Sevillanas, and you'll be a winner.

3 Meet & Greet

Greet the other people present when entering a shop, bar or office. A general 'Buenos días/tardes/noches.' (Good morning/afternoon/evening) gives a friendly first impression, plus a 'Hasta luego' (See you later) on leaving.

buenos días

4 Child-Friendly

Children are welcome in bars and restaurants, where running around and playing are tolerated with good grace. However, most rooftop terrace bars don't allow under-18s.

5 Sensitive Subjects

The Spanish Civil War (1936–39) and Franco's Dictatorship (1939–75) are still highly controversial, divisive and sensitive subjects in Andalucía, especially among the older generation. The Pacto de Olvido (Pact of Forgetting), when democracy was restored after Franco died, meant that the events during those five decades were not spoken about openly for many years, and victims and their families felt that justice had been denied them. Under the Ley de Memoria Historica (Law of Historical Memory), passed by the socialist government in 2007, local authorities were obliged to locate war graves, and exhume and identify victims of the dictatorship. This has, inevitably, reopened old wounds within communities and families. Read up on the subject, be aware of the region's complicated history, and be careful about talking to locals, as they are likely to either express strong opinions or prefer to avoid the subject entirely.

7 Kissing Clever

It's normal to kiss on both cheeks (right cheek first) when meeting someone for the first time, either socially or in a business environment. Post-Covid, some people may still be cautious and shake hands, but Andalucians are highly tactile, so they enjoy the *dos besos* (two kisses).

6 Local Lingo

Andalucian Spanish drops or alters the final syllable, so *cansada* (tired) becomes *cansa* or *cansao*.

Some Andalucian expressions:

una jartá – a lot; for example, '*Te quiero una jartá*' (I love you very much).

una mijita – a little; like '*Una mijita más de leche, porfa*' (A little more milk, please).

no ní ná – a triple negative; meaning 'definitely [yes]'.

▶ For more on language, go to p254

Read, Listen, Watch & Follow

 READ

Andalus: Unlocking the Secrets of Moorish Spain
(Jason Webster; 2005) The Arab ancestry of modern Spain: food, language and culture.

The Factory of Light: Tales from My Andalucian Village (Michael Jacobs; 2003)
Engaging adventures in deepest rural Jaén.

The Seville Communion
(Arturo Pérez-Reverte; 1995) Literary thriller by the best-selling novelist, filmed as *The Man from Rome* (2022).

Gypsy Ballads
(Gabriel García Lorca; 1928) Lyrical poetry collection by the celebrated Granadino writer.

 LISTEN

Almoraima
(Paco de Lucia and Camarón; 1975) The birth of 'new flamenco' from the collaboration between legendary guitarist and singer.

Blues de la Frontera
(Pata Negra; 1986) Ground-breaking flamenco blues from Sevillano brothers, Raimundo and Rafael Amador.

Milagro
(Dellafuente; 2021) Spanish-Brazilian rapper from Granada, mixing hip-hop, reggaeton and flamenco, plus classical in this latest work.

La Portada podcast
(2022) Co-presented by the former editor of *El País* in English – Spanish current affairs, politics and culture.

Verde Mar
(Chambao; 2002) Soulful 'flamenco chill': accessible electronic pop from the now-defunct Málaga group.

▷ WATCH

La Trinchera Infinita/The Endless Trench (Jon Garaño, Aitor Arregi and Jose Mari Goenaga; 2019) Republican man hides in his marital home for 33 years.

Isla Mínima/Marshland (Albero Rodríguez; 2015) Police thriller set in Guadalquivir town.

Carmen (Vicente Aranda; 2003) New take on the classic tragic tale.

La Peste (Alberto Rodríguez and Rafael Cobos; 2018) TV drama set in Seville during the bubonic plague.

Flamenco Flamenco (Carlos Saura; 2010) Mesmerising showcase of top artistes.

PHOTO 12/ALAMY STOCK PHOTO ©

GENERAL DE PRODUCCIONES Y DISEÑO/ALAMY STOCK PHOTO ©

FOLLOW

@andaluz foodandtravel
Food writer Fiona Dunlop's mouth-watering snaps.

@inglesandaluz
An English teacher's take on Andalucian expressions.

Alisoninandalucia
(alisoninandalucia.com) Informative blog about the region.

Surinenglish
(Surinenglish.com) English version of Costa del Sol newspaper.

Andalucia.com
(andalucia.com) Comprehensive website covering entire region.

Sate your Andalucía dreaming with a virtual vacation

SEVILLE

FIERY | HISTORIC | CHARMING

Experience
Seville
online

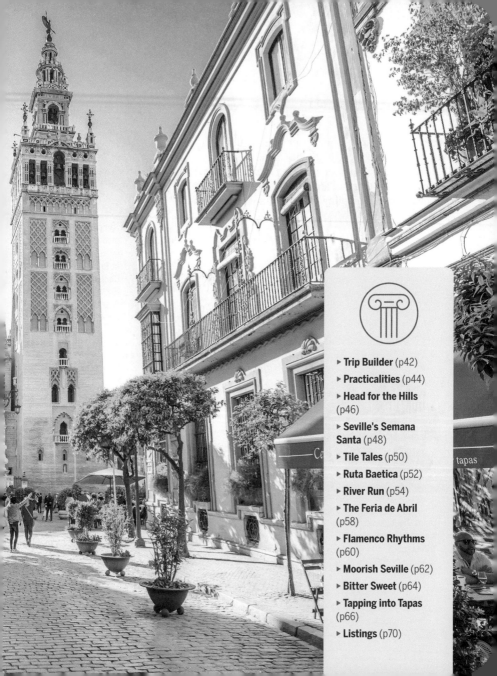

SEVILLE
Trip Builder

▬ The old adage 'Don't think; feel' could be written about Seville: the intense joy and pain of flamenco, the high-octane partying of the Feria, the lofty drama of Semana Santa, the intense colour of tiles or the mind-boggling choice of tapas. Surrender yourself.

ISLA DE LA CARTUJA

C Leonardo da Vinci

Camino de los Descubrimientos

C Marie Curie

Sample fresh market produce and learn to cook tapas at **Taller Andaluz de Cocina** (p68)
🚶 20 min from Puerta Jerez metro station

Av Carlos III

Puente de la Cartuja

C Marques de Paradas

Puente del Cachorro

C Arjona

C Alfarería

Puente de Isabel II

Learn about glazed ceramic tiles at **Centro Cerámica Triana** (p50)
🚶 20 min from Puerta Jerez metro station

Explore Seville's **Río Guadalquivir** and paddleboard past the Nao Victoria (p54)
🚶 10 min from Puerta Jerez metro station

C San Jacinto

C Pagés del Corro

C Evangelista

TRIANA

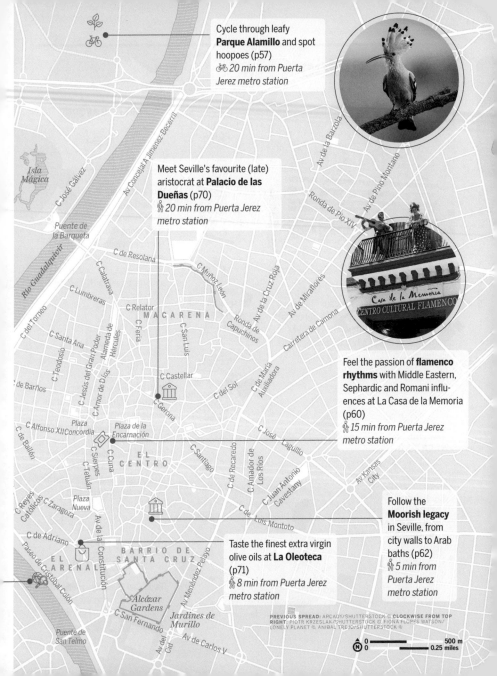

Cycle through leafy **Parque Alamillo** and spot hoopoes (p57)
🚲 20 min from Puerta Jerez metro station

Meet Seville's favourite (late) aristocrat at **Palacio de las Dueñas** (p70)
🚶 20 min from Puerta Jerez metro station

Feel the passion of **flamenco rhythms** with Middle Eastern, Sephardic and Romani influences at La Casa de la Memoria (p60)
🚶 15 min from Puerta Jerez metro station

Follow the **Moorish legacy** in Seville, from city walls to Arab baths (p62)
🚶 5 min from Puerta Jerez metro station

Taste the finest extra virgin olive oils at **La Oleoteca** (p71)
🚶 8 min from Puerta Jerez metro station

Isla Mágica

Río Guadalquivir

Puente de la Barqueta

C José Gálvez

C de Torneo

C del Torneo

C Santa Ana

C Teodosio

C de Baños

C Alfonso XII

C de Bailén

C Reyes Católicos C Zaragoza

C de Adriano

EL CARENAL

Paseo de Cristóbal Colón

Puente de San Telmo

C de Resolana

C Calatrava

C Lumbreras

C Relator

MACARENA

C Feria

Alameda de Hércules

C Jesús del Gran Poder

C Amor de Dios

Plaza Concordia

Plaza de la Encarnación

C Sierpes

C Cuna

C Tetuán

Plaza Nueva

Av de la Constitución

BARRIO DE SANTA CRUZ

EL CENTRO

C Muñoz León

C de la Cruz Roja

C San Luis

Ronda de Capuchinos

C Castellar

C Gerona

C del Sol

C de María Auxiliadora

C Santiago

C de Recaredo

C Amador de los Ríos

C José Laguillo

C Juan Antonio Cavestany

C de Luis Montoto

Av de Miraflores

Carretera de Camona

Av Kansas City

Alcázar Gardens

Jardines de Murillo

C San Fernando

Av Menéndez Pelayo

Av del Cid

Av de Carlos V

Av Concejal A Jiménez Becerril

Av de la Barzola

Av de Pino Montano

Ronda de Pío XIV

🧭 N 0 ____ 500 m
0 ____ 0.25 miles

Practicalities

ANIBAL TREJO/SHUTTERSTOCK ©

ARRIVING

Sevilla San Pablo airport Located 7km from the city centre. The EA (Especial Aeropuerto) bus leaves every 15 to 30 minutes to Plaza de Armas bus station. A taxi takes around 20 minutes.

WHEN TO GO

MAR–MAY
Spectacular wildflower meadows, streets perfumed with orange blossom, Easter and the Feria (spring fair)

SEP–OCT
Warm weather with mild nights for hiking and exploring the city

NOV–FEB
Cool but sunny days, lower accommodation prices, fewer crowds; beware of rain showers

HOW MUCH FOR A

Caña (small glass) of beer
€1.30

Cafe cortado (espresso with steamed milk)
€1.30

Toast with olive oil, tomato and jamón
€2.60

GETTING AROUND

Bus Tussam city buses are efficient; bear in mind that much of the centre is pedestrianised. Many stops show arrival times on electronic displays and the app is excellent for trip planning. A ticket costs €1.40, or you can get a tourist travel card (one/three days) for €5/10.

Metros run from Ciudad Expo (Aljarafe area) in the west to Olivar de Quintos in the east. Handy stops include Puerta Jerez for the cathedral, Puerta de Cuba for Triana and Prado de San Sebastian for Parque María Luisa. A ticket for one zone costs €1.35, and a one-day travel card €4.50.

Taxis Can be easily hailed in the street, or use apps like Uber and Cabify. A city-centre journey will cost €5 to €8.

EATING & DRINKING

Taste Seville's Jewish heritage (the city had one of Spain's biggest Sephardic communities until the 15th century) in the deliciously oily *espinacas con garbanzos* (spinach and chickpeas, seasoned with cumin and served with fried bread).

In Seville, craft beer is popular in the hip Alameda and Macarena areas, vermouth has an established following, and sherry is almost local. But lager is the all-round favourite, and *sin alcohol* (alcohol-free) or 0.0% ('zero-zero') is ubiquitous.

Best *montadito de pringá* (pork roll; pictured above right) Bodeguita Romero (p69)

Best *tortas de aceite* Inés Rosales (p71; pictured right)

CONNECT & FIND YOUR WAY

Mobile phones Most European mobile phone plans include Spain; otherwise, buy a prepaid SIM with Lobster, an English-language mobile service, or Movistar, Vodafone or Orange.

Navigation When walking around Seville's historic centre, you'll find that some streets will change direction several times keeping same name, while straight ones may have two or three name changes. All part of the charm.

WHERE TO STAY

Seville is brimming with stylish, historic hotels, as well as good, well-priced hostels and chic furnished apartments.

Neighbourhood	Pro/Con
Santa Cruz	The old Jewish quarter with beautiful converted palaces. Gets crowded with tourist groups.
Triana	Strong local identity; visible flamenco and ceramics roots. Some resentment of tourists.
Alameda/ Macarena	Hip, alternative area with trendy vibe. Can be noisy.
Centre	A mix of boutique and larger, modern chain hotels. Vehicle access tricky.

SEVILLE CARD

Various options (24/48/72/100 hours) including free entry to certain museums, a boat trip on the river, hop-on hop-off tour buses and more *(citypassguide.weebly. com/sevilla-card.html)*.

MONEY

Nearly everywhere accepts cards; mobile device payment systems like Apple Pay and Google Pay are becoming more widespread. Always take cash, especially for tips.

01

Head for
THE HILLS

CYCLING | NATURE | LANDSCAPES

■■■■ Tear yourself away from Seville's alluring beauty, and as you travel north, the flat, dry plain turns into the rolling tree-covered hills of the Sierra Norte. Sparsely populated, this beautiful national park has small, pretty towns among oak-covered hills that stretch as far as the eye can see. Pigs, sheep and goats roam, and you might spot otters, eagles and vultures.

🗺 How To

Getting here/around The main town, Cazalla, is 82 km from Seville. The best way to get around is by car or by train to Cazalla-Constantina station. Rent bikes from Bicicletas Via Verde (bicicletas verdevia.com). TurNature (*turnature.es*) does nature and cultural tours in the area.

When to go In spring, days are warm and the meadows are carpeted in wildflowers, while in autumn nights are still mild.

Beware Some country roads are extremely narrow, such as the A7101 from Cazalla-Constantina train station to San Nicolas. Proceed with caution.

Map showing Parque Natural Sierra Norte de Sevilla, Cascadas de Huéznar, San Nicolás del Puerto, Batan de las Monjas, Ribera de Huéznar, Via Verde de la Sierra Norte, Isla Margarita, Ribera de Huéznar. Scale 0–2 km / 0–1 miles.

Cycle an Old Railway

Immerse yourself in nature, cycling next to a river through shady pine forests filled with birdsong. The **Ribera de Huéznar** is one of the many smaller rivers that feeds the mighty Guadalquivir – its banks are covered with willows and alders. Listen out for nightingales.

The **Via Verde de la Sierra Norte** cycle path runs for 19km from near Cazalla through San Nicolás del Puerto to Cerro de Hierro, a vast jagged limestone outcrop that was mined for its iron. On an old railway, this Via Verde (greenway) offers an easy route with a gentle climb (2.5% gradient) and spectacular

views. Plus, it's downhill all the way back!

The route starts close to Cazalla-Constantina train station, running next to woodland and then winding through pasture dotted with holm oak and chestnut trees; look out for dazzling fields of poppies in spring. Even when you can't see the river, you can

✕ Best Lunch Stop

An idyllic place for lunch, the Batán de las Monjas is a former woollen mill and now a restaurant with cabins and campsite at Km 8 on the Via Verde. On a large wooden balcony, shaded by climbing vines, friendly staff serve imaginative salads (chickpea, avocado and matured sheep's cheese) and hearty *revuelto serrano* (eggs, potatoes and chorizo), as well as home-reared lamb. Try the locally produced wines: Fundus is a tempranillo, cabernet sauvignon and merlot (Fuente Reina winery) and Cueva la Sima (La Margarita) is made from chardonnay and airen varieties, and aged in barrels of home-grown chestnut wood. Both are from Constantina.

still hear its gentle burbling. After crossing the Huéznar on a wooden bridge, you pass between golden granite cliffs and then through a tunnel.

A few kilometres on, is the **Cascadas de Huéznar** – this idyllic spot, with a series of rushing crystalline falls, gets crowded on summer weekends, unsurprisingly. The streams and pools are popular for cooling off, even though swimming isn't strictly allowed. Also try **Isla Margarita**, near the start, especially with kids who are happy paddling in shallow streams.

Above Via Verde de la Sierra Norte

Seville's Semana Santa

THE AGONY AND ECSTASY OF SEVILLE'S HOLY WEEK

In spring, orange blossom fills the city with its intoxicating scent, the sun warms the streets, and Seville prepares for Semana Santa (Holy Week). An estimated million people come to watch the processions over eight days from Palm Sunday to Resurrection Sunday. If you don't mind crowds, it's an unmissable experience.

Left Brotherhood in procession through Seville. **Middle** Float featuring the Virgin Mary. **Right** Musicians at Semana Santa.

What Is it & Who's Who?

Semana Santa, which takes place between late March and mid-April, consists of 60 processions snaking their way down the city's narrow streets, with beautifully garbed statues swaying to mournful trumpets and steady drumbeats.

At first sight, it's intimidating and bizarre: rows of tall, hooded figures dressed in robes, with eyes visible through holes and wearing white gloves and a cord around their waist. The origin of the *nazarenos'* hoods was for anonymity during penance (ignore urban legends connecting them to the Klu Klux Klan).

The largest *hermandades,* the Catholic brotherhoods made up of *nazarenos, costaleros* and other roles, have upwards of 2500 members in their processions. Each procession features at least two *pasos* (floats), the Virgin Mary and Jesus Christ; add on a couple of marching bands, and you'll understand why it takes more than an hour for many of them to file past.

If you see a man with a ring of padded fabric on his head, he's a *costalero,* and is one of a team of around 30 to 50 sharing the 1000kg-plus weight of a *paso* on his neck. The *costaleros* work in shifts, enjoying a well-earned beer in between.

Route Master

Each procession leaves its own parish church and makes its way to the Catedral. In mid-afternoon, there could be as many as nine in the streets at any one time, so careful logistical planning is needed.

If it rains, as is common in spring, the *hermandades* take shelter in the nearest church to protect the statues, many of which are centuries-old priceless artefacts.

Get in Position

To feel the emotion, you need to get into the crowds. At the *salida,* when the Virgin leaves its church, carefully manoeuvred so that the *palio* fits though the often low baroque archway, tearful cries of *'¡Guapa!'* (Beautiful!) ring out.

Watching the processions from a high vantage point such as a balcony can be equally thrilling, especially when rose petals rain down. If your budget allows, book a bed on the official route that all processions take (La Campana, Calle Sierpes, Plaza de San Francisco, Avenida de la Constitución, Plaza Virgen de los Reyes). Look out for free printed guides in shops and bars that show the processions' timings and routes, as well as the Llamador app.

> At first sight, it's intimidating and bizarre: rows of tall, hooded figures dressed in robes...

Sacred Music & Silence

For weeks beforehand, Semana Santa music can be heard blasting out of people's cars, as anticipation builds. Slow, rhythmical and mournful, a uniformed marching band follows each *paso*. In addition, the *paso* may stop when a man or woman on the balcony breaks into song. He or she will address the Virgin or Jesus directly in their suffering, before a hushed crowd. This *saeta* (literally, arrow) is a heartfelt lament with Jewish and flamenco roots. At the other extreme, one of the *hermandades* which goes out on the Madrugá (Thursday night/Friday morning), Jesús del Gran Poder, has no music. The effect is electric – especially in a normally noisy, rumbustious city like Seville. If you're not here in Semana Santa, **Garlochi** bar in Alfalfa, gives a taste of the dramatic decor and atmosphere.

 Gold Standard

Among the most eye-catching features of the Semana Santa processions are the sumptuous **mantos** (cloaks) worn by Virgin Mary statues, along with the *techos de palio* (decorative canopies over the statues). Painstakingly hand-embroidered with gold thread by skilled artisans, a single garment can take as long as two years to create. The **embroidery workshop** at Francisco Carrera Iglesias in Alfalfa, led by the revered maestro Paquili, has created pieces for the Macarena *hermandad's* Virgen de la Esperanza, one of Seville's most popular statues, as well as for the fashion house Loewe. You can visit his workshop by appointment (carreraiglesias.es).

02 Tile TALES

CULTURE | ARTS | HISTORY

▬▬▬ You can't miss them as you walk around Seville, whether in antique car advertisements on walls, adorning resplendent palaces, lining park benches or declaring street names. *Azulejos* (glazed ceramic tiles) are an eye-catching and colourful element that is intrinsically linked with the city, and specifically the neighbourhood of Triana. Learn how they are made and seek out the finest examples.

MARC HILL/ALAMY STOCK PHOTO ©

🖾 How To

Getting here The best tiles can be seen on foot around Seville centre. Start at the **Centro Cerámica Triana**, then wander around the *barrio* spotting examples, from market stall signs to religious imagery. **Plaza de España** in Parque

María Luisa is a ceramics showcase extraordinaire, with tile panels from each province of Spain.

Best places to buy For antique pieces, go to **Populart** in Santa Cruz, while **Tentiles** (San Vicente) has contemporary homewares featuring classic designs.

ANIBAL TREJO/SHUTTERSTOCK ©

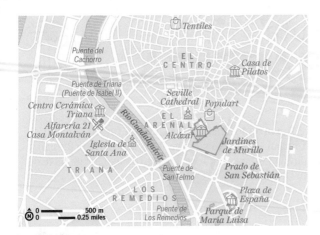

Left Plaza de Espana.
Bottom left Casa Mensaque.

SEVILLE EXPERIENCES

Ceramic Masterpieces

Triana is the main centre of production of Seville's ceramics tradition, and these are two of our favourite buildings.

Alfarería 21 Casa Montalván Located in the former Montalván ceramics factory, this restaurant is decorated with old ceramic pieces recycled to create unique contemporary architecture with delightful patios and fountains.

Casa Mensaque This Regionalist building in Calle San Jacinto, dating from 1905, features work by the finest ceramicists of the time, including Manuel Rodríguez and Pérez de Tudela. It constitutes a splendid ceramic catalogue of Triana, from Renaissance-inspired tiles to English-style hunting scenes. The building houses the Triana district government office, although visitors can enter.

■ Recommended by Antonio Librero, _art historian, and_ **Paula Felizon**, _ceramicist and anthropologist,_ @barroazul

Mosaic Magic

Ceramic pieces were first produced here in Roman times, using mud from the Guadalquivir riverbank. The Moors decorated their palaces with vibrant tiles, although Seville's finest _azulejos_ are in Mudéjar buildings (Moorish-Christian): the **Alcázar** palace boasts salons lined with vibrant alicatado tiles. Look closely, as each tiny glazed piece – in vivid blue, green or yellow – was cut by hand to fit into an intricate geometric pattern, such as a star. As well as their aesthetic value, these tiles are practical too, keeping rooms cool in summer and guarding against damp.

Top Techniques

Less time-consuming methods were _cuerda seca_ (dry rope), to separate areas of colour, and then later, moulds (_arista_ or _cuenca_) to imprint the design. Visit **Casa de Pilatos** for stunning examples of floral and leaf motifs. Niculoso Pisano, an Italian ceramicist, gave his name to a style of panel painted with religious and mythological images; check out his work in Triana's **Iglesia de Santa Ana**, the **Catedral** and the **Museo Bellas Artes**.

Factory Visit

More than 20 factories operated in Triana in the early 20th century. Explore inside one at the **Centro Cerámica Triana** (icas. sevilla.org/espacios/centro-ceramica), a little-known museum housed in the former Cerámica Santa Ana factory, with original kilns of different sizes, as well as a collection of beautiful painted tiles and bowls. Don't miss the video interviews with _trianero_ (people of Triana) who worked in the factory.

03 Ruta BAETICA

ROMAN HISTORY | RUINS | MUSEUMS

Two great emperors, Trajan and Hadrian, were born in Italica, the first Roman city outside Italy. You can explore part of the Ruta Baetica (the Roman name for the lower Guadalquivir Valley), renowned centuries ago for its olive oil, wine and silver production.

🏛 Trip Notes

Getting here/around Italica is located in Santiponce, near Seville. Take the M170A/M170B bus from Plaza de Armas bus station; then carry on to Carmona through the Campiña, past wheat fields and olive groves. Écija is a further 55 km away. Alsa buses link Seville's Prado de San Sebastián bus station with Carmona and Écija .

Top Tip Every June an international dance festival (festivalitalica.es) is held at the Roman theatre in Italica.

🏛 Hadrian's Home

Emperor Hadrian added a grand *nova urbs* (new city) with huge mansions to his childhood home town of Italica. Its mighty amphitheatre (pictured) seated 25,000, which was unusually large for a provincial town. Gladiators fought each other here as a ritual sacrifice for the emperor's health. Later on, the games became entertainment, with wild animal hunts – you can see the pits where their cages were kept.

TRABANTOS/SHUTTERSTOCK ©

■ **By Alvaro Jimenez PhD**, *archaeologist*

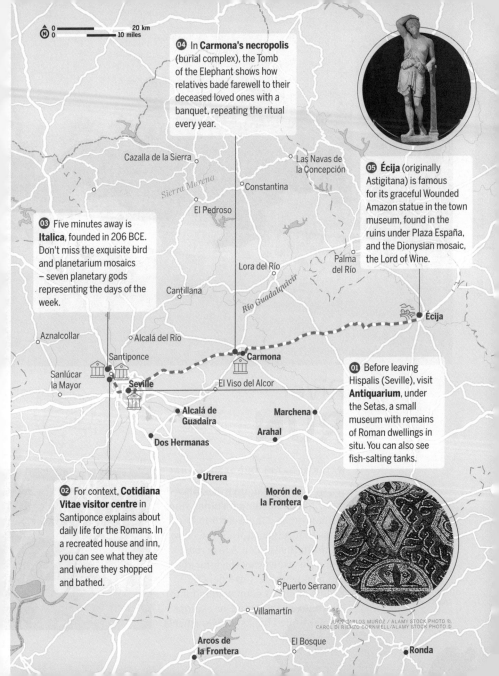

04 In **Carmona's necropolis** (burial complex), the Tomb of the Elephant shows how relatives bade farewell to their deceased loved ones with a banquet, repeating the ritual every year.

05 **Écija** (originally Astigitana) is famous for its graceful Wounded Amazon statue in the town museum, found in the ruins under Plaza España, and the Dionysian mosaic, the Lord of Wine.

03 Five minutes away is **Italica**, founded in 206 BCE. Don't miss the exquisite bird and planetarium mosaics – seven planetary gods representing the days of the week.

01 Before leaving Hispalis (Seville), visit **Antiquarium**, under the Setas, a small museum with remains of Roman dwellings in situ. You can also see fish-salting tanks.

02 For context, **Cotidiana Vitae visitor centre** in Santiponce explains about daily life for the Romans. In a recreated house and inn, you can see what they ate and where they shopped and bathed.

Cazalla de la Sierra
Las Navas de la Concepción
Constantina
Sierra Morena
El Pedroso
Lora del Río
Palma del Río
Cantillana
Río Guadalquivir
Écija
Aznalcollar
Alcalá del Río
Santiponce
Sanlúcar la Mayor
Seville
Carmona
El Viso del Alcor
Alcalá de Guadaira
Marchena
Arahal
Dos Hermanas
Utrera
Morón de la Frontera
Puerto Serrano
Villamartín
Arcos de la Frontera
El Bosque
Ronda

0   20 km
0   10 miles

JUAN CARLOS MUÑOZ / ALAMY STOCK PHOTO ©; CAROL DI RIENZO CORNWELL/ALAMY STOCK PHOTO ©

04 River **RUN**

WATER SPORTS | BRIDGES | NATURE

Río Guadalquivir has played a key role in Seville's fortunes since Roman times – the wealth-laden ships that returned from the New World in the Golden Age arrived along this waterway, docking at the port near the Torre del Oro. Paddle along its calm waters for an alternative perspective or explore its plant-filled banks on two wheels.

Above The Torre del Oro on the Río Guadalquivir.
Left Puente Isabel II.

TRAVELERPIX/GETTY IMAGES ©

🏛 How To

Getting here The river is within walking distance of most areas of central Seville.

When to go The air temperature on the water is always cooler, so on hot summer days it's a respite, while in winter it may feel chilly.

Getting around Use two-wheeled transport for exploring the city sustainably: regular or electric bikes, Segways, and regular or electric scooters are great options. You can also book a tour at **Surf The City** (surfthecity.es), **Sevilla Bike Center** (sevillabikecenter.es) *or* **ElecMove** (elecmove. com).

All Aboard

If you want to enjoy the river without other craft to disturb your journey, especially as a beginner, go **paddleboarding at sunset**. The sun gleams pinky-orange across the water, as the breeze gently ripples the surface. You can focus on your surroundings and, literally, go with the flow. Rent from Paddle Surf Sevilla (paddlesurf sevilla.com) or h2go Sevilla (h2gosevilla.com).

The wide river means everyone has their own space and you can stay close to the riverbank. Paddleboarding experience is not necessary; you'll gradually find your balance, learning to move and steer the board with the paddle. Any movement on the water can affect your craft, so when a boat comes along you need to adjust your board accordingly.

Bridge Views

Passing beneath famous bridges is always a thrill, and Seville's oldest one, **Puente Isabel II**, with its iconic cast-iron circles, is no exception. When it is lit up at night, the effect is magical. Look out for wildlife on the river, such as ducks

with their ducklings; on the riverbank, oleanders dazzle with their brilliant pink flowers.

You also get a riverside view of the life-size replica of **Magellan's ship**, *Nao Victoria* (fun dacionnaovictoria.org), which departed from Seville to make the first circumnavigation of the world, returning in 1522.

On Your Bike

With its sunny weather, lack of gradients and 175km network of bike lanes, Seville is an ideal city for cycling. You can follow the river along most of the east bank and part of the west. Start at the Torre del Oro and cycle along the wide promenade for a picturesque view of Calle Betis across the water, with its houses of traditional *albero*-yellow, vivid turquoise and terracotta red. You'll pass Chillida's Monument to (religious) Tolerance sculpture on the left, just before Puente Isabel II. Opposite, in Triana, is the **Castillo de San Jorge** (*visitasevilla.es/ monumentos-y-cultura/castillo-de-san-jorge*)

📖 River of Fortune

The port was located in the Arenal district (*arena* meaning sand) by the Torre del Oro. Ships were built in the Atarazanas Reales, the Royal Shipyards next to the Hospital de Caridad; the 13th-century building is being converted into a cultural centre. Río Guadalquivir brought Seville untold wealth, thanks to the city's monopoly on trade from the Americas, making it one of Europe's richest cities. But the river also caused a dramatic reversal of fortune. By 1717, ships could no longer navigate its waters due to silting and Cádiz took on the mantle of main port, while Seville declined in both status and splendour.

⛵ Canal Dreams

The waterway that passes through central Seville is the **Alfonso XIII canal**, which ends beyond the Puente Alamillo. The actual river was rerouted for Expo '92 due to persistent flooding in the city. The canal is wide and largely straight, with no current, making it ideal for water sports.

which houses a museum about the Inquisition.

Cross the river at the next bridge, Cristo de la Expiración, and after Torre Sevilla you'll find yourself in the jungly **Jardín Americano**, dating from Expo '92, with fishtail palms and prickly pear; the cycle lane is bordered by huge purple bougainvillea.

After leaving this garden, the cycle path takes you along a riverbank lined with elm and poplar, and under the **Puente Barqueta**. On the next section, don't miss the viewing platforms over the river.

Park Life

If you're still riding, you'll soon enter the **Parque Alamillo** (juntadeandalucia.es/avra/parque-alamillo). At 120 hectares, it's the city's largest park and has willow-fringed lakes and streams; look out for bitterns, and hoopoes with their distinctive black and white tails. Stop at an outdoor cafe for a well-earned *refresco*, then follow the snaky path high up onto the **Puente Alamillo**, with wonderful views back down the river, and return along the riverside Calle Rey Juan Carlos I. Reward yourself with a *tinto de verano* at **Embarcadero** bar, hidden away on Calle Betís.

Left Replica of the Nao Victoria.
Top Alfonso XIII Canal. **Above** Castillo de San Jorge.

THE FERIA
de Abril

01 Portada
The Feria entrance gate, with a new design chosen each year. Lit up spectacularly at midnight on Saturday (the *alumbrao*).

02 Caseta
Families, groups of friends and companies entertain guests in these striped tents, complete with bar – there are 1000-plus in total.

03 Farolillos
Orange and white paper lanterns strung along the sandy pavements, illuminated by 200,000-odd bulbs at night.

04 Pescaito frito
A dish of fried fish – crispy battered hake, small sole, anchovies and calamari – traditionally eaten on Saturday night.

05 Traje de flamenca
Tightly fitted over bust and hips, with a ruffled skirt, flamenca dress cut and colour trends that change annually.

06 Sevillanas
Performed in pairs at the Feria, this was designed as a courting dance, with plenty of flirtatious glances over the shoulder.

Distrito Norte

Macarena

Este-Alcosa-Torreblanca

Triana Casco Antiguo San Pablo-Santa Justa

Nervión Cerro-Amate

Distrito Sur

Los Remedios

Bellavista-La Palmera

07 Rebujito
A mix of dry Manzanilla sherry and lemonade, served in a jug with ice and drunk from small glasses.

08 Calle del Infierno
Funfair next to the *casetas* with bumper cars, big wheels and waffle stands; very popular with children and teenagers.

09 Albero
The yellow sand on the Feria ground pavements, which turns muddy when it rains (as often happens in April in Seville).

10 Recinto or Real de la Feria
The area in Los Remedios district where the Feria takes place. It covers 275,000 sq metres and has 15 streets named after bullfighters.

11 Paseo de Caballos
The procession of gleaming carriages and elegant horse riders, with women riding side-saddle, that parades around the Feria every afternoon.

05 Flamenco **RHYTHMS**

CULTURE | FLAMENCO | ARTS

▬▬ Few art forms encapsulate Seville like flamenco. The *baile* (dance), *cante* (singing) and *toque* (guitar) convey all the extremes of raw emotion that you expect in the fiery southern city of Seville: joy, pain and grief, enacted with mesmerising technical brilliance. Flamenco swirls around you seductively, but also grabs you by the throat. It is strong yet delicate and not easily forgotten.

📱 How To

Getting there You can see flamenco at *tablaos* (shows) and *peñas* (clubs) in Seville. Avoid those where you eat and ideally buy your ticket in advance.

When to see it Flamenco shows are available most of the year, although some venues may close for July or August; call ahead.

Top tip Some shows, like **Flamenco Esencia** in Triana (flamenco-esencia.com), provide an explanation in English. Also check out the excellent **Museo del Baile Flamenco** (museodelbaileflamenco.com).

Map showing: ISLA DE LA CARTUJA, Río Guadalquivir, La Peña Flamenca Torre Macarena, MACARENA, Casa de la Memoria, Plaza de la Encarnación, EL CENTRO, Plaza Nueva, Museo del Baile Flamenco, EL ARENAL, La Casa del Flamenco, Flamenco Esencia, Teatro Flamenco Triana, Jardines de Murillo, TRIANA, Plaza de España. Scale: 500 m / 0.25 miles

Flamenco Origins

Flamenco was probably brought from India by gypsies around the 14th century; they arrived in Seville 200 years later, living outside the city walls. Today, the art form incorporates elements of Andalucian folk songs, as well as Arabic, Sephardic-Jewish, African and gypsy music, an authentic melting pot revealing the cultural influences within Seville.

Declared **UNESCO Intangible Heritage of Humanity** in 2010, flamenco is performed around the world, but its spirit lives in Seville.

Watching a Show

Ta-taka-tak... A flamenco performance starts with the dancer tapping their foot on the wooden stage. The guitarist keeps pace, as the *bailaor/a* builds up speed to a crescendo of sound, movement and emotion, spinning on a penny with their arms

𝒦 Best Flamenco Shows

La Casa del Flamenco A typical Sevillan patio with seats around the stage and three daily performances – go for the second one, when the performers are warmed up but not tired.

La Peña Flamenca Torre Macarena A flamenco association with a beautiful outdoor patio and high-quality, authentic performances on Wednesday and Friday.

Teatro Flamenco Triana An intimate theatre with the performers on a curtained stage. The artistes are top-notch.

La Casa de la Memoria Good performers, although the visibility is not ideal. The museum upstairs (under refurbishment at time of publication) has antique dresses, hand-painted fans, shawls, castanets and paintings.

gracefully curved above their head.

Most shows in Seville have a singer, two dancers and a guitarist. While one is performing, the others will clap along (known as *palmas*) to keep the rhythm, at a velocity to make your head spin; they will also shout '*Óle!*'.

During a show, you will see just a few of the many *palos* (styles) of flamenco; *alegrías* are happy, while *soleás* (loneliness) are sad. That's why you need to watch the dancers' faces – while the lightning-fast feet are astonishingly impressive, it's the facial and hand expressions that portray the centuries-long delight and suffering.

■ **Recommended by Eva Izquierdo**, *flamenco teacher specialising in beginners @ishowusevilla*

Above La Casa del Flamenco.

06 Moorish SEVILLE

HISTORY | ARCHITECTURE | CULTURE

In 711 CE, the Moors arrived from North Africa and successive dynasties ruled Isbyllia (Seville) until the mid-13th century, culminating with the Almohads. Follow the Moorish legacy in Seville, from the mighty fortified city walls to the emblematic Giralda minaret/bell tower.

🗺 Trip Notes

Getting around You can easily walk from the centre to most sites, although the Macarena city walls are a little further – catch the C3 circular bus from Puerta Jerez or the C4 from Juzgados (next to Prado de San Sebastián).

Entry Tickets are needed for the Alcázar and the Catedral and can be booked online in advance. The Catedral ticket includes access to Iglesia Colegial del Divino Salvador church (known as El Salvador). Torre del Oro admission can be bought at the door.

🏛 Tracing History

Follow the route of the **old defensive walls**. From the Torre del Oro, take Pasaje José María del Rey to Torre de Plata, through the Postigo del Carbón, onto Calle Santander, past Torre Abdel Aziz to the Alcázar.

For a taste reminiscent of Moorish sweets, try the *alfajores* from **Convento Santa Paula**.

■ **By Claudia Dobler**, *official tourist guide*, @claudiadoblersevilla

02 The cathedral's belltower, the **Giralda** with its horseshoe arches and geometric latticework, was formerly a minaret. Walk among the courtyard's orange trees where the faithful once washed before praying at the-then Aljama mosque.

03 Tuck into tapas at **Bar Giralda**, beneath beautiful 12th-century Moorish painted walls and ceilings, discovered in this former hammam during restoration work in 2020. They are the only such decorated Arab baths on the Iberian Peninsula.

04 Walk along the impressive 400m section of crenelated **Muralla** (city walls) by the Macarena gate, complete with entrances and guard towers. The walls originally had around 15 gates; you can still see four.

C Alemanes

C San José

C Abadés

Plaza Virgen de los Reyes

C Mateos Gago

BARRIO DE SANTA CRUZ

Av de la Constitución

Plaza del Triunfo

Patio de las Banderas

C Santo Tomás

C Miguel de Mañara

EL ARENAL

Paseo de Cristóbal Colón

Alcázar Gardens

Jardines de Murillo

C Almirante Lobo

Puerta de Jerez

Río Guadalquivir

Av de Roma

Puente de San Telmo

01 While most of the **Real Alcázar** dates from the 14th century onwards, the Patio del Yeso was built by Mudéjar craftsmen and retains exquisite Almohad plasterwork.

05 The dodecagonal riverfront **Torre del Oro** (pictured left), now a naval museum, may owe its name to its gleaming exterior or gold stored inside. Climb up for panoramic city and river views.

Prado de San Sebastián

07 Bitter
SWEET

FOOD | LOCAL PRODUCE | FARMS

▬▬▬ Even if you're not a fan of marmalade, you'll have heard of Seville oranges – and when you come to the city, you'll see the trees lending much-needed shade in almost every street. At Christmas, their fruit stands out like bright orbs against the green leaves and a few months later the city is bathed in their heady fragrance.

KIRK FISHER/SHUTTERSTOCK ©

🗺 How To

Getting here You can see and smell orange trees all over Seville. Take the 1260/M126 bus to Mairena El Alcor from San Bernardo.

When to go Bitter oranges are picked in January. Orange blossom comes out in early spring (February/March).

Local producers Try **Caprichos del Gua-**

dalquivir (caprichos delguadalquivir.com), **Obrador Valle de la Osa** (facebook.com/Obrador ValleDeLaOsa) and **La Golosa** marmalade or buy direct at **Convento Santa Paula** (santapaula.es). Get Seville orange pastries, drinks and Benditaluz body lotions at **Orange Tree** (orangetreesevilla. com).

MIRIAM HEPPELL/ALAMY STOCK PHOTO ©

Left Orange trees, Alcázar.
Bottom left Seville oranges.

Fragrant Streets

Although Seville is famous for its 50,000 orange trees, the aromatic bitter fruit and the sweet scent of *azahar* (orange blossom) that pervades the city in spring, *naranjas amargas* (bitter oranges) aren't popularly consumed here. In fact, Paddington Bear's favourite sandwich ingredient was invented in Scotland.

The Moors first brought orange trees to Isbyllia (Seville). Enjoy the fruits of their labour as you stroll through beautiful outdoor spaces cooled by pools and fountains and lined with citrus trees at the **Alcázar** and **Jardines de la Buhaira**, as well as the patios of former mosques, two of which remain today as the **Catedral** and **Iglesia Colegial del Divino Salvador**.

Pithing Off

Small, aromatic and with a thick layer of pith, these *citrus aurantium* oranges look completely different from the sweet varieties like navel and salustiana. In January, the ripe fruit grown on farms is picked and sent to England, France and other countries. However, in the city streets, many oranges are left on the pavements.

On the Farm

You can visit family-run organic orange farms in the town of **Mairena del Alcor**, east of Seville. The lower Guadalquivir valley offers the ideal conditions: sandy, phosphorus-rich soil, plenty of sun, cool winters and hot summers. At **Huerta Ave María** (huertaavemaria.com), supplier to UK supermarket Waitrose, walk through the orange grove and learn about caring for the trees and then taste the homemade marmalade. **Gospa Citrus** (gospacitrus.com) offers cooking workshops.

Clean, Green, Orange Power

Oranges are so supercharged, they can even generate power. A pilot scheme to produce electricity sustainably from the 5.7 million kilos of unwanted bitter oranges left on Seville's streets was launched in 2021 by Emasesa, the municipal water company.

From 1000kg of fruit, 500kg of peel and 500L of juice are extracted. The citrus liquid is fermented to produce methane, which powers a water purification plant. According to Emasesa, a tonne (1000kg) of fruit generates 50kW of energy, the equivalent of what five homes would consume in one day. A neat way to recycle waste fruit and produce clean energy.

08 Tapping into **TAPAS**

TAPAS | WINE | COOKING

Seville is where the tapa (a small plate of savoury food was invented. Whether it's simple fried *boquerones* (anchovies), a plate of sliced *jamón ibérico*, prawns with chilli and garlic, or an exquisitely plated creation of *mojama* (dried tuna), watermelon and Payoyo cheese, this is the place to spoil your taste buds!

🗺 How To

Getting here You won't have to walk far to find a tapas bar, whether a tourist joint or a local haunt. Good areas to *tapear* (go on a tapas crawl) are Calle Mateos Gago, the Arenal around Calle Gamazo and Arenas, Plaza Alfalfa, Calle Feria including the market, and the Alameda de Hércules.

When to go Lunchtime is around 2pm, dinner around 9pm.

Eat with a local Take a tapas tour with **A Question of Taste** (*aqot. com*) or **Sevilla Tapas** (sevilla-tapas.com).

How to Tapear

Traditionally, you go elbow to elbow with the locals standing at the bar, but you can also sit down at a small table. Order from the menu, which could be a sheet, chalkboard or QR code; prices for a tapa range from around €2.50 to €6. Share a table-full of tapas without looking greedy – if your friend's *solomillo al whisky* (pork loin in garlic and whisky sauce) is mouth-wateringly tasty, order one for yourself. Be aware that in some bars you can only order large dishes, not tapas, on the terrace.

Make Your Own

If you want to try your hand at making tapas in a bustling market atmosphere,

Aove left Casa Morales (p69).
Left Taller Andaluz de Cocina (p68).
Above Calle Mateos Gago.

Taller Andaluz de Cocina (tallerandaluz decocina.com) in Triana market will have you producing two Andalucian classics (both vegan-friendly too): *salmorejo* and chickpeas with spinach. It also offers market tours and tastings, where you try *jamón ibérico* and other cold meats, cheese, olives, pastries and seasonal local fruit such as chirimoya (custard apple).

Perfect Pairing

What to pair with your tapa? Northern Seville province has produced wine for centuries – Emperor Carlos V insisted on Cazalla wine at his wedding. **Colonias de Galeón** (colonias degaleon.com) uses different blends of grape varieties each season to fit the wine's character (Soplagaitas is a fresh, fruity chardonnay/viogner); its shop is near Plaza Nueva. **Tierra Savia** (bodegastierrasavia.com) ferments

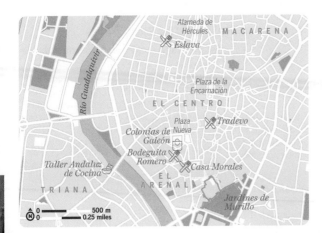

Left Bodeguita Romero.
Below Eslava.

and ages its zaranda viejo tempranillo in antique *tinajas* (clay jars) and also uses native varieties like mollar.

Seville's Top Tapas Bars

Casa Morales A stone's throw from the cathedral and with 170 years of family tradition, this essential tapas experience offers rustic charm, friendly service and great food.

Bodeguita Romero The *montadito de pringá* (pork roll) and marinated potatoes are recognised as the best in Seville, but everything is great at this third-generation family-run bar.

Eslava Seville's original innovative tapas bar. From the popular honey pork ribs to the award-winning 'Becquer's cigar', the focus is on quality ingredients and excellent service.

Tradevo Tradition and evolution. Expect delicious modern takes on classic Mediterranean cooking, such as avocado and prawn 'cannelloni', from one of the best kitchen teams in Seville.

■ **"Seville's Top Tapas Bars" recommended by Shawn Hennessey**, *food and wine writer and Sherry Educator*
@sevillatapas

Listings

BEST OF THE REST

Astonishing Interiors

Catedral & Giralda

The largest Gothic cathedral in the world, this vast edifice houses a stunning gold altarpiece, masterpieces by Murillo and Goya, Columbus' tomb and a former minaret that you can climb.

Casa de Pilatos

With exquisite tiles and *artesonado* wooden ceilings, this Gothic-Mudéjar-Renaissance palace is home to the Dukes of Medinaceli. It was partly inspired by Don Fadrique's trip to Jerusalem in 1519.

Palacio de las Dueñas

The Duquesa de Alba was Spain's best-known aristocrat; she adored Semana Santa, Feria and bullfighting. See her personal mementoes as well as art and furniture in this majestic yet intimate palace.

Museo de Bellas Artes

Formerly the Convent of the Orden de la Merced, this museum houses outstanding works from Seville's 17th-century Golden Age. Look out for Murillo's vast *Inmaculada Concepción* and Zubaran's sumptuous saints.

Monasterio de Santa María de las Cuevas-Centro Andaluz de Arte Contemporáneo

Popularly known as La Cartuja, this former Carthusian monastery hosted Columbus before his second voyage, then became an English-owned ceramics factory (the prestigious brand still exists). It is now a contemporary arts centre.

Iglesia de Santa Catalina

This beautifully eclectic 13th-century church has a Gothic facade from another temple covering the original Mudéjar door. Blink at the blingy baroque chapel by Leonardo de Figueroa, then climb the brick bell tower.

Good for Kids

Espacio Primera Vuelta al Mundo/Nao Victoria

Climb aboard this replica of Magellan's ship, which completed the first circumnavigation of the world in 1519–22. A compact but informative visitor centre tells of challenges and dangers on the voyage.

Pabellón de Navegación

Get the feel of life at sea in a light display that mimics sailing on a wide ocean. Smells, sounds and stories of life aboard are fun, while ship-themed video games will obviously delight.

Acuario de Sevilla

Complementing the marine theme, the aquarium is comparatively small, but its 7000 specimens of 400 species still appeal. The hypnotic Sala de Medusas (Jellyfish Room) will delight all ages.

CaixaForum

This superb arts centre puts on world-class exhibitions, each with fun, tailored, hands-on children's activities. The excellent shop has gorgeous creative books, toys and gifts.

Isla Mágica

For a full day out of white-knuckle rides, as well as swimming in Agua Mágica's pools – especially during Seville's sweltering summer – this theme park is a good bet.

Isla Mágica

Artisanal Shops

Tentiles

Choose pretty, practical pieces with medieval Sevillano tile designs and colourful modern graphic prints, including charger plates, trays and tea towels at this shop on Calle Jesús del Gran Poder.

Juan Foronda

Since 1923 this Seville institution, whose main branch is on Calle Sierpes, has been supplying traditional Feria items to *sevillanos*. Choose from simple fans to hand-embroidered silk fringed manila shawls.

La Oleoteca

In this Arenal shop, you can try and buy premium Andalucian extra virgin olive oils such as Oro Bailén and Castillo de Canena. Try the latter's *arbequina* finished in sherry butts.

Inés Rosales

As well as olive oil biscuits, this shop on Plaza San Francisco is brimming with local goodies, such as elderflower and orange gin from Carmona and convent pastries from Constantina.

Outdoor craft markets

Every weekend you can browse handicrafts at Triana's Paseo de Arte market, while the Zoco in Parque María Luisa (third Sunday) tempts with everything from crocheted bags to handmade jewellery.

Outstanding Eateries

Palo Cortao €

Tuck into creative tapas and more than 30 sherries at this small restaurant with a quiet terrace near Plaza Cristo de Burgos. Friendly and knowledgeable service; ask for the daily specials.

Basque €€€

Three-Michelin-starred Eneko Atza produces sophisticated, strong flavours: the tuna tartare tartlet is a standout. With refined yet warm service and intimate curved booths, this is one of the city's best.

La Cochera del Abuelo €€

The Arzak-trained chef of this award-winning homey bistro in San Lorenzo, with wood-fired grill and attentive service, eschews fusion and fads, focusing instead on prime ingredients: Andalucian venison, Iberian pork and sea bass.

Cañabota €€€

Winning a Michelin star in 2022, to no one's surprise, this temple to fish and seafood has tasting menus starting at €90. The tapas bar next door is similarly impressive.

T Espacio Gastronómico €€

An offshoot of the slow food movement standard-bearer, ConTenedor in Macarena, this place features a single communal semi-circular table and the famous duck rice, as well as scallop and veggie versions.

Condende €

Inside Feria market, this lively bar-stall specialises in pastries, from South American *pao de queijo* and Venezuelan *arepas* to Japanese gyozas and Indian samosas, with fillings to suit all tastes.

Casa Ozama €€

Eating outside at this elegant modernist villa with a bougainvillea and jasmine-filled garden in El Porvenir is a joy. Everything on the menu is good, but service can be slow. Over-18s only.

El Disparate €€

With terrace tables on the buzzing Alameda, this place serves contemporary Mediterranean fare like tomato, watermelon, smoked sardine and basil salad, or lamb kofta with houmus and eggplant.

 Scan to find more things to do in Seville online

HUELVA

ADVENTURE | MOUNTAINS | FOOD

Experience
Huelva
online

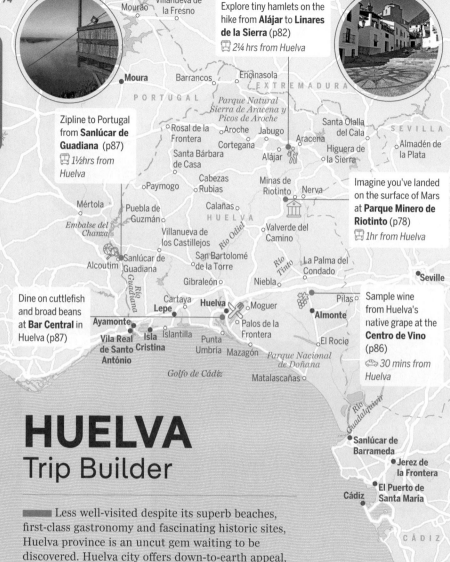

Explore tiny hamlets on the hike from **Alájar** to **Linares de la Sierra** (p82)

🚶 2¼ hrs from Huelva

Zipline to Portugal from **Sanlúcar de Guadiana** (p87)

🚍 1½ hrs from Huelva

Imagine you've landed on the surface of Mars at **Parque Minero de Riotinto** (p78)

🚍 1hr from Huelva

Dine on cuttlefish and broad beans at **Bar Central** in Huelva (p87)

Sample wine from Huelva's native grape at the **Centro de Vino** (p86)

🚗 30 mins from Huelva

PORTUGAL

EXTREMADURA

Parque Natural Sierra de Aracena y Picos de Aroche

SEVILLA

HUELVA

Mourão
Villanueva de la Fresno
Moura
Barrancos
Encinasola
Rosal de la Frontera
Aroche
Jabugo
Aracena
Santa Olalla del Cala
Almadén de la Plata
Cortegana
Higuera de la Sierra
Santa Bárbara de Casa
Alájar
Paymogo
Cabezas Rubias
Minas de Riotinto
Nerva
Mértola
Puebla de Guzmán
Calañas
Embalse del Chanza
Villanueva de los Castillejos
Valverde del Camino
Alcoutim
Sanlúcar de Guadiana
San Bartolomé de la Torre
La Palma del Condado
Gibraleón
Niebla
Seville
Cartaya
Pilas
Lepe
Huelva
Moguer
Almonte
Ayamonte
Islantilla
Palos de la Frontera
Vila Real de Santo António
Isla Cristina
Punta Umbría
Mazagón
El Rocío
Parque Nacional de Doñana
Matalascañas

Golfo de Cádiz

Río Guadiana
Río Odiel
Río Tinto
Río Guadalquivir

Sanlúcar de Barrameda

Jerez de la Frontera

El Puerto de Santa María

Cádiz

CÁDIZ

HUELVA
Trip Builder

Less well-visited despite its superb beaches, first-class gastronomy and fascinating historic sites, Huelva province is an uncut gem waiting to be discovered. Huelva city offers down-to-earth appeal, while hill villages have unspoiled charm and cultural heritage in bucketloads.

Atlantic Ocean

0 — 20 km
0 — 10 miles
Ⓝ

Practicalities

ARRIVING

The bus and train stations in Huelva city are both centrally located; high-speed trains go to Madrid via Córdoba. The nearest airport is in Seville, 90 minutes away by train or up to two hours by bus.

FIND YOUR WAY

Huelva province consists of Parque Nacional de Doñana, the coast, El Condado, El Andevalo, the Cuenca Minera (Mining Area) and the Sierra de Aracena y Picos de Aroche.

MONEY

Make sure you bring cash to the Sierra, as not everywhere accepts cards and ATMs are scarce.

WHERE TO STAY

City/town	Pros/cons
Huelva city	Handy for travel connections. Stylish places are limited.
Aracena	Good base for visiting villages, but you need a car.
Aya-monte	Handy for popping over the border to Portugal. No beach within walking distance.
Mazagón	Lovely long beach; great for families. Hugely crowded in summer.
Punta Umbría	Lively town with several beaches. Beware of parking fines in high season.

EATING & DRINKING

Huelva city is famous for its *chocos* (cuttlefish; pictured top left) – in fact, the natives are known as *choqueros*. The province is renowned for its fabulous gastronomy including free-range pork and *jamón ibérico* from the mountains and superb freshly caught seafood like *gambas blancas* (white prawns) and great wines from El Condado.

Best Iberian pork Arrieros (p85)

Must-try wine Barredero (pictured bottom left)

GETTING AROUND

Bus Nine EMTUSA bus lines cover Huelva city. Buses are also the best way to get around Huelva province, whether climbing up into the mountains or shimmying down the coast. Damas runs services to Palos, Moguer, Matalascañas and Aracena. There are also services from Aracena to the villages of the Sierra.

Train Services link the capital with Jabugo-Galaroza, Almonaster-Cortegana and Palma del Condado.

JAN–MAR	APR–JUN	JUL–SEP	OCT–DEC
Sunny days, cool nights, rainy inland.	Warm with some showers – best time for hiking, with fabulous spring flowers.	Swelteringly hot and dry; beaches are packed. The mountains offer respite.	Mild days; good for mushroom-hunting in the hills.

09 Endangered DOŇANA

WILDLIFE | BIRDWATCHING | BIODIVERSITY

▰▰▰▰ Think safari, but with sand dunes, pine forests and marshes bursting with wildlife. In birdwatchers' paradise Parque Nacional de Doñana, which hosts the largest number of aquatic bird species in Western Europe, you can see flamingos and spoonbills, and, if you're lucky, the endangered Iberian lynx. It's a glimpse of an untouched world, a delicate ecosystem under threat from human development.

SANTIAGO URQUIJO/GETTY IMAGES ©

🗺 How To

Getting here/around
Most tours start in either Matalascañas, El Rocio or El Acebuche Visitor Centre; try donanavisitas. es or donana-nature.com (Damas runs buses to the first two).

When to go Spring is popular, as many birds arrive to breed. Book well in advance and avoid visiting during El Rocio pilgrimage in May/June. In winter, you can see wildfowl migrating south. Be super-vigilant for lynx if driving; over 100 are killed by cars every year.

RAMN CARRETERO/EYEEM/GETTY IMAGES ©

Far left Wild horses, El Rocío. **Bottom left** Iberian lynx. **Near left** Western swamphen.

Over the Dunes

Visits that depart on or near the coast head along the beach and over the dunes. These are no ordinary sand dunes; they are blown around two to five metres inland every year by the *foreño* (south-westerly wind). You can walk down between the dunes to *corrales*, small valleys where *junca* rushes and pine trees grow until they're enveloped by an advancing dune.

Into the Pines

Keep your eyes peeled in the *coto* (woodland with scrub) and you might spot the endangered Iberian lynx slinking between the mastic bushes; numbers are happily recovering, with more than 100 in the park. In spring, wild boar piglets scamper after their mother; look up for an imperial eagle, with an impressive 2m wingspan.

Watch the Marsh

Covering half of Doñana, the *marismas* (marshlands) host an incredible 360 species of aquatic birdlife – look out for marbled teal, red-crested pochard and brilliant purple swamphen – as well as wild horses. This landscape changes seasonally with islands appearing as the water level drops as the spring rains abate. Groundwater pumping for nearby farms and lower rainfall threaten the unique habitat.

Living in the Park

At **Poblado de la Plancha** on Río Guadalquivir, you can see how people used to live in Doñana in rush-thatched houses called *chozas*. They collected pine nuts, farmed horses and cattle, hunted duck, collected clams, wove baskets and made charcoal.

🏠 El Rocío

One of Spain's biggest pilgrimages, this sees the wild-west village of El Rocío, with sandy streets and wild horses roaming in nearby marshes, fill to bursting with over 100 *hermandades* (brotherhoods), arriving on horseback, in 4WDs, and in pretty ox-drawn wagons. After days of fervent celebrating and praying Andaluz-style in their houses, on early Monday morning the brotherhoods compete to carry the adored 13th-century statue of La Paloma Blanca (the White Dove) to their houses.

El Rocío takes place at Whitsun (seven weeks after Easter) and causes heavy traffic in the area, so it's best avoided then unless you want a close-up look at the action.

10 Mining LIFE

GEOLOGY | LANDSCAPE | HISTORY

Gold, silver and copper have been mined around Río Tinto for more than 5000 years. With similar mineral properties to Mars, the area's surreal rust-coloured terrain and river have been used by NASA to carry out research. Today you can visit vast open-cast mines, ride in a train alongside the 'coloured river' and see the red planet landscape up close.

JOE MCUBED/SHUTTERSTOCK ©

🗺 How To

Getting here Damas buses go to Minas de Riotinto from Plaza de Armas station. Both the Mars on Earth visit and railway ride leave from outside the town.

When to go Open all year round; with little shade or vegetation, in summer it is extremely hot. While written information and tours are largely in Spanish, you can rent an audio guide in English at the museum.

FRANK SANCHEZ/ALAMY STOCK PHOTO ©

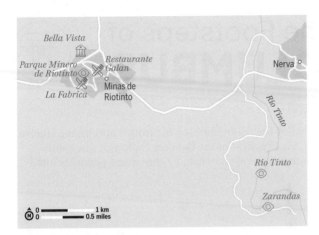

More Ore The 230km-long Iberian Pyrite Belt has yielded metallic mineral riches for millennia. Walls of rock streaked with golden-yellow copper pyrite, and orange and red ores give clues to the millions of tonnes extracted. The **Río Tinto river** is highly acidic and can only support bacteria similar to those possibly existing on Mars, which cause the water's vivid ochre and rust colours.

Ride the Rails At the **Parque Minero de Riotinto**, you can ride in wooden train carriages along a 19th-century railway line, built by the British to transport the ores to Huelva city's port. The train follows the river through the lunar landscape of bare escarpments, with former stations and rusting locomotives. As well as the excellent museum, the park also includes the colossal **Corta Atalaya** open-cast mine, complete with spiralling railway terraces. Nearby **Restaurante Galan** and **La Fabrica** are good lunch spots.

Life on Mars You can also visit the waste deposit from the copper foundry at **Zarandas**, used for NASA and ESA research. The YEMO exploration rover, SHEE deployable habitat dome and Gandolfi 2 space suit were tested here; you can see replicas, before following a short wooden boardwalk through the red landscape.

British Influence In addition to modern mining techniques, the British Río Tinto Company introduced golf and football to Spain. A Victorian house in **Bella Vista**, the *barrio inglés* (English neighbourhood), furnished in period style, shows how a family would have lived, complete with jars of Twinings tea and a tricycle.

Left Mines, Río Tinto. **Bottom left** Parque Minero de Riotinto.

El Año de los Tiros (Year of the Shots)

On 4 February 1888, thousands of striking miners held a demonstration in the town square. Among other demands, such as improved pay and shorter working hours, the men wanted the British mining company to stop using *teleras*, open-air calcination of mineral ores (refined by being burned), which produced noxious sulphurous fumes. Scores of protestors, who also included local farmers, were killed by soldiers. *El corazón de la tierra* by Minas de Riotinto native Juan Cobo Wilkins is a novel based on these events; it was also made into a movie.

11 In the Footsteps of
COLUMBUS

HISTORY | SHIPS | CHURCHES

▬▬▬▬ In 1492, Columbus sailed the ocean blue, leaving from a port on the Huelva coast, Palos de la Frontera. Visit replicas of the Genoese explorer's three ships, find out what supplies they carried and see where he stayed and prayed before leaving.

🏞 Trip Notes

Getting here/around The M402 or M403 bus from Huelva city will take you to the **Monumento** (Punta Sebos stop) and then to **La Rabida** monastery, high above the Río Tinto. From there, walk down the hill to **Muelle de las Carabelas**. Continue on the M402/M403 from La Rabida to Palos, and back to Huelva. For Moguer, take the M403. Take the bus 3 to the **Sanctuario** in El Conquero *barrio*.

📖 Controversial Columbus

The topic of Columbus is a divisive one. While he is celebrated in Spain (the day he arrived in the New World, 12 October, is a national holiday), and his elaborate tomb in Seville cathedral is popular with visitors, native peoples across the Americas see the explorer as an exploitative coloniser rather than an audacious visionary.

04 Columbus was highly religious – before sailing from Palos, he is said to have prayed at the **Sanctuario de Nuestra Señora de la Cinta**, 3km north of the city, overlooking the Odiel wetlands.

03 **La Fontanilla** in Palos de la Frontera is the well from which water taken on board was drawn. Two ships, *Pinta* and *Niña*, and their captains, the Pinzon brothers, hailed from the town.

o Huelva

Río Tinto

o Palos de la Frontera

05 This 37m-tall **Monumento a la Fe Descubridora**, of a figure leaning on a cross by American sculptor Gertrude Vanderbilt Whitney, is said to represent either Columbus or a La Rabida monastery friar.

Odiel

La Rabida

02 At the **Muelle de la Carabelas**, you can see how life was during the voyage on board full-sized replicas of the *Pinta*, *Niña* and *Santa María* (pictured opposite), and in the excellent visitor centre.

Isla de Saltes

o Punta Umbria

01 Columbus stayed at **Santa María La Rabida**, the 15th-century hilltop Franciscan monastery, while planning his first voyage – the friars helped him to secure funding from Queen Isabella. Murals depict his departure.

Golfo de Cádiz

12 Through the
CORK OAKS

RURAL SCENES | VILLAGES | HIKING

▰▰▰ Verdant, thickly forested hills of oak and chestnut, streaked with hiking trails and dotted with white towns unchanged over centuries, the Sierra de Aracena y Picos de Aroche is a stunning natural park where you can escape from modern life. Pull on your walking boots, grab your water and head off on a trail.

CONTI MAURO/SHUTTERSTOCK ©

🗺 **How To**

Getting here Damas runs buses from Huelva to Aracena, and then a daily service to Linares and Alájar. It's worth hiring a car to stop for breathtaking views and to visit out-of-the-way villages and hamlets. Note that the A470 from Aracena to Linares Alájar is very narrow and windy; the N433 is faster but less scenic.

When to go Spring wildflowers are a sheer delight; autumn is pleasantly mild.

JOSERPIZARRO/SHUTTERSTOCK ©

Left Alájar. **Bottom left** Hiking, Sierra de Aracena y Picos de Aroche.

A Different Pace

Life moves slowly in the Sierra de Aracena. Roads are serpentine but spectacular, and most villages are best navigated on foot. If you're driving, leave your car near the village entrance and walk down the steep, narrow, twisty cobbled streets and into an earlier era. In **Linares de la Sierra**, look out for the *llanos*, intricate mosaic designs in white and black pebbles on the floor outside houses.

Walk On By

Well-signposted trails lead from one village to the next – head out of **Alájar** east on the PR-A434, forking left to follow a high path with spectacular views called **El Caracol** (4.3km). Then turn right down to **Los Madroñeros**, a tiny hamlet of white houses with just five residents, or alternatively continue to **Linares** (9.7km total loop). Return to Alájar between ancient drystone walls looking onto the **Corchero Valley**. For an easy stroll, head west from Alájar on the **Camino de los Molinos** (3.3km), a flat trail along the Río Alájar, past old watermills.

Nature's Bounty

Foragers will delight in picking mushrooms from September to May – the most prized is the orange-capped *tana*, or Caesar's mushroom. In spring, the landscape is tinged pink with peonies and rockrose – also spot the white variety (gum rockrose), with red landing pad spots on the petals for insect pollinators. Look up and listen for woodpeckers and exquisitely-hued bee-eaters and golden orioles.

⚜ Most Unusual Festivals

Almonaster La Real is renowned for its *fandango*, a folkloric flamenco song and dance performed at the **Cruces de Mayo** (flower-festooned crosses) festival in early May.

On 7 September, the townsfolk of Alájar commemorate the transfer of ownership of the hilltop Peña de Arias Montano from church to village in the **El Poleo** horseback pilgrimage.

Olive branches skewered with dried sweet chestnut leaves create homemade sparklers, or *rehiletes*, which are lit from bonfires at **La Pura** festival in Aracena on 7 December.

Belenes vivientes are scenes from the nativity story enacted by costumed villagers, along with animals, on weekends before Christmas.

■ By Lucy Arkwright and Angel Millán, *owners of eco-hotel Posada San Marcos in Alájar, @posadasanmarcos*

13 Jamón
JAMÓN

TRADITION | GASTRONOMY | WILDLIFE

Considered by many to be the finest ham in the world, *jamón ibérico de bellota* comes from Spanish acorn-fed purebred pigs that graze freely in the Sierra de Aracena. Small, athletic and perfectly adapted to the terrain, their cured legs can be seen hanging in good bars all over Andalucia.

JESUS SIERRA/GETTY IMAGES ©

🗺 How To

Getting here Jabugo is ham central; take a Damas bus to Aracena, then a daily local service to Jabugo, or a train to Jabugo-Galaroza. A car will afford you more flexibility.

When to go Spring and autumn have the most pleasant temperatures – you'll see the porkers in the *dehesa* from late October/early November to March.

MAVV/SHUTTERSTOCK ©

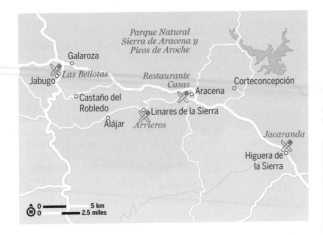

Left *Jamón ibérico de bellota.*
Bottom left Pigs in the *dehesa.*

Home on the Dehesa

The *pata nega* (black-footed) purebred Iberian pig roams free around the *dehesa* (pastureland dotted with oak trees), with more than a soccer pitch of land per animal. With their long snouts, they are closer in DNA to wild boar than white pig breeds. During *la montanera,* the five or so months that these grey porkers spend rooting out *bellotas* (acorns) and other tasty treats, they double their body weight.

Healthy Ham

The melt-in-the-mouth texture and nutty taste of *jamón iberico de bellota,* cured for three years, make it a Spanish national obsession. (*Jamón serrano,* the mountain ham that makes up 93% of Spanish cured ham, is from larger, more intensively farmed white-hoofed pigs.) The glistening ruby-red delicacy is full of oleic acid and omega-6 fatty acids from the acorns, which reduce bad cholesterol.

Balanced Ecosystem

Around the oaks of the *dehesa* – the *encina* (holm or holly oak), with its big, round crown, and the *alcornoque* (cork oak), whose bark is stripped every nine years – you can see lynx, deer, booted eagles and black-winged kites. Look out for jays collecting and storing acorns; those they forget grow into trees, helping to maintain this ancient landscape.

Several ham producers, such as Cinco Jotas (*cincojotas.es*) and Jamones Eíriz Jabugo (*jamoneseiriz.com*), offer tours to meet the pigs, see how the ham is salted and cured, and taste a variety of Iberian cold cuts like *jamón, salchichón* and chorizo.

The Sierra's Best Jamón Ibérico

Las Bellotas In Jabugo, the capital of *jamón ibérico,* and famous for its *carne a la brasa* (grilled meat); also try the *carrillera* (pork cheeks).

Restaurante Casas Terrace tables on a pretty Aracena cobbled street with a stream. The speciality is San Jacobo (breaded and fried ham and cheese).

Arrieros The region's most renowned restaurant; in Linares. Experimental, beautifully plated dishes include pig's tongue and saliva glands with curry.

Jacaranda Located in Higuera de la Sierra, the low-temperature *secreto* (pork skirt) here is sublime, as is the *pistou* (vegetable stew).

■ Recommended by Maria Castro, *communications director,* @cincojotas

Listings

BEST OF THE REST

Beach Life

Flecha del Rompido

This long, narrow spit of sand is as unspoiled as it gets. Take the ferry *(flechamar.es)* from El Rompido across the Río Piedras, then walk across a 200m boardwalk to the pristine beach.

Cuesta Maneli

Located between busy Mazagón and Matalascañas (km39 A494), this wide, cliff-backed beach is accessed via the Asperillo dunes dotted with yellow gorse, and then down wooden steps.

Punta Umbría

Popular with Spanish holidaymakers, this is the closest beach to Huelva city, while still being near the Marismas del Odiel nature reserve. Head to riverfront Avenida de la Ría for fresh seafood.

Matalascañas

It's not the most attractive at first sight, with tower blocks lining the beach, but turn right and you'll find a gloriously empty stretch of sand. Only an hour from Seville.

Huelva City Industrial Heritage

Restored Railway Tracks

Follow the raised final section of the 84km railway, built to transport mineral ores from the Río Tinto mines to the pier. Look out for the magnificent neo-Mudéjar Estacion de Sevilla train station, now sadly abandoned.

Muelle del RíoTinto

At sunset, stroll along this curved 1165m pier stretching out in the Río Odiel, from where 130 million tonnes of minerals were loaded from trains onto ships bound for Britain.

Barrio Reina Victoria

This curious neighbourhood of British-style houses with pitched rooves and front gardens, also known as the Barrio Obrero, was built in 1917 for the mine workers of Río Tinto.

Casa Colón

Huelva prospered massively due to the mines. This grand pink confection, built as a luxury hotel, is now used as a conferences and exhibition centre. The elegant gardens are worth visiting.

Constructed & Natural Wonders

Gruta de la Maravillas

Take a guided tour through these astonishing limestone caverns in Aracena, formed naturally by karstification. Marvel at the other-worldly red, blue and green-tinged stalactites, stalagmites and columns.

Centro de Vino

At this interactive centre in Bollullos Par Del Condado, learn about wine-making in the Condado de Huelva area using the native *zalema* grape. Have a tasting and find out about wineries to visit.

Al-Munastyr Mosque, Almonaster La Real

In this perfectly preserved 10th-century hilltop mosque near the Portuguese border, you can still see the pillared *haram* (prayer hall), *mihrab* (prayer niche) and granite ablutions basin.

Cuesta Maneli

Dolmens

All over Huelva province, you can see these megalithic tombs: in Berrocal, Valverde del Camino and Zalamea Real. The most impressive is the Dolmen del Soto, in Trigueros, with its 21m-long corridor.

Centro de Visitantes La Rocina

Close to El Rocio, this Parque Nacional de Doñana visitor centre has a display of native flora and fauna, and a *choza* (traditional thatched dwelling). Spot birds from a walking trail through pine forests.

Get Active

Wing Foil

Try this thrilling new water sport in El Portil, using a short, wide board with a hydrofoil underneath. The lightweight handheld 'wing' catches any slight breeze, making it easier to jump.

Via Ferrata

Climb on the via ferrata El Morante in Santa Barbara de Casa, with steps and cables fixed into the rock – perfect for all ages and levels of experience.

Cross-border zipline

After shooting down the 720m line over the Río Guadiana to Alcoutim, explore the Portuguese village; then you'll be taken back to Sanlúcar de Guadiana by boat.

Cycling by the Odiel

Hire bikes and follow the 22km cycle lane along the bank of the Río Odiel to Punta Umbría, via La Bota beach and campsite and through the *marismas* (marshland).

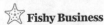 Fishy Business

Finca Alfoliz   €€€

A new rural venture in Aljaraque near Huelva city, by Xanty Elias of Michelin-starred Acanthum. Wood-fired grill is king – Huelva prawns and Iberian pork loin; for veggies, hummus with grilled eggplant.

Dolmen del Soto, Trigueros

Bar Central   €

A no-frills joint with terrace next to Huelva's Mercado del Carmen serving well-priced food including *chocos* (cuttlefish), *habas enzapatás* (broad beans with garlic and herbs) and local sherry-type wine.

Berdigón 14   €

An atmospheric bar in a 15th-century fisherman's house with a pretty patio. Open from breakfast to night-time (late on weekends). Exhibitions, live music and literary events.

Costa Colón €   €€

At this *chiringuito* (beach restaurant) in Mazagón, try a Huelva classic with a twist: cuttlefish meatballs with couscous. Cocktails, live music and DJs get the party vibe going. Rents sunbeds and parasols.

Taberna La Botánica   €€

Tuck into sushi of tender bluefin *almadraba* tuna (sustainably caught) at this charming tavern in seaside El Rompido. Salads are good too; reservations essential on weekends.

El Choco   €€

Try m*ojama* (dried tuna) and *coquinas* (small clams) at this classic town centre restaurant in Mazagón. Prawns are good but pricey. Excellent service and good wine list.

 Scan to find more things to do in Huelva online

CÁDIZ &
GIBRALTAR

WILD | BEACHES | FLAMENCO

Experience
Cádiz &
Gibraltar
online

0 — 20 km
0 — 10 miles

Taste *manzanilla* and tour a bodega in **Sanlúcar de Barrameda** (p94)
🚗 + 🚆 *30min from Jerez*

Río Guadalquivir

Trebujena

Dive into flamenco and sherry at Jerez's lively **tabancos** (p96)
🚗 + 🚆 *15min from Jerez airport*

Golfo de Cádiz

Sanlúcar de Barrameda

Chipiona

Jerez de la Frontera

Uncover the diverse *barrios* of the cheery capital **Cádiz** (p100)
🚗 + 🚆 *30-45min from Jerez*

Rota

El Puerto de Santa María

Bahía de Cádiz

Cádiz

Isla de León

Puerto Real

San Fernando

Chiclana de la Frontera

Sancti Petri

Atlantic Ocean

Conil de la Frontera

CÁDIZ & GIBRALTAR
Trip Builder

Savour the local food scene in **Zahara de los Atunes** (p104)
🚗 *30min from Vejer de la Frontera*

Mainland Spain's soulful southernmost province is a laid-back, unbelievably beautiful Andalucian jewel with an unstoppable food scene, a strong flamenco legacy and one of the county's most magical coastlines. This is a place where drinking in the urban buzz and escaping into wide-open natural spaces go hand in hand.

SEVILLA

Almargen

Lebrija

Soak up the white-town beauty of **Vejer de la Frontera** (p114)
🚗 + 🚌 *50min from Tarifa or Jerez*

Villamartín

Olvera

Algodonales

Embalse de Záhara

Záhara de la Sierra

Hike down gorges or into the mountains in the **Sierra de Grazalema** (p110)
🚗 + 🚌 *1½hr from Cádiz*

Bornos

Embalse de Bornos

El Torreón (1648m)

Grazalema

Arcos de la Frontera

El Bosque

Jedula

Ronda

Benaoján

Río Guadalete

Embalse de Guadalcacín

Ubrique

Parque Natural Sierra de Grazalema

Río Guadiaro

MÁLAGA

CÁDIZ

Cortes de la Frontera

El Aljibe (1091m)

Gaucín

Medina Sidonia

Alcalá de los Gazules

Jimena de la Frontera

Casares

Benalup de Sidonia

Embalse de Barbate

Parque Natural Los Alcornocales

Manilva

Río Barbate

El Palmar

Vejer de la Frontera

Castellar de la Frontera

Guadiaro

Zahora

San Roque

Barbate

Los Barrios

Dig into **Gibraltarian history in the** Upper Rock Nature Reserve (p116)
🚗 *50min from Tarifa*

Los Caños de Meca

Zahara de los Atunes

La Línea de la Concepción

Gibraltar (UK)

Atlanterra

Facinas

Parque Natural del Estrecho

Bahía de Algeciras

Algeciras

Bolonia

Pelayo

Parque Natural del Estrecho

Fall under the Costa de la Luz's spell on secluded **Playa del Cañuelo** (p102)
🚗 + 🚶 *30min from Tarifa*

Tarifa

Go kitesurfing, kayaking, paddleboarding and more in **Tarifa** (p102)
🚗 + 🚌 *1¼hr from Cádiz*

Wander around ancient Roman ruins at **Baelo Claudia** (p108)
🚗 *20min from Tarifa*

Strait of Gibraltar

MOROCCO

Mediterranean Sea

Practicalities

NIGEL JARVIS/SHUTTERSTOCK ©

ARRIVING

Aeropuerto de Jerez The province's only airport, with trains to/from the city centre and bus station (from €1.40), as well as Cádiz (from €3.90, 35 to 50 minutes) and El Puerto de Santa María (from €1.70, 10 to 18 minutes). Taxis cost €15 to the centre.

Gibraltar and other airports Gibraltar airport (pictured) is a good option for southern Cádiz province; a five-minute walk leads across the Spanish border into La Línea de la Concepción for onward bus services. Seville and Málaga airports are also useful for Cádiz province, with good transport links.

HOW MUCH FOR A

Tortilla de camarón tapa €1.50

Glass of sherry €2

City walking tour from €12

GETTING AROUND

Train Renfe services link Cádiz with El Puerto de Santa María, Jerez, Jerez airport and on to Seville, with tickets starting from €1.40 for a quick hop on a *cercanía* service.

Bus and boat Buses cover most destinations at affordable prices; the main companies are Comes (tgcomes.es), Damas (damas-sa. es), Monbus (monbus.es) and CMTBC (cmtbc.es). CMYBC also runs frequent catamarans between Cádiz and El Puerto de Sana María.

Car For maximum flexibility, hire your own wheels. There are rental outlets at Jerez airport; rates vary hugely and it's wise to book well ahead.

WHEN TO GO

MAR–JUN
Excellent springtime hiking; tuna/*almadraba* festivals; warmer climate

JUL–AUG
Peak beach season (book everything ahead!), whale-spotting, local fiestas

SEP–OCT
Warm weather, fewer crowds, grape harvest, hiking – a great time to visit

NOV–FEB
Some places close/reduce hours over winter – a quieter, cooler, more affordable season

TOP: JOSE Y YO ESTUDIO/SHUTTERSTOCK ©
BOTTOM: JOSE Y YO ESTUDIO/SHUTTERSTOCK ©

EATING & DRINKING

Cádiz's lively food scene has grown into one of Andalucía's unmissable highlights, with cooking fuelled by the freshest local produce – from wild *almadraba* tuna and smooth artisanal cheeses to unique sherries and delicate spices inherited from Spain's time under Moorish rule. Fuss-free seafood *chiringuitos* (beach bars) and family-owned tapas bars rub shoulders with creative Michelin-starred addresses, each as seductive as the next. There are countless regional dishes to tempt you: start with a glass of crisp *manzanilla* paired with a just-fried *tortillita de camarones* (prawn fritter; pictured bottom right) in Sanlúcar de Barrameda.

Best winery Bodegas Tradición, Jerez (p95; pictured top right)

Must-try tapas El Lola, Tarifa (p106)

CONNECT & FIND YOUR WAY

Wi-fi Pretty much everywhere has wi-fi, including hotels, cafes, restaurants, tourist offices and so on. Cádiz city has its own free wi-fi network *(wifi.cadiz.es)*.

Navigation Resist the urge to follow driving-navigation apps into narrow-laned city centres and tiny village streets; it's better to park and walk a few minutes.

WHERE TO STAY

The main decision is between city, beach or mountains – or a few nights in each! Summer along the Costa de la Luz is particularly expensive.

Place	Pro/Con
Cádiz	Fabulous food, nightlife, shopping, sights and galleries; good transport links
Tarifa	Perfect for beaches/water sports; good shopping, dining and nightlife; original hotels; near Gibraltar airport
Vejer de la Frontera	Beautiful boutique hotels; great food scene; very busy in July/August; limited public transport
Jerez	Main transport hub with airport; flamenco; nightlife; sherry scene; limited accommodation
Sierra de Grazalema	Best for outdoors lovers; small country hotels in white villages; limited public transport
Sanlúcar de Barrameda	Laid-back vibe; best for Parque Nacional de Doñana; small boutique hotels; outstanding gastronomy

MUSEUM MONDAYS

Most Spanish museums close on Mondays, so it's best to double-check opening hours in advance.

MONEY

It's worth carrying a few euros in cash as some smaller restaurants and shops don't take card payments. To reduce costs, sidestep the summer season, when accommodation prices skyrocket.

14 Sherry WORLD

WINE | FOOD | ARCHITECTURE

Discover a wine made nowhere else on earth on this adventure around Cádiz's fabled Sherry Triangle, which centres on ancient Jerez de la Frontera and its lively neighbours Sanlúcar de Barrameda and El Puerto de Santa María. From sipping sherries as the sun sinks over the vines to soaking up flamenco fervour at a classic *tabanco* (sherry tavern), the local sherry scene reveals the province's soul.

JG JONES/SHUTTERSTOCK ©

🗺 How To

Getting here/around It's easy to hop between the sherry towns, and many bodegas sit in the town centres. Jerez has its own airport, plus good train and/or bus connections. For El Puerto de Santa María, there are trains and buses. Only buses serve Sanlúcar.

When to go The vineyards look most spectacular in July and August with vines blooming (though it's hot). September is grape-harvest time. Visit off-season (November to February) for quieter tours.

CARON BADKIN/SHUTTERSTOCK ©

Left Las Banderillas. **Bottom left** Bodega Hidalgo-La Gitana.

Tours & Tastings Explore local bodegas, where calming hidden patios and lush gardens lead to cathedral-like halls stacked with three-tiered rows of barrels. Beyond introductory tours there's a whole world of unique experiences: a sunset sherry-tasting out in a vineyard at Sanlúcar's **Bodega Hidalgo-La Gitana**; an after-dark bodega visit with wine-sampling at El Puerto's **Bodegas Gutiérrez-Colosía**; or the magical combination of a spectacular Spanish art collection with VORS wines at Jerez's **Bodegas Tradición**.

Tabanco Time Flamenco, sherry and tapas collide in Jerez's *tabancos*: traditional 20th-century taverns that have recently been revived by ambitious new owners. Savour a *palo cortado* or a *fino* with some *payoyo* goat's cheese at locally loved *tabancos* **El Pasaje**, **Plateros** and **Las Banderillas**.

Stay Overnight Jerez's celebrated **Bodegas González-Byass** has transformed a 19th-century building within its grounds into the romantic **Hotel Bodega Tio Pepe** (tiopepe.com), the world's first 'sherry hotel', a luxe hideaway with a dreamy rooftop pool. During summer, the bodega's gorgeous gardens host **pop-up restaurants** in collaboration with some of the province's top chefs.

Wine Festivals Sanlúcar throws its own *manzanilla*-fuelled fiesta each May, while El Puerto celebrates sherry with its April/May **Fiestas del Vino Fino**. Jerez's September **Fiestas de la Vendimia** combine flamenco, sherry and the start of the harvest; catch the first treading of the grapes on the cathedral's steps.

🍷 Sherry Secrets

Sherry is a wine with so much character and such incredible notes and aromas that you don't need to be an expert to recognise it. To become a sherry, a white wine is aged in contact with the air inside an old sherry cask, using the labour-intensive *solera* and *criadera* system. This ageing process needs to be inside the 'sherry triangle' of Jerez–El Puerto–Sanlúcar. The winery's microclimate, the type of ageing (oxidative or biological) and the grape variety give the sherry its identity: *fino*, *manzanilla*, *amontillado*, *oloroso*, *palo cortado*, Pedro Ximénez and so on.

■ **By Carmen Gutiérrez Pou**, *winemaker at Bodegas Gutiérrez-Colosía and owner of Bespoke sherry bar in El Puerto de Santa María*, @carmengutipou

Flamenco

ANDALUCÍA'S MOST EVOCATIVE CREATION IS A FIERY, COMPLEX AND UNIQUE ART ROOTED IN THE REGION'S HISTORY.

No art captures Andalucía's essence like feisty flamenco, and the heartland of Spain's flamenco scene revolves around the three intensely soulful cities of Seville, Cádiz and Jerez de la Frontera. Countless flamenco greats have emerged from the Roma *barrios* (neighbourhoods) of San Miguel and Santiago in Jerez, Santa María in Cádiz and Triana in Seville.

Left Paco de Lucía. **Middle** Festival de Jerez. **Right** Flamenco at a *tablao*.

A Short History

Flamenco originally emerged from the mingling of Andalucía's oppressed Roma, Moorish and Jewish communities in the wake of the Reconquista (Christian conquest), particularly in Seville, Cádiz and Jerez. Over the centuries, this gave birth to *cante jondo,* the raw and emotive purist version of flamenco, with dancing and guitars added into the mix in the 19th century, around the same time that flamenco began to be documented (until then it had been passed on vocally). It was also in the mid-19th century that flamenco entered its so-called golden era, becoming a professional performance art across Andalucía, particularly at the famous *cafés cantante* – though, for many aficionados, this in turn diluted *cante jondo* as it began to mix with other genres. After fading from the 1920s onwards, flamenco experienced a great rebirth in the mid-20th century, largely thanks to two *gaditano* greats, the guitarist Paco de Lucía and the *cantaor* (singer) Camarón de la Isla. Today, this renaissance shows no signs of slowing down.

The Essentials

Flamenco in its purest incarnation is a highly interactive and unrehearsed art, ideally with an informal environment and plenty of audience participation, though these days there are plenty of planned performances. The key components are song, dance, guitar and the often-overlooked *jaleo* (clapping etc by the audience), which when combined, if you're lucky, lead to the elusive *duende,* an intangible heightened state of emotion typically associated with flamenco. Flamenco's many, varied *palos* (song types) range

from fast-paced *bulerías* (a Jerez speciality) and Cádiz's cheery *alegrías* to deep, despairing *siguiriyas*.

Festivals

Almost every Andalucian fiesta involves flamenco, from headline acts such as Seville's Feria de Abril (p58) and the Feria de Málaga (p130) to small-scale village parties. The world's greatest dedicated flamenco celebration happens each February/March with the two-week **Festival de Jerez**.

Seeing Flamenco

The easiest way to catch a flamenco performance is at a professional, rehearsed *tablao;* although *tablaos* can lack the spontaneity associated with 'pure flamenco', they host top-quality performers in dramatic venues (ancient caves, urban taverns etc), often offering dinner and drinks.

> Flamenco in its purest incarnation is a highly interactive and unrehearsed art.

Run by local aficionados, traditional *peñas* are typically private clubs with an authentic flamenco atmosphere. While most are closed to non-members, there are a few that welcome outsiders for particular sessions; ask around locally. Jerez's peña scene is at its liveliest during the Festival de Jerez.

Jerez's lively *tabancos* (sherry bars) are intimately linked with the city's flamenco scene, and several of them cram regular performances into their clamorous confines, where you can soak up the song over a glass of *fino* or even join a dance class (*facebook.com/rutadelostabancosdejerez*).

🏛 Flamenco Museums in Cádiz

Centro de Interpretación Camarón de la Isla (San Fernando) Launched in 2021, this innovative multimedia gallery explores the life and legacy of beloved local flamenco singer Camarón de la Isla. Born here in 1950 as José Monge Cruz, Camarón became one of Spain's flamenco legends, famously collaborating with the great guitarist Paco de Lucía, from nearby Algeciras.

Centro Andaluz de Documentación de Flamenco (Jerez) A beautiful 15th-century palace in central Jerez is the setting for Spain's only flamenco library, whose shelves burst with musical and print works. The Centro also screens flamenco performances and offers details about upcoming shows, dance academies and more.

Welcome to
CARNAVAL

ARTS | CULTURE | HISTORY

Join the *gaditanos* (Cádiz residents) for their humorous 10-day February Carnaval, one of Spain's greatest carnivals and famous for its satirical costumed performing groups. Celebrated in one shape or another since the 15th century, the Carnaval de Cádiz is a deep-dive into the region's sunny psyche, with rainbows of floats carried around town, witty political commentary and a fiercely contested competition.

ANDREAS POERTNER/SHUTTERSTOCK ©

🗺 How To

Getting here/around
Cádiz is well connected by train and/or bus to destinations across the province, as well as to Seville, Málaga and beyond. Once here, explore on foot or by bike.

When to go Cádiz's Carnaval usually kicks off in February, though dates vary according to when Easter falls.

Tip Book accommodation as far ahead as possible and expect soaring prices. Alternatively, stay nearby and travel into Cádiz.

Local language Knowing a little Spanish will help you make sense of performances.

JOSE GOMEZ SANCHEZ/ALAMY STOCK PHOTO ©

JOSERPIZARRO/SHUTTERSTOCK ©

Far and near left Carnaval de Cádiz.
Bottom left Gran Teatro Falla.

Street Performers

The Carnaval fun revolves around the hundreds of *murgas* (groups of costumed performers) that you'll spot parading around town, often carried on tractors or floats but also simply strolling and bursting into song. Don't miss the *chirigotas:* these 12-person *murgas* are loved for their satirical wit.

Barrio de la Viña

Jump right into Cádiz's Carnaval 'capital' – a vineyard turned down-to-earth fishing neighbourhood, wedged between Playa de La Caleta and the Mercado Central. Tapas bars overflow, floats are paraded down the street and the *murga* scene is at its liveliest (including plenty of unofficial groups!), particularly on pastel-painted Calle Virgen de la Palma. Other spots to catch a glimpse include Plaza de Topete, Calle Ancha and outside the Catedral.

The Great Competition

The city's official Concurso de Agrupaciones (group competition) sees 300 or so *murgas* face off in a lively battle at the 1905 Mudéjar-inspired Gran Teatro Falla, designed by Andalucian architect Adolfo Morales de los Ríos. It can be tricky for visitors to get involved, with spectator tickets selling out well in advance; your best bet is to ask locally about last-minute tickets.

Year-Round Carnaval

For anyone who can't make it during the festivities, a sequin-clad taste awaits at Cádiz's much-awaited **Museo del Carnaval** (scheduled to open in early 2023), set inside the 18th-century Palacio de Recaño, while **Cádiz Experiences** (cadizexperiences.com) runs Carnaval-themed tours.

☆ The Carnaval Backstory

With Tenerife's Caribbean-influenced carnival as its main Spanish rival, Cádiz's Carnaval is thought to have first emerged in the late 15th century thanks to the arrival of Genoese merchants and, later, the boom in trade with the Americas. Today, beyond the lighthearted fancy-dress scene, it's a satire-rich fiesta packed with social and political commentary. Carnaval was officially banned from 1937 until 1947 during the Spanish Civil War and Franco's ensuing dictatorship, though it continued illegally behind closed doors, especially in the Barrio de la Viña. Then for three decades it was held each May as the tightly controlled Fiestas Típicas Gaditanas. It wasn't until 1977 that Carnaval returned to its full splendour.

16

Cádiz's Buzzing
BARRIOS

NEIGHBOURHOODS | CITIES | CULTURE

As one of Europe's oldest continuously inhabited cities (founded by the Phoenicians around 1100 BCE), over the centuries Cádiz has grown into a clutch of distinctive *barrios* (neighbourhoods), all with their own own personalities. On a wander around the evocative old city, you'll discover flamenco-filled streets, ancient watchtowers, lively plazas, dynamic markets and more.

✂ Mentidero Meals

Off the tourist trail, the Barrio del Mentidero has excellent dining spots.

Almanaque Classics with a twist by *gaditano* chef Juan Carlos Borrell (p120).

La Taberna del Anteojo Prawns with salsa verde, fabulous seafood *fideuà* and traditional fish.

Nuevo Labra Great breakfast *tostadas* with *jamón*, tomato and olive oil.

📔 Trip Notes

Getting here/around Cádiz is best explored by walking or cycling, and has urban buses (turismo.cadiz.es). There are good train and/or bus connections to destinations beyond, plus catamarans to/from El Puerto de Santa María (cmtbc.es).

When to go March to June, September and October combine warm days with fewer crowds and mid-season prices. February is Carnaval time. Winter months offer quieter, cooler explorations.

Walking tours Delve into Cádiz's *barrio* scene on an expert-guided tour; **Cadizfornia Tours** (cadizforniatours.com) is highly recommended.

■ Recommended by **Annie Manson**, *owner of Annie B's Spanish Kitchen in Vejer de la Frontera, @anniebspain*

05 Once a vineyard, then the city's fishing quarter, the **Barrio de la Viña** is Cádiz's liveliest corner, home to the greatest Carnaval celebrations and beloved tapas haunts such as **El Faro** and **Casa Manteca**.

04 In the city's affluent north, the **Barrio del Mentidero** sprung up in the 18th century. Highlights here include the 1920s **Alameda Apodaca garden** and its summer kiosk bars. Don't miss the 126 watchtowers set up across town during the 17th- and 18th-century trade boom.

03 Just northwest, the **Barrio de San Juan** sprawls around flower-filled **Plaza de Topete** (pictured opposite) and the **Mercado Central de Abastos**, with its fabulous gastronomic corner.

02 Crammed with historic buildings, today's **Barrio del Pópulo** has been the heart of the city since Phoenician times and centres on the baroque-neoclassical **Catedral**, begun in 1772. Drink in the views from pastel-walled **Campo del Sur**.

01 Wander the meandering alleys of the **Barrio de Santa María**, Cádiz's original flamenco quarter and one of the city's oldest neighbourhoods, dating from the 15th century. Here, intricately adorned churches mingle with tempting gastronomic streets such as Calle Plocia.

Map labels:

Bahía de Cádiz

Paseo de Carlos III
Parque del Genovés
Av Doctor Gómez Ulla
Alameda
Alameda Apodaca
La Taberna del Anteojo
Almanaque
Plaza de Mina
C Enrique de las Marinas
Plaza de España
Nuevo Labra
C Cervantes
C Sacramento
C Torre
C Sagasta
Av Ramón de Carranza
Av del Puerto
C San José
C Hospital de Mujeres
Plaza Candelaria
Av Duque de Nájera
C Rosa
Plaza de la Reina
Plaza de la Libertad
Plaza de la Catedral
C Compañía
C Pelota
C Plocia
Cuesta de las Calesas
Av de Astilleros
Playa de la Caleta
Plaza de la Reina
C Sagasta
C San Juan de Dios
C Sopranis
C Pericón de Cádiz
Campo del Sur
Campo del Sur
Plaza de la Constitución

Atlantic Ocean

0 — 500 m
0 — 0.25 miles
N

17

The Coast
OF LIGHT

BEACHES | FOOD | NATURE

▬▬▬ Stretching from kitesurf-loving Tarifa to the golden shores of Huelva's Parque Nacional de Doñana, Cádiz's 200km-long Costa de la Luz is one of Spain's most beloved beach destinations. Many beaches sit within fiercely protected nature reserves, where you can't help but feel Andalucía's raw natural beauty, and it's perfectly possible to escape the crowds and find your own patch of Atlantic-washed paradise.

JOSERPIZARRO/SHUTTERSTOCK ©

🗺 How To

Getting here/around
Make the most of your visit by using a hire car; summer parking is a nightmare, so arrive early. Tarifa, Bolonia and the beaches between them are linked by summer buses (horizontesur.es).

When to go May/June and September/October for warm weather without summer crowds. For July and August, book ahead (and expect soaring prices).

Chiringuitos Among the greatest joys of Cádiz's coast are its lively *chiringuitos* (beach bars), open May to October.

FERNANDOALONSOGSTOCKFILMS/SHUTTERSTOCK ©

Left Bolonia. Bottom left Kite surfing, Costa de la Luz.

Superstar Strands

In Tarifa, head to **Punta Paloma**, **Playa de Valdevaqueros** and sweeping **Bolonia**. **El Palmar** is beloved by surfers, while neighbouring **Caños de Meca** has golden-white kitesurf beaches and pine-forest walks. Or seek out the cliff-edged **Calas de Roche** just outside Conil de la Frontera.

Walk-in Beaches

Northwest from Tarifa, isolated **Playa del Cañuelo** is a dreamy, elemental place: a golden-blonde naturist sweep bordered by pine groves, accessible only by walking 2km along a dirt track above Bolonia or clambering down from southern Zahara de los Atunes. Between Los Caños and surf-loving El Palmar, **Playa de la Mangueta** is another untouched nudist beauty with honey-white sand folding into natural rock pools; follow a dirt path for a kilometre. In Los Caños, walk past the rippling dunes to **Playa del Faro** beside Trafalgar lighthouse.

Escape to Doñana

As the summer months heat up in Sanlúcar de Barrameda, savvy *sanluqueños* slip across the Guadalquivir by boat to the 28km-long, dune-backed strand bordering the ethereal Parque Nacional de Doñana – one of the wildest, most magical back-to-nature beaches in southern Spain.

Urban Havens

Even the lively provincial capital has its own tucked-away sandy stretches, such as powder-soft **Playa de la Cortadura**.

Best Chiringuitos

Tangana Near Tarifa's dune, this classic surfers' bar combines great food, sunset cocktails and views of North Africa; the province's best poke bowls are made with local avocados and Barbate tuna.

Feduchy Playa Backed by Conil's sandstone cliffs, Feduchy is perfect for a beachside meal and fiery sunsets. Local favourites such as *tortitas de camarones* mix with Japanese tuna-and-papaya nigiri.

Chiringuito El Nio An almost-deserted beach, a backdrop of Trafalgar lighthouse and the limitless Atlantic, just a 20-minute walk across the dunes from Los Caños. Order freshly grilled sardines with tomato salad, or a sunset mojito.

Chiringuito Serenade This thatch-roofed spot, on eastern Bolonia beach, is all about the chilled vibe with live music or DJs most weekends, dancing on the sand and strawberry daiquiris.

■ **Recommended by James Stuart**, *founder of Califa Vejer hotels and restaurants, @califavejer*

18 Glorious Gaditano
DINING

FOOD | WINE | CULTURE

Fabulous food is a key part of Cádiz's essence, and fresh-as-it-gets produce, traditional recipes and creative twists all collide on the local gastronomic scene. With a clutch of inspired, dive-right-in gastronomic experiences now on the table, this is one of Spain's most thrilling regions for food lovers.

Above Mercado de Abastos Andalucía. **Near right** Ruta del Atún. **Far right** Bajo de Guía.

🗺 How To

Getting here/around
A great way to dive into Cádiz cuisine is on a local tapas crawl. If you're planning to string together a few different foodie towns, hiring a car is best.

When to go Anytime, though some coastal restaurants close over winter (November to February). Save May/June for *almadraba* events.

Seafood capital Sanlúcar de Barrameda's riverside **Bajo de Guía** neighbourhood is one of Andalucía's greatest spots for seafood restaurants.

Almadraba Time

Cádiz's gastronomy is intimately linked to the famous *almadraba,* a wild-tuna-fishing technique developed by the Phoenicians. Today, this sustainable method lives on in only four Costa de la Luz fishing towns: Tarifa, Barbate, Zahara de los Atunes and Conil de la Frontera.

During the May/June *almadraba* season, you can join a trip to see the *almadraba* in action, with its famous *levantá* (lifting of the nets) out in the Atlantic, thanks to **Cádiz Atlántica** (cadizatlantica.com), a pioneering sustainable-tourism initiative that showcases the region's rich maritime heritage. At this time of year local villages host **Ruta del Atún festivals**, with restaurants competing to create the greatest tuna-based tapa; Zahara's festival is one of the headliners (ruta delatun.com). And at Barbate's mural-walled **Mercado de Abastos Andalucía**, you can often see tuna auctions in full swing.

🍴 Michelin-Starred Meals

Aponiente (El Puerta de Santa María) Andalucía's first three-Michelin star, by chef Angel León, with its laid-back **Taberna del Mar** offshoot.

LÚ, Cocina y Alma (Jerez) Jerezano chef Juan Luis Fernández's Michelin-starred venture; don't miss sister gastrobar **Bina Bar.**

Mantúa (Jerez) Cádiz-inspired cooking by local chef Israel Ramos, who also runs tapas favourite **Albalá**.

For a taste of the prized catch, seek out **El Campero** in Barbate (Cádiz's self-styled 'tuna temple'), **Casa Varo** in Vejer de la Frontera (a family-owned delight), **Restaurante Antonio** in Zahara (known for its tuna tartare), **Cooking Almadraba** in Conil (by Mauro Barreiro) and beloved tapas hangout **El Lola** in Tarifa.

Markets & Fresh Bounty Smooth artisanal cheeses, golden olive oils, local-grown vegetables, *retinto* beef, king prawns – this is just a taste of the province's natural bounty. In recent years, several *gaditano* markets have undergone a gastronomic makeover with food stalls, sherry bars and more. **Cádiz's Mercado Central de Abastos** and **Vejer's Mercado de San Francisco** are among the best, while **Sanlúcar's market** hosts a museum devoted to *manzanilla* sherry.

Tapas & Global Flavours The road to Cádiz's soul is paved with tempting tapas, from punchy *papas aliñás* (potato salad) and silky *chicharrones* (slow-roasted pork

 ⭐ **The Almadraba Story**

The history of Cádiz has always been intertwined with its relationship with the ocean and the world of fishing. From the Phoenicians, Carthaginians, Romans and Moors to modern-day Japan, many cultures have marked the evolution of Cádiz's coastal villages, where the gastronomy revolves around the great Atlantic red tuna and the millennia-old *almadraba* fishing technique. The *almadraba* was traditionally a world of its own, mysterious and tricky to access for outsiders, but now we have helped rescue ancient *almadrabero* buildings and opened up this art to visitors by sailing out into the heart of the fishing experience.

 ■ **By Ignacio Soto,** *director of Cádiz Atlántica,* *@cadizatlantica*

Left *Almadraba* fishing technique.
Below Tuna, Mercado Central de Abastos.

belly) to crispy-fresh *tortillitas de camarones* (prawn fritters). Start with Sanlúcar's **Plaza del Cabildo** (don't miss **Casa Balbino**) and Cádiz's old city (try **Taberna La Sorpresa** and the **Barrio de la Viña**), and don't miss the small-town tapas scenes in Vejer, Tarifa, Zahara, Barbate, Conil and Grazalema. Jerez's *tabancos* are another tapas staple.

Meanwhile, the region's Moorish influence shines in the use of spices, dried fruits and citrus flavours, and many restaurants pull in world-roaming flavours, particularly around Tarifa and Vejer. At Vejer's **El Jardín del Califa** (califavejer.com), exquisite North African and Middle Eastern cuisine arrives in a magical centuries-old building.

Immersive Gastronomy Celebrated Spanish chef José Pizarro opens up his designer oceanside home, **Iris Zahara** (josepizarro.com/iris-zahara), in Atlanterra, for overnight stays and exclusive culinary retreats, involving activities from hands-on cooking classes to sherry-tasting tours. In nearby Vejer, **Annie B's Spanish Kitchen** *(anniebspain. com)* is a culinary haven where you can master Andalucian specialities over a week-long retreat, take a Moroccan-cooking day class, join tapas tours, learn about sherries and more.

In the Sierra de Grazalema, visit olive-oil-makers such as Zahara's **Oleum Viride** (oleum viride.com) and taste local cheeses at Grazalema's **Queso Payoyo** (payoyo.com).

19

In the Romans'
FOOTSTEPS

HISTORY | CULTURE | CITIES

▬▬ Deep-dive into Cádiz's history on a spin through the province's evocative Roman-era jewels, stringing together abandoned ocean-side cities, serene hillside settlements, ruins hidden among the urban sprawl and a lively capital where archaeological wonders await right beneath your feet. For many *gaditano* villages, things first started with the Romans.

JAPHOTOS/ALAMY STOCK PHOTO ©

🗺 How To

Getting here/around
Some (but not all) of these Roman-era sites are accessible by bus, though a car is most convenient. In the Sierra de Grazalema area, exploring by hiking or cycling is a joy.

When to go The best months are March to May, September and October, for fewer crowds and pleasant weather; avoid July and August, when temperatures and crowds soar.

Detour If you're passing through the Bahía de Algeciras/Gibraltar area, there are more Roman relics at Phoenician-founded Carteia in San Roque.

HANS GEORG ROTH/GETTY IMAGES ©

Left Teatro Romano. **Bottom left** Forum, Baelo Claudia.

By the Atlantic Fresh rosemary wafts through the air as you wander past crumbling aqueducts, ancient fish-salting factories, thermal baths, a porticoed forum and a sprawling basilica at one of Andalucía's major Roman sites, the ruined ocean-hugging city of **Baelo Claudia**. During July/August, the Roman theatre here springs back to life hosting concerts, plays and dance shows.

Roman Cádiz Once known as Roman Gades, Cádiz reveals Roman-era delights beneath modern-day theatres, hotels and urban homes standing tall since Moorish times. Worthwhile stops include the 1st-century-BCE **Teatro Romano** (unearthed under a ruined 10th-century castle), the **Fábrica de Salazones** (a fish-salting factory used until the 4th century) and the relic-filled **Museo de Cádiz**.

To Assido-Caesarina A short detour inland from Cádiz, whitewashed **Medina Sidonia** was both an important Roman settlement called Assido-Caesarina and, later, the home of the powerful Duques de Medina Sidonia. Local curiosities include the excavated 1st-century Cardo Maximus and a ruined Roman fortress.

Into the Hills Just outside the leather-making town of **Ubrique** in the Sierra de Grazalema, expert-led tours dive into the Roman city of **Ocuri**, which thrived until the 3rd century CE. Combine with a hike down from the hillside white village of **Benaocaz** along the old Roman road, through fragrant olive groves and cork forests. Don't miss the chance to taste Ubrique's prize-winning artisanal cheeses.

Baelo Claudia's History

Let your imagination wander beyond today's excavated ruins surrounded by white-gold sands to the Baelo Claudia that was a key commercial hub for Roman Hispania. Founded back in the 2nd century BCE, the city thrived on fish-salting, tuna-fishing and trade with North Africa, which is clearly visible across the Strait of Gibraltar. It reached its maximum splendour under the rule of Emperor Claudius, but a slow decline followed by a devastating earthquake led to it being completely abandoned in the 3rd century. The whole place is still being excavated and fresh treasures emerge each year.

20 Mountain
THRILLS

HIKING | ADVENTURE | NATURE

━━━━ Sprawling 534 sq km across Cádiz province's northeast corner, the Parque Natural Sierra de Grazalema offers rugged peaks, glinting lakes, plunging gorges, eerie caves, rare *pinsapo* (Mediterranean fir) forests and beautiful old *pueblos blancos*. The entire place is an adventure lovers' paradise

Above Garganta Verde. **Right** *Pinsapo.*

ROBERT HARDING/ALAMY STOCK PHOTO ©

GRACEENE/SHUTTERSTOCK ©

🗺️ How To

Getting here/around
There are buses to/from Grazalema, Zahara de la Sierra and other towns. Once here, it's easy to explore by walking and cycling, though a car offers more freedom.

When to go May, June, September and October are best for outdoor adventures; avoid busy weekends and bank holidays.

Permits and restrictions Four of the park's most exciting hiking trails require prebooked permits from the **Centro de Visitantes El Bosque** (☎956 40 97 33; cvelbosque@reservatuvisita.es). Some routes are off-limits from June to mid-October.

Heavenly Hikes

Outstanding hiking is the Sierra de Grazalema's speciality, with routes ranging from an easy-breezy 5km shaded walk along the **Río Majaceite** to the tough 3km ascent of the province's tallest peak, **El Torreón** (1648m). Part of the fun of walking here is discovering the ancient whitewashed villages sprinkled around the mountains, many of which are linked by scenic paths that have been used for centuries.

For the park's four standout routes (including El Torreón), you'll need to request permits at least 15 days ahead from park's visitor centre in El Bosque. The 2.5km **Garganta Verde** route near Zahara de la Sierra is a spectacular descent into a lush river-washed canyon, whose crags are watched over by

Europe's largest colony of griffon vultures; it's also a popular canyoning spot. On the soothing **El Pinsapar** trail you'll track 12km between the white villages of Grazalema and Benamahoma through a fiercely protected pinsapo forest, with views stretching across to

Sevilla and Málaga provinces. For expert-led hikes with a focus on the local environment, flora and fauna, link up with Grazalema-based **Horizon** (*horizonaventura.com*).

On Two Wheels

Although this is serious mountainous terrain, the beauty of exploring the Sierra de Grazalema by cycling is that there are rewarding routes for all levels. Steep climbs emerge on majestic mountain passes, while off-road mountain-biking routes plunge across shady valleys.

Grazalema Cycling Adventures (grazalema cycling.com) runs excellent guided rides, and rents out bikes with self-guided routes set up.

Over in Olvera, you can pick up the **Vía Verde de la Sierra** (viasverdes.com), a 36km-long cycling, walking and horse-riding route created from a disused 1920s railway line (with some wheelchair-accessible-sections). There are bike-hire spots, restaurants and accommodation at reimagined train stations along the way.

🚲 Cycling Routes

When asked about my favourite local cycling route, it's hard to pick just one, because there are so many beautiful options in the Sierra de Grazalema. One highlight is, for sure, the Puerto de las Palomas (1357m). This 12.5km climb has nothing to envy from famous cycling cols in the Alps or Pyrenees, as the views of Zahara's reservoir and surrounding mountains are simply stunning. It's a real challenge for road cyclists, while e-bikes mean it's also possible to enjoy it on a more leisurely ride. Then there are mountain-bike routes for both technically skilled and less-experienced riders through the natural park, with, every once in a while, a white village to explore.

■ **Recommended by Agnieta Francke**, *founder of Grazalema Cycling Adventures,* *@grazalemacyclingadventures*

⛰ Mountain Restaurants

La Maroma (Grazalema) A creative twist on classic tapas.

Al Lago (Zahara de la Sierra) Mediterranean flavours with a gourmet touch (and a boutique hotel).

El Refugio (Benaocaz) Updated mountain-style cooking with divine views.

Cafetería Rumores (Grazalema) Traditional breakfasts and fuss-free tapas on Grazalema's lively square.

Out on the Water

When temperatures start to rise, head out kayaking or paddleboarding across the shimmering turquoise lake at the foot of Zahara de la Sierra, where **Discovery Aventura** (discovery-8.com) has its own nautical base. During summer, the full-moon kayaking tours shine a whole new light on the region's rugged beauty. There's even a locally loved lakeside beach to relax on, the **Playita de Arroyomolinos**, open during July and August.

Paragliding, Horse-Riding & More

From canyoning downriver to exhilarating via ferrata routes over near Ronda (in Málaga province), the adventure-activity line-up here is endless. **Algodonales** village is a popular paragliding hub, with companies such as **Zero Gravity** (paraglidingspain.eu) offering classes and flights with instructors. Horse-riding through the pine forests and cork groves is also a delight; the creative, sustainably run **Tambor del Llano** hotel (tambordelllano.es) offers day rides and multiday trips with glamping under the stars, as well as astronomy nights.

Left Puerto de las Palomas.
Top right Cafetería Rumores.
Bottom right Paragliding, Algodonales.

21

Roaming Cádiz's
WHITE TOWNS

HISTORY | NATURE | HIKING

▬▬▬ Head from the sunny Costa de la Luz to the rugged Sierra de Grazalema to discover Cádiz's beautiful *pueblos blancos* (white towns), where gleaming-white streets are dressed with hot-pink bougainvillea, glinting lakes sit beneath ancient Moorish castles and Andalucía's long, turbulent history springs to life.

🗺 Trip Notes

Getting here/around If you aren't cycling or hiking, the best way to explore is with your own car. Buses serve most villages, but services are limited.

When to go Spring (March to June) and autumn (September and October) are best for warm (not sweltering) weather. For fewer crowds, avoid weekends, summer and bank holidays.

Tip Stay a few nights at one of the charming rural hotels in/near Grazalema or Zahara de la Sierra to soak up the mountain serenity.

🏘 A Long History

The *pueblos blancos* are living pieces of history. Villages like Zahara, Grazalema and Olvera feel chiselled into the rock and have been inhabited for thousands of years. In the afternoon you can hear the hiss of pressure pots cooking chickpeas for *potaje* (stew), and doors are often wide open with people wandering into geranium-lined patios.

By Mona Arain Crites, *owner of hotel-restaurant Al Lago in Zahara de la Sierra,* @al_lago_andalucia

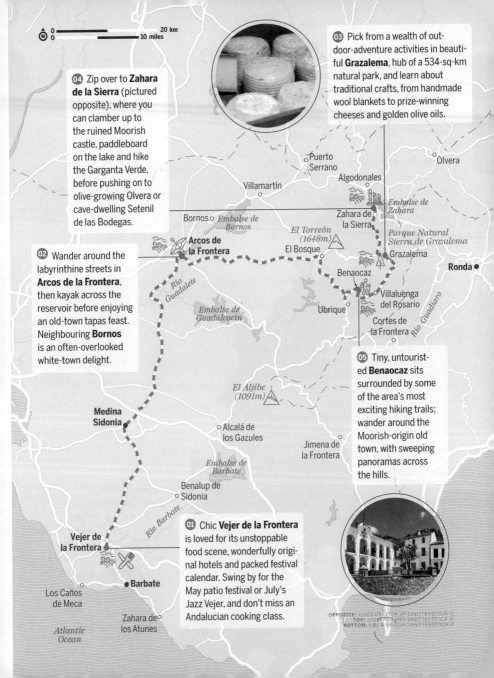

04 Zip over to **Zahara de la Sierra** (pictured opposite), where you can clamber up to the ruined Moorish castle, paddleboard on the lake and hike the Garganta Verde, before pushing on to olive-growing Olvera or cave-dwelling Setenil de las Bodegas.

03 Pick from a wealth of outdoor-adventure activities in beautiful **Grazalema**, hub of a 534-sq-km natural park, and learn about traditional crafts, from handmade wool blankets to prize-winning cheeses and golden olive oils.

02 Wander around the labyrinthine streets in **Arcos de la Frontera**, then kayak across the reservoir before enjoying an old-town tapas feast. Neighbouring **Bornos** is an often-overlooked white-town delight.

05 Tiny, untouristed **Benaocaz** sits surrounded by some of the area's most exciting hiking trails; wander around the Moorish-origin old town, with sweeping panoramas across the hills.

01 Chic **Vejer de la Frontera** is loved for its unstoppable food scene, wonderfully original hotels and packed festival calendar. Swing by for the May patio festival or July's Jazz Vejer, and don't miss an Andalucian cooking class.

0 — 20 km
0 — 10 miles

Puerto Serrano
Olvera
Villamartín
Algodonales
Embalse de Zahara
Bornos · *Embalse de Bornos*
Zahara de la Sierra
Parque Natural Sierra de Grazalema
El Torreón (1648m)
Arcos de la Frontera
El Bosque
Grazalema
Benaocaz
Ronda ●
Río Guadalete
Villaluenga del Rosario
Embalse de Guadalcacín
Ubrique
Cortes de la Frontera
Río Guadiaro
El Aljibe (1091m)
Medina Sidonia
Alcalá de los Gazules
Jimena de la Frontera
Embalse de Barbate
Benalup de Sidonia
Vejer de la Frontera
Río Barbate
Los Caños de Meca
● **Barbate**
Zahara de los Atunes
Atlantic Ocean

22 Up On the ROCK

HISTORY | OUTDOORS | ARCHAEOLOGY

▬▬▬ Strategically perched at the jaws of Europe, Gibraltar has been warred over for centuries, eventually becoming a British overseas territory under the Treaty of Utrecht in 1713. And yet it remains a world of its own, where the southern-Spanish sun casts its bright glow across British-flavoured streets, people speak in the local *llanito* and thrilling history awaits around every corner.

🗺 How To

Getting here/around Gibraltar airport has good connections. From Spain, Gibraltar is a quick walk away across the border from La Línea de la Concepción in Cádiz province (border queues mean it's best not to drive in). Remember your passport!

When to go March to June, September and October are best weather-wise and for migration-season bird-watching. July and August bring summer festivals.

Food From perfect Andalucian tapas to Punjabi-style curries, Gibraltar has a wonderfully varied culinary scene.

Marina Bay
Eastern Bay
Gibraltar National Museum
Cathedral of the Holy Trinity
Catalan Bay
Upper Rock Nature Reserve
Alameda Botanic Gardens
Sandy Bay
Gibraltar Town
Mediterranean Steps
Rosia Bay
Gorham's Cave Complex
Camp Bay
Bahía de Algeciras
Little Bay
0 — 500 m
0 — 0.25 miles
Europa Point

Colourful Capital

Stroll along **Gibraltar Town's** pastel-painted streets for a taste of the Rock's swash-buckling history, with a stop at the **Gibraltar National Museum** and a peek at the 15th-century **cathedral's** Alhambra-flavoured courtyard (testament to its former life as a mosque), all surrounded by a distinctive blend of Spanish, British, Genoese and Portuguese architecture. This is where most of Gibraltar's 32,700 inhabitants live.

Early inhabitants Join a boat tour with a local historian for a glimpse of the Unesco-listed **Gorham's Cave Complex** on Gibraltar's southeast tip. These four sea-level caves hidden in the limestone cliffs were inhabited by Neanderthals for over 100,000 years, with rare rock etchings dating from around 39,000 years ago.

Moorish times It was through Gibraltar that the

⚠ Natural Havens

Beyond its historical intrigue, Gibraltar is also a naturally spectacular place – a 5km-long limestone outcrop rising to 426m, almost entirely encircled by the Mediterranean.

Upper Rock Nature Reserve Along with concealing a string of military sites, Gibraltar's lush nature reserve is threaded with hiking paths.

Mediterranean Steps Hike to 419m above sea level on this spine-tingling climb up the southern end of the Rock, with views sprawling across to North Africa and, in spring, a world of colourful blooms.

Alameda Gardens Founded in the early 19th-century, Gibraltar's botanic gardens are a wonderland of wild olive trees, stone pines and other autochthonous plants.

Islamic conquest of the Iberian peninsula began in 711 CE. With its roots thought to spin back to the 9th century, Gibraltar's fortress was rebuilt in 1333 after the Moors recaptured the Rock from the Spanish.

Military relics Gibraltar's upper reaches are dotted with ancient military sites, many within the **Upper Rock Nature Reserve**, from isolated gun batteries to tunnels carved from the rock during the Great Siege of 1779–83. With a Nature Reserve pass (visitgibraltar. gi) you can visit them all on a refreshing hike, on which you'll inevitably spot Gibraltar's most famous inhabitants – troops of Barbary macaques.

Above Upper Rock Nature Reserve

Listings

BEST OF THE REST

 Moorish Architecture

Alcázar de Jerez

Soothing Alhambra-flavoured gardens, an octagonal tower and an ancient mosque with horseshoe arches await at Jerez's unparalleled Almohad fortress, dating from the 11th or 12th century.

Castillo de San Marcos

El Puerto de Santa María's much-reworked 13th-century castle was built on the site of a Moorish mosque and still conceals an original *mihrab* (prayer niche). It's now part of Bodegas Caballero, offering tours and tastings.

Castillo de Vejer

The magical *pueblo blanco* of Vejer de la Frontera is topped by a hibiscus-filled castle from the 10th or 11th century, which later became the home of the powerful Duques de Medina Sidonia.

Castillo de Guzmán

Though Tarifa's imposing castle was taken by the Christians in 1292, it was originally built for the Córdoban caliph Abd ar-Rahman III in the 10th century; join a guided tour for an insight into the town's layered history.

 Special Stays

La Casa del Califa   €€

Savour Vejer's design scene at one of southern Spain's most magical boutique retreats: a rambling collection of 16th-century town houses with arty styling and Moorish-era roots. Book ahead for the unmissable garden restaurant (see p107).

Cortijo Bablou   €€

Escape the world at this French-owned 19th-century farmhouse just outside Arcos

de la Frontera, where boho-chic design meets glamping yurts, homegrown breakfasts and a dreamy pool.

Finca La Donaira   €€€

Near El Gastor in the Sierra de Grazalema mountains, this boho-luxe hideaway is part equestrian centre, part organic farm and part soothingly rustic countryside retreat with its own spa.

Riad   €€

Get a taste for Tarifa's intriguing backstory at a fabulous 17th-century old-town mansion where restored frescoes and red-brick alcoves mingle with Morocco-inspired design and a calming hammam.

Local Crafts & Chic Boutiques

Casa LAMAR

A creative wonderland in Cádiz's historic centre, devoted to bringing local artisanal crafts into contemporary design, from Jerez-made ceramics to Grazalema blankets and *esparto*-grass homewares.

Azogue Art & Vintage

Uncover a vintage-filled haven in the heart of Tarifa's old town, where flamenco dresses sit beside denim jackets, Hawaiian shirts and interior-design pieces.

Cestería Tradicional

The owner of this delightful workshop, Juani Marchán, crafts beautiful bags, baskets, fans and more from palm leaves, wicker and other all-natural materials, among the whitewashed streets of Vejer's old town.

Quesería La Abuela Agustina

Step into a tempting world of artisanal mountain food products in lovely Grazalema: orange-blossom honey, small-scale Olvera olive oil and the family's own prize-winning *payoyo* cheeses, made with rosemary and other local herbs.

Ar-monía

The eco-conscious rainbow-coloured rugs, throws, cushions covers and other homewares at this cheery Tarifa boutique are handcrafted in Almería reusing materials leftover from Spain's textile industries.

Zahir

Pick up Scandi fashion labels, Andalucian ceramics, breezy beachwear, beautiful home-decor pieces and other goodies at one of Vejer's chicest independent boutiques, just off the main square.

Artesanía en Lana

The cosy blankets, scarves, ponchos and other soul-warming pieces in this small Grazalema shop are all made locally, celebrating the village's former life as one of Spain's wool-making hubs.

No Ni Ná

A mother-daughter duo is behind this Zahara de los Atunes haven that fuses local crafts (including Ubrique-made leather bags) with forward-thinking fashion.

Seafood with a View

Casa Bigote €€

This legendary seafooder on Sanlúcar's Bajo de Guía boulevard has a wood-beamed dining room for digging into salt-baked fish with locally grown potatoes, along with an always-busy river-view tapas bar.

El Pez Limón €€

Catch the sunset with your toes in the sand on Zahara's Playa del Carmen, where locally loved *chiringuito* El Pez Limón serves *espetos* (skewers) of sardines, wild-tuna *arroz* (rice) and superb seafood tapas.

El Cuartel del Mar €€€

Hidden at the southern end of Chiclana's Playa de La Barrosa, this former Guardia Civil barracks has been reimagined as one of the Costa de la Luz's chicest restaurants, with fabulous Andalucian-fusion cooking by Asturian chef Manuel Berganza.

Las Rejas €€

Among the clutch of superb seafood restaurants in tiny beachside Bolonia, Las Rejas specialises in perfect *arroces* (rice dishes), fruits-of-the-sea tapas and fresh fish of the day.

Flamenco

Pena Flamenca La Perla

Cádiz's Barrio de Santa María hosts the city's liveliest and most respected *peña,* where guests are welcome to enjoy weekly performances (usually on Friday night).

Centro Cultural Flamenco Don Antonio Chacón

For a deep-dive into Jerez's thriving flamenco scene, enquire locally (at the tourist office or Centro Andaluz de Documentación de Flamenco) about performances at this standout *peña.*

Bodegas & Wine Bars

Bodegas Lustau

On an intimate tour of Jerez's Lustau winery you'll taste elegant sherries as you stroll around the vine-shaded 19th-century bodega; the team produces wines in all three Sherry Triangle towns, as well as excellent vermouth.

Bodegas Gallardo

Try Vejer's famous orange wine at the town's original bodega, founded in the 1980s; today the local drop is made with organic oranges and the winery offers occasional tasting sessions (ask ahead).

Magerit

One of Andalucía's greatest wine boutiques, just off the Alameda Apodaca in northern Cádiz city, specialising in sherries, Vinos de la Tierra de Cádiz and other Spanish drops, as well as local artisanal food products.

Bodegas Barbadillo

Sanlúcar's prestigious Barbadillo winery, hidden away in the ancient Barrio Alto, runs in-depth tours of its 19th-century bodega building, where *manzanilla* has been made since the 1820s.

Taberna La Manzanilla

With original beams and arches, this reimagined pharmacy evokes its 1930s wine-tavern roots and serves exclusively Sanlúcar sherries, including *manzanilla en rama* (straight from the barrel).

Bodegas Osborne

El Puerto de Santa María's most respected bodega was founded in 1772 by the British wine-maker Thomas Osborne Mann; you can tour its Bodega de Mora building, which also has a gourmet tapas restaurant.

Natural Spaces

Parque Natural Bahía de Cádiz

The rippling marshes, dunes, lagoons and salt flats that surround Cádiz city make up a 105-sq-km nature reserve known for its rich birdlife, with walking and cycling trails weaving through. Don't miss **Salinas de Chiclana**, an old salt factory turned open-air summer spa (salinasdechiclana.es).

Parque Natural del Estrecho

There's more outstanding birdwatching in this 191-sq-km natural park sweeping from Tarifa to Zahara de los Atunes, where you can enjoy Atlantic-view coastal hikes, go whale-watching in the Strait of Gibraltar, and more.

Parque Natural Los Alcornocales

One of Cádiz's least-known corners, the 1746-sq-km Los Alcornocales nature reserve is a wonderland of whispering cork forests, with just a few low-key *pueblos blancos* as tempting bases for hiking the trails.

Visitas Doñana

To explore the wild expanses of the Parque Nacional de Doñana from the Sanlúcar side, book a 2½-hour boat-and-4WD tour from Bajo de Guía (visitasdonana.com).

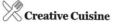 Creative Cuisine

Corredera 55 €€

Fresh, organic, local ingredients fuel the innovative cooking at this soothingly styled Vejer jewel. Grab a perch on the dreamy terrace for spiced cauliflower steaks, oven-baked cheese with rosemary or coconut-laced fish curry.

El Francés €€

Arrive early to snag a terrace table under the bougainvillea at one of Tarifa's top tapas haunts; goat's-cheese-stuffed eggplant, braised octopus and divine *patatas bravas* often grace the regularly changing menu.

Almanaque €€

Rare, ancient regional recipes are given a creative makeover by chef Juan Carlos Borrell at this rustic-chic *casa de comidas* (meals house), which occupies part of an 18th-century Cádiz mansion. Try a succulent *arroz* (rice) with red tuna, *percebes* (goose barnacles) or KmO vegetables.

La Carboná €€

Jerez's 'Chef del Sherry', Juan Muñoz Soto, pairs wonderfully original fresh seafood, grilled Cantabrian meats and other market-fired creations with a world of sherries in an elegantly converted bodega.

RaíZes €€

A Basque-*madrileño* (Madrid) chef duo is at the helm of this boundary-pushing Cádiz-inspired kitchen near Tarifa's port, where the menu arrives on an old vinyl and local-produce specialities swing from baked-pear tortellini to hazelnut-butter oysters.

Taberna Jóvenes Flamencos €

The top pick among Arcos' old-town tapas bars for its flamenco-inspired decor, lively vibe and traditional-rooted creations, including *retinto* burgers and *tagarnina* (thistle) tortilla.

Yoga & Outdoors

Suryalila

Hidden out in the countryside between Arcos and the Sierra de Grazalema, this respected yoga centre is an inspiring place for specialised retreats, in-depth trainings and home-cooked plant-based meals in a cosily converted century-old *cortijo*.

Aventura Ecuestre

Catch the blazing Tarifa sunset on horseback while trotting along one of the golden-white beaches with well-established Aventure Ecuestre, based near northern Playa de Los Lances.

Ion Club

If you're keen to tackle kitesurfing or windsurfing, Ion is one of Tarifa's most established academies, with over 30 years on the scene and a raft of courses catering to different experience levels.

FIRMM

Going strong since 1998, this not-for-profit Tarifa-based organisation researches whale behaviour, and also offers responsible half-day whale-watching excursions as well as more specialised courses.

 Tarifa's Vegan & Breakfast Havens

Chilimosa €

A cosy all-vegetarian hub tucked into Tarifa's old town, offering fabulous fresh falafel, Indian-style curries, perfectly spiced samosas and home-baked cakes, with some ingredients plucked from the home garden.

Café Azul €

On the Tarifa scene since the 1990s, 'el Azul' delivers divine breakfasts in a Morocco-inspired setting just steps from the old town. Pop in before the brunch-time crowds for artful fruit salads, fresh juices and tomato-topped *molletes* (flat round rolls).

Power House €€

Join Tarifa's yogis and kitesurfers at this roadside garden cafe, with a boho-chic feel and world-wandering bites that include creative brunches, market-fresh salads and punchy poke bowls.

 White Villages

Benamahoma

On a drive (or cycle) between El Bosque and Grazalema, make a stop in beautiful white-washed Benamahoma, a 350-person hamlet clinging to the mountainside, surrounded by willow trees and *pinsapos* (Spanish firs).

Castellar & Jimena de la Frontera

In eastern Cádiz's Parque Natural Los Alcornocales, Castellar is a dramatic walled white village high above a reservoir, while Jimena has a crumbling 13th-century Nasrid castle on the site of Roman ruins.

Villaluenga del Rosario

Some of the province's most prized artisanal cheeses are made in tiny Villaluenga, between Benaocaz and Grazalema. Now home to 400 inhabitants, it was once an important Moorish settlement and has its own cheese museum.

 Cave Art

Centro de Interpretación Cádiz Prehistórico, Benalup–Casas Viejas

Between Vejer and Alcalá de los Gazules, the Benalup area conceals Cádiz's most important prehistoric relics; around 900 Neolithic cave paintings have been unearthed here. Though the caves themselves are off-limits, you can visit the interactive museum.

 Scan to find more things to do in Cádiz & Gibraltar online

MÁLAGA

OUTDOORS | FOOD | BEACHES

Experience
Málaga
online

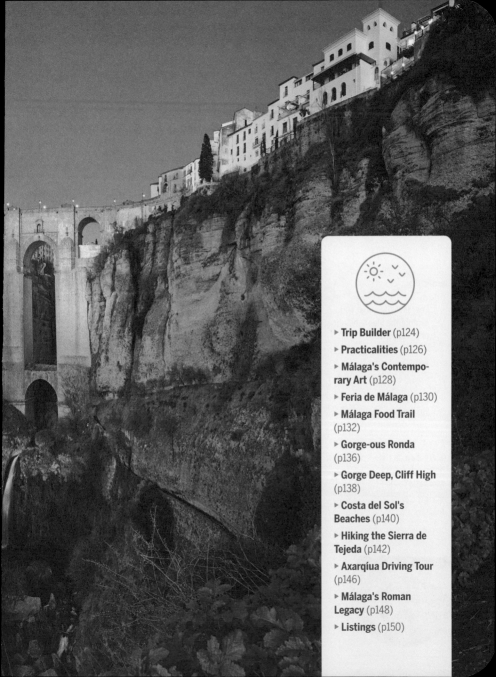

MÁLAGA
Trip Builder

Málaga is much more than a gateway to the spectacular Costa del Sol beaches. Multifaceted city aside, there are the natural wonders of El Chorro and Torcal, photogenic *pueblos blancos*, superb hiking in Málaga's mountain ranges and plenty of food, glorious food (and wine).

Scale sheer rock faces or a via ferrata in **El Chorro** (p138).
🚍 / 🚗 + 🥾 1hr from *Málaga*

Fuente de Piedra

Laguna de Fuente de Piedra

Campillos

Teba

Embalse del Conde del Guadalhorce

El Chorro

Villamartín

Algodonales

Setenil de las Bodegas

Ardales

Peer into the gorge and explore the Moorish heritage of **Ronda** (p136)
🚋 / 🚗 + 🥾 1hr from *Málaga*

Arriate

El Burgo

Alozaina

Ronda

CÁDIZ

Parque Natural Sierra de Grazalema

Ubrique

Río Guadiaro

Torrecilla (1918m)

Parque Natural Sierra de las Nieves

Coín

Cortes de la Frontera

Istán

Ojén

Glam it up on the beaches of glitzy **Marbella** (p140)
🚗 + 🥾 1½hrs from *Málaga*

Gaucín

Benahavís

Marbella

Mijas Costa

Jimena de la Frontera

San Pedro de Alcántara

Puerto Banús

Costa del Sol

Estepona

Manilva

Discover your perfect beach along the **Costa del Sol** (p140)
🚗 + 🥾 1-2hrs from *Málaga*

Guadiaro

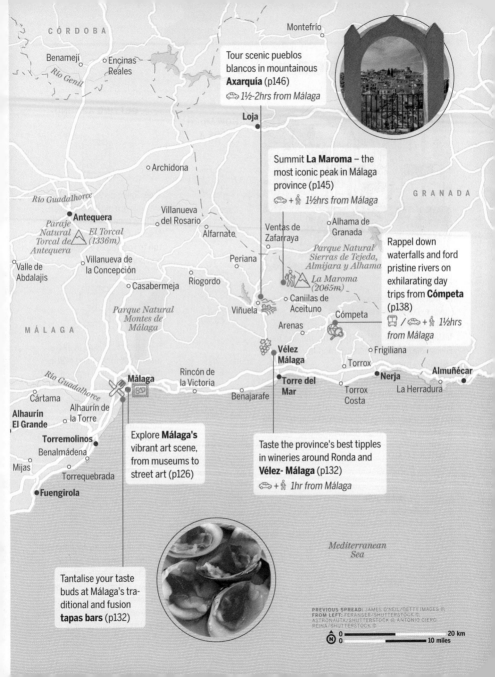

CÓRDOBA

Montefrío

Benamejí
Encinas Reales

Río Genil

Tour scenic pueblos blancos in mountainous **Axarquía** (p146)
🚗 *1½-2hrs from Málaga*

Loja

Archidona

Summit **La Maroma** – the most iconic peak in Málaga province (p145)
🚗+🥾 *1½hrs from Málaga*

GRANADA

Río Guadalhorce

Antequera

Paraje Natural Torcal de Antequera
El Torcal (1336m)

Villanueva del Rosario

Alfarnate

Ventas de Zafarraya

Alhama de Granada

Valle de Abdalajís

Villanueva de la Concepción

Periana

Parque Natural Sierras de Tejeda, Almijara y Alhama

La Maroma (2065m)

Rappel down waterfalls and ford pristine rivers on exhilarating day trips from **Cómpeta** (p138)
🚆 / 🚗+🥾 *1½hrs from Málaga*

Casabermeja

Riogordo

Caniilas de Aceituno

Parque Natural Montes de Málaga

Viñuela

Cómpeta

MÁLAGA

Arenas

Frigiliana

Vélez Málaga

Torrox

Río Guadalhorce

Málaga

Rincón de la Victoria

Torre del Mar

Nerja

Almuñécar

Cártama

Benajarafe

Torrox Costa

La Herradura

Alhaurín de la Torre

Alhaurín El Grande

Explore **Málaga's** vibrant art scene, from museums to street art (p126)

Taste the province's best tipples in wineries around Ronda and **Vélez- Málaga** (p132)
🚗+🥾 *1hr from Málaga*

Torremolinos

Benalmádena

Mijas

Torrequebrada

Fuengirola

Mediterranean Sea

Tantalise your taste buds at Málaga's traditional and fusion **tapas bars** (p132)

N 0 _____ 20 km
   0 _____ 10 miles

Practicalities

ARRIVING

Aeropuerto de Málaga Main international gateway *(aena.es)* to Andalucía, 9km west of Málaga city centre. Connected by *cercanías* (local) trains to Málaga train station, the city centre and also to Fuengirola (€2.70, 45 minutes) and Torremolinos (€1.80, 20 minutes).

Málaga-María Zambrano Train Station (pictured) Multiple daily trains to Cádiz (3½ hours), Córdoba (one hour), Seville (2¾ hours) and Madrid (2½ hours). Tickets for high-speed AVE trains to Seville and Madrid tend to cost double.

HOW MUCH FOR A

Cazón adobo tapa
€4

Glass of wine
€2.50

Cup of coffee
€1.50

GETTING AROUND

Train Renfe services connect Málaga with most major destinations around Andalucía, plus Madrid. *Cercanías* (local trains) run to Fuengirola via Torremolinos and Benalmádena.

Bus Málaga is linked to all the main cities in Spain, as well as numerous smaller, regional destinations. Main bus companies are Alsa *(alsa.es)* and Portillo *(avanza bus.com)*. Long-distance buses depart from the main bus station while Costa del Sol buses stop at the more central Muelle Heredia bus stop in the city centre.

Car To visit remote destinations around the province and for maximum flexibility, hire a car. Málaga airport has the cheapest car rentals in Andalucía if you book well ahead; otherwise rates tend to vary considerably.

WHEN TO GO

MAR–JUN
Balmy hiking weather; uncrowded beaches

JUL–AUG
Very hot; packed beaches. Starlite Festival (Marbella); Feria de Málaga; Noche de Vino (Cómpeta)

SEP–NOV
Fewer crowds, warm weather, warm sea; grape harvest; excellent hiking

DEC–FEB
Olive harvest; cool weather; affordable accommodation prices; almond blossoms

EATING & DRINKING

Málaga's dining scene is undoubtedly one of the highlights of anyone's visit, from the freshly grilled and fried fish at its *chiringuitos* (beach restaurants) to sophisticated fusion and Michelin-starred cuisine, as well as tantalising tapas in the likes of Málaga (the city), Marbella, Nerja and Ronda. Regional dishes include *porra antequerana* (local spin on *salmorejo*, topped with tuna, ham and hard-boiled eggs; pictured bottom right) and *salpicón* (summer salad consisting of finely chopped red and green pepper, cucumber and onion); wash them down with a crisp dry muscat (pictured top right) or a Ronda tempranillo.

Best winery Bodegas Ordóñez Málaga, Vélez-Málaga (p146)

Must-try tapas La Tranca, Málaga

CONNECT & FIND YOUR WAY

Wi-fi Free wi-fi is ubiquitous in hotels, restaurants, cafes, tourist offices etc. There are free wi-fi hotspots around Málaga city centre and Marbella.

Navigation Historic city centres and *pueblos blancos* are serpentine mazes of one-way, narrow lanes. Save yourself a lot of stress (and your wing mirrors!) by parking at designated car parks elsewhere and walking.

WHERE TO STAY

Málaga province has accommodation to suit all budgets. Since attractions are fairly spread out, base yourself where you plan to spend the most time.

Town/City	Pro/Con
Málaga	Museums, varied dining, festivals, accommodation options, great transport connections; crowds.
Marbella	Great beaches, numerous restaurants, transport connections; expensive.
Ronda	Sightseeing, scenic viewpoints, museums, good restaurants; busy in summer, few trains.
Nerja	Great beaches, water sports, ample dining; little budget accommodation, limited transport links.
Antequera	Great access to hiking and rock climbing, transport links; limited accommodation and dining.
Cómpeta	Traditional village life, great hiking; limited accommodation, transport and dining.

MÁLAGA PASS

This pass (*malagapass.com*) includes entry to the city's main museums, lets you skip the entry queue and provides discounts at restaurants, hotels, shops etc.

MONEY

Cash is still king in the smaller, more remote villages, so it's good to have some euros on you. Coins are handy for paying parking attendants at beaches along the Costa del Sol.

23 MÁLAGA'S
Contemporary Art

ART | CULTURE | HISTORY

The birthplace of Picasso, one of the 20th century's most iconic artists, Málaga has long been an art heavyweight. Deep-dive into Picasso's work that encompasses all his artistic periods, visit his childhood home and explore the city's other artistic offerings, from cutting-edge installations as CAC, Museo Carmen Thyssen and offshoot of Paris' Pompidou Centre to the urban-renewal street art project.

CLASSIC IMAGE/ALAMY STOCK PHOTO ©

🗺️ How To

Getting here/around
All the museums and the urban-renewal project are within easy walking distance of each other.

When to go Year-round, though bear in mind that the museums are busiest in the summer months when the city throngs with visitors.

Top tip Due to the huge popularity of Museo Picasso, in peak season it's essential to book your timed entry slot online.

DAVID MG/SHUTTERSTOCK ©

Left Museo Carmen Thyssen.
Bottom left Museo Picasso.

Picasso's Málaga The **Museo Picasso** runs through the artist's career in chronological order, from Picasso's paintings from his teenage years to a quick trot through cubism, and detours into sculpture. While short of show-stopping works (which are in Barcelona and Paris), this museum is a much more intimate foray into Picasso's life. Continue your exloration at the nearby **Casa Natal de Picasso** – the artist's childhood home, complete with personal objects, such as his christening gown, family photos, lithographs and sketches.

Museo Carmen Thyssen See works by Joaquín Sorolla, Ignacio Zuloaga and other 19th-century Spanish artists in the 16th-century palace. These glimpses of *andaluz* life through the lens of *costumbrismo* (Spanish folk art) – bullfighting, flamenco and bar-room brawls – are fascinating.

Centro de Arte Contemporáneo A former 1930s market building on the east bank of Río Guadalmedina is now Málaga's main exposition centre for modern art. International names (Damien Hirst, Louise Bourgeois) are well represented, but otherwise the interior highlights the revolving cast of thought-provoking paintings and installations by Spanish artists.

Centre Pompidou Málaga This hard-to-miss building by the port, topped by a giant multi-coloured cube, hosts frequently changing contemporary art exhibitions by Spanish and international names. The permanent collection alone includes works by the likes of Antoni Tàpies and Frida Kahlo, plus the powerful *Ghost* by Kader Attia – a truly extraordinary use of aluminium foil.

✿ MAUS: Urban Renewal in SOHO

The triangle-shaped neighbourhood of SOHO, near the port, was run-down for decades until local street artists conceived MAUS (Málaga Arte Urbano en el Soho) in 2015 as a way of injecting new life into the *barrio*. Street art is a big part of the project, and a walk around SOHO lets you view the seven-storey mural of a fighter pilot by D*Face (aka Dean Stockton), looming behind the CAC; a giant chameleon by environmentally minded Belgian artist ROA on Calle Casas de Campos; and a work by local artist Dadi Deuscol, depicting a half-nude, bearded man who rejects the rules at Calle Tomás Heredia 12.

Feria de Málaga

NEED-TO-KNOW INFO ABOUT EUROPE'S BIGGEST SUMMER PARTY

The Feria de Málaga is an exuberant week-long celebration that literally starts with a bang – a huge fireworks display and a concert by the bay – before segueing into days of sherry-fuelled traditional dancing, funfairs, horse shows, live music and bullfighting. Here's the lowdown on how best to participate in Europe's biggest party.

Left Fireworks, Feria de Málaga.
Middle Flamenco, Feria de Málaga.
Right Horse and carriage parade, Feria de Málaga.

Brief History

Dating back to 1487, the Málaga Fair commemorates the reconquest of the city from the Moors by King Ferdinand and Queen Isabella – Los Reyes Católicos. While the fair has been celebrated in one form or another since 1491, over the centuries it has grown into Spain's biggest summer party, traditionally held for a week from Saturday to Sunday over the third week in August.

The Proceedings

The party kicks off in style with the 'Big Bang' at midnight on the Friday, followed by a free concert by a top Spanish performer or band on Malagueta Beach. From the following day, the festivities are split between the **Feria de Día** (Day Fair), which is concentrated around Calle Larios in Málaga's city centre from around noon to 6pm daily, and **Feria de Noche** (Night Fair), which takes place nightly at El Real – a giant fairground west of the A-7 near the Palacio de Congresos from 9pm until dawn.

Where to See the Fireworks

Make sure you've sorted out an excellent vantage point for watching 'Big Bang' in advance. Options include the following:

Catedral de Málaga rooftops Buy tickets online a week in advance for great views of the port. Steep climb up lots of steps.

Gibralfaro viewing platform Fantastic bird's-eye views of Málaga. Small and crowded.

Muelle Uno Excellent ground-level views. Get here early to nab a spot.

Lighthouse Pretty much as close as you can get to the fireworks and the lighthouse beam. Extremely crowded.

Rooftop terraces Allows you to combine drinking with the light show. Book the likes of AC Palacio in advance or grab a seat early.

From a boat Several boat companies departing from Muelle Uno run firework-watching trips; superb unobstructed views. Very limited tickets.

Malagueta Beach Ideal for the post-fireworks concert. Massive crowds.

Feria del Día

During the day, smartly dressed men and women in flamenco dresses throng the streets to dance the foot-stomping, finger-clicking *Sevillanas* (traditional Seville dance). Dine at the packed restaurants and stalls dotting the city centre, groove to the live bands in Málaga's Plaza de la Constitución, Plaza de las Flores, Plaza de la Merced and Plaza Mitjana, and admire the Andalucian horses during daily horse and carriage parades.

> During daylight hours, smartly dressed men and women in flamenco dresses throng the streets to dance.

Feria de Noche

When darkness falls, crowds head to El Real, where *malagueños* (Málaga residents) gather to gossip, dance, strike business deals and drink at the 180 semi-private *casetas* (marquees), amid a merry hubbub of children getting underfoot, swirling dancers and waiters carrying platters of *pescaíto frito* (battered, fried small fish) and trays of *fino* (sherry), Málaga Dulce (sweet dessert wine) and *rebujito* (sherry shandies). Outside the private *casetas,* you can catch the free live music shows at the 'Caseta Municipal', open to all revellers, or simply wander around, people-watch and take in the non-stop assault on the senses: careering dodgem cars, brilliantly lit ferris wheels, loud music and dazzling lights.

♨ Feria Survival Tips

Use public transport Line F bus (€1.50 for a single ticket, €10 for 10) runs round the clock between the centre of Málaga and the fairground.

Dress the part Women can buy dresses (around €100) for the *feria* at numerous shops in the centre; second-hand dresses are sold at Cudeca charity shops on Plaza María Guerrero and Calle Puerta Nueva.

Protect yourself from the heat Drink plenty of water, wear light clothing and save yourself for night-time festivities.

Be prepared for big crowds To experience the fair without being overwhelmed, check out El Real during the day.

24 Málaga Food
TRAIL

FOOD | WINE | CULTURE

Málaga province is a gastronavigator destination par excellence. There's a superb tapas scene in Málaga proper, along with Latin fusion dining and Michelin-starred establishments. Dotted around the province, *chiringuitos*, award-winning bodegas and the world's first ecological caviar producer beckon.

🗺 How To

Getting here/around
Restaurants in Málaga are walkable; most *chiringuitos* along the coast and some bodegas are reached by bus. Visiting the sturgeon farm and some of the bodegas is easiest with your own wheels.

When to go Year-round. Visitor numbers spike during the summer (book restaurants well ahead). The best time to visit bodegas is September, during the grape harvest.

Best tour Spain Food Sherpas (spainfood sherpas.com) offers superb Málaga food tours.

Tantalising Tapas

The city of Málaga excels in the art of *tapear*. Local flavours not to miss include *porra antequerana* (similar to *salmorejo* but topped with tuna, ham and hard-boiled eggs), *ajoblanco* (cold almond soup with garlic), *gazpachuelo* (fish soup with potatoes and mayonnaise), *concha fina* (giant clams, eaten raw), *pipirrana malagueña* or *salpicon* (chopped red and green pepper, cucumber and onion salad) and *tortilla de camarones* (prawn fritters). Try them all at Málaga's best tapas bars (p151).

Málaga's Wines

Málaga province has been producing wine for almost 3000 years, with the best wines earning the 'Málaga' and 'Sierras de Málaga' Designation of Origin (DO) labels of excellence. Defined by mountainous topography,

🍴 Sabores Latinos

In recent years, Málaga has really begun to shine with the introduction of flavours from Latin America – Mexican, Peruvian, Colombian, Argentinian and Venezuelan – to its culinary repertoire. Whether you're looking for freshly made tacos, ceviche and expertly mixed pisco sours, superlative steaks or pillowy *arepas*, you'll find them all here.

Top left Mercado Atarazanas (p150).
Top right Las Merchanas (p151).
Left *Ajoblanco*.

Axarquía wines mostly use the muscat grape, with Botani and Dimobe brands winning international awards. Small wineries in the Ronda mountains produce characterful cabernet, merlot, syrah and tempranillo, while the microclimates in the Málaga mountains result in excellent dessert wines, made from Pedro Ximénez and muscat grapes. Look out also for Andresito and Al Fresco wines made from doradilla grapes, grown in the nutrient-rich soil of northern Málaga. You can visit some of the bodegas (p151) or else taste the local vintages in Málaga's wine bars (p151).

La Fritura Malagueña & Espetos

For *malagueños*, a day out at the beach is synonymous with a long lunch at a *chiringuito*, feet in the sand and a glass of *tinto con limón* to wash down two of Málaga's signature dishes. Dating back centuries, *fritura Malagueña* (fish fry) is a typical Sephardi Jewish dish that comprises lightly battered fish and shellfish fried in olive oil. Ingredients include

🐟 Know Your Caviar

'We produce three types of caviar: organic, Russian-style and traditional or Iranian-style. Organic is the most natural style – we add salt and seal it inside glass containers. When you eat it, you feel it pop against the roof of your mouth. Russian-style is caviar that's undergone a two-month maturation process in a special cylinder – a stronger flavour, but it still pops. The taste of traditional-style caviar – which is what most Russian customers associate with caviar – is achieved by letting it age for four to five months. Its flavour is the most pronounced, it's blacker in colour and it has a buttery texture.'

■ **Carmen Arriaza,** *guide/caviar expert at Riofrío Caviar, lives in Granada,* @riofriocaviar

GERARDVANDEWERKEN/SHUTTERSTOCK ©

MÁLAGA EXPERIENCES

Far left Caviar de Riofrío. **Near left** Sardines *espeto*. **Below** Sturgeon, Caviar de Riofrío factory.

boquerones (fried anchovies), *calamaritos* (baby squid), *salmonete* (red mullet), whiting, mackerel and *cazón adobo* (marinated dogfish). Another dish synonymous with Málaga is the *espeto*, a skewer of fresh sardines, roasted over coals in a barbecue pit, often on an old fishing boat.

World's First Organic Caviar

A tiny village in the Loja mountains has become an unlikely destination for casual gourmets and Michelin-starred chefs alike. Founded in 1963 as a trout farm by fish farming pioneer Dr Domezain, Caviar de Riofrío branched out into breeding critically endangered sturgeon in the 1980s and now produces some of the world's best caviar. Proximity to the source of the River Frío keeps the running water in the sturgeon pools a constant 14 to 15 degrees, and high standards of animal welfare and use of river plants to filter any waste has earned the farm the world's first 'organic' certification. Most of the caviar comes from Nacarii and Osetra species, along with some from Beluga. Everything – from spawning to packaging – is done on the premises, ensuring that this caviar is genuinely a '0 Km' foodstuff. Caviar and champagne tastings are available for visitors.

LEFT: PICTURE ALLIANCE/GETTY IMAGES ©. RIGHT: JOSÉ LUIS ROCA/STRINGER/GETTY IMAGES ©

25 Gorge-ous
RONDA

HISTORY | CULTURE | ARCHITECTURE

Its whitewashed houses tumbling down into the dramatic gorge that splits Ronda in two, the birthplace of modern bullfighting is intensely dramatic. Settled by the Celts, Phoenicians and Romans, Ronda was transformed by the Moors, whose influence is felt still.

🗺 Trip Notes

Getting here/around Ronda's tangle of Moorish lanes is a joy to wander. The town is well-connected by bus to numerous Andalucian destinations, and there's a daily train to Málaga.

When to go Year-round, though November and March are the rainiest months. Winters are crisp and cool and the busiest months (July and August) are relatively mild due to Ronda's lofty location.

Walking tours Freetours Ronda (freetoursronda.com) offers engaging themed perambulations.

🍴 Best Lunch Stops

Bodeguita El Coto Tiny bar serving ice-cold beer and tapas – *migas Rondeñas*, garlicky *caracoles* and hearty tortilla.

Albacara Ronda-style stewed oxtail and sea bream baked in salt served with epic side orders of gorge views.

Almocábar Imaginative spins on Rondeña cuisine, such as *ajoblanco* (cold almond soup with garlic) with melon sorbet, plus superb wines.

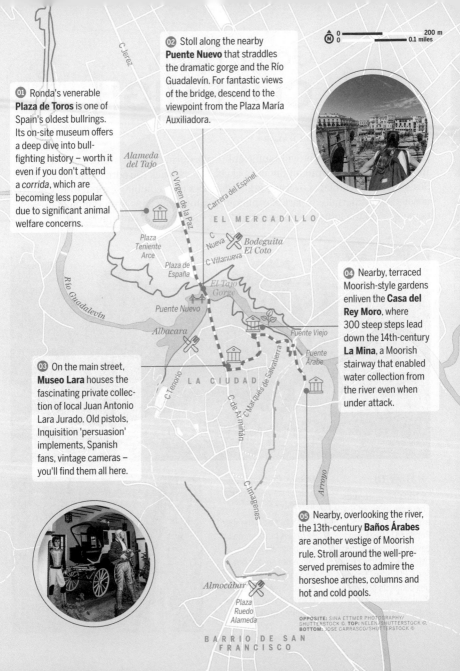

01 Ronda's venerable **Plaza de Toros** is one of Spain's oldest bullrings. Its on-site museum offers a deep dive into bullfighting history – worth it even if you don't attend a *corrida*, which are becoming less popular due to significant animal welfare concerns.

02 Stoll along the nearby **Puente Nuevo** that straddles the dramatic gorge and the Río Guadalevín. For fantastic views of the bridge, descend to the viewpoint from the Plaza María Auxiliadora.

04 Nearby, terraced Moorish-style gardens enliven the **Casa del Rey Moro**, where 300 steep steps lead down to the 14th-century **La Mina**, a Moorish stairway that enabled water collection from the river even when under attack.

03 On the main street, **Museo Lara** houses the fascinating private collection of local Juan Antonio Lara Jurado. Old pistols, Inquisition 'persuasion' implements, Spanish fans, vintage cameras – you'll find them all here.

05 Nearby, overlooking the river, the 13th-century **Baños Árabes** are another vestige of Moorish rule. Stroll around the well-preserved premises to admire the horseshoe arches, columns and hot and cold pools.

0   200 m
0   0.1 miles

C. Jerez

Alameda del Tajo

Carrera del Espinel

EL MERCADILLO

Plaza Teniente Arce

C Nueva
Bodeguita El Coto

C Villanueva

C. Virgen de la Paz

Plaza de España

El Tajo Gorge

Río Guadalevín

Puente Nuevo

Albacara

Puente Viejo

Puente Árabe

C. Tenorio

LA CIUDAD

C. de Armiñán

C. Marqués de Salvatierra

C. Imágenes

Arroyo

Almocábar

Plaza Ruedo Alameda

BARRIO DE SAN FRANCISCO

26 Gorge Deep, CLIFF HIGH

ADVENTURE | OUTDOORS | NATURE

If hiking doesn't provide sufficient thrills during your active exploration of the Málaga province's mountainous pockets, you can kick the adrenaline up a notch. Scale the sheer cliff faces overlooking Andalucía's rock climbing capital of El Chorro, abseil down waterfalls as part of exhilarating canyoning trips from Cómpeta or come play on the lofty steel playgrounds near Comares and Antequera.

ALBERTO JOSE MORENO JURADO/GETTY IMAGES ©

🗺 How To

Getting here/around
There are frequent trains from Antequera and Ronda to Málaga and excellent bus connections; twice-daily Málaga trains serve El Chorro. Loymerbus connects Málaga to Cómpeta (two to four daily) and there's a daily Málaga–Comares bus; a car gives you greatest flexibility.

When to go September to May is best for rock climbing/via ferratas; summers are too hot. Canyoning season is May to September, with cold river pools ideal for escaping the heat.

PECOLD/VSHUTTERSTOCK ©

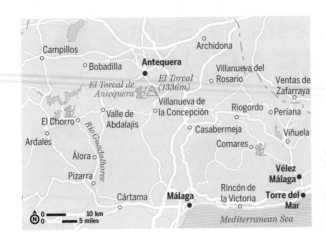

Left Torcal de Antequera.
Bottom left Rock climbing, El Chorro.

Canyoning

For the uninitiated, canyoning is an exhilarating way of exploring the beautiful, pine-fringed, mountainous river gorges of Málaga province. Don a wetsuit and helmet, then slide down natural water slides, jump off cliffs into refreshing, deep pools of crystal-clear water, rappel down waterfalls and swim through caves. Canyoning routes range from easy to seriously demanding, so good river guides are a must. **Titan Aventura** (titanaventura. com) offer superb trips down Río Verde and Lentegí.

Rock Climbing

The limestone gorge next to the village of **El Chorro** is a world-famous climbing destination. Its 1500+ routes range from mid-grade pitches to world-class hard ascents, while the limestone pinnacles and spires of the **Torcal de Antequera** also throw down the gauntlet to experienced climbers. Beginners can learn the ropes with **Climbing Malaga** (climbingmalaga.com).

Via Ferrata

Málaga province abounds in lofty steel playgrounds, bolted to sheer rock faces. They'll have you shimmying up vertical ladders and balancing on wire tightropes above the abyss. Route difficulty ranges from A (beginner) to E (incredibly challenging). Tiny **Comares** is home to three via ferrata, navigated with the help of **Vive Aventura** (viveaventura.es), with three more routes near **Ronda** suitable for beginners. Challenge yourself with an intermediate Tyrolean traverse near **El Chorro**, while the two half- and full-day routes in **El Torcal de Antequera** are as challenging as any in the Alps.

⚠ Best Canyoning Thrills

'Out of all the gorges where we take people canyoning – Río Verde, Lentegi, Bermejo, Nigüelas, La Bolera and Almanchares – my favourite is the upper section of the Río Verde. It's stunningly beautiful and offers an excellent mix of exhilarating natural water slides (down waterfalls), rappels and jumps. Lentegi is interesting as well – it's got fewer jumps but it's more technical, so you do more abseils and down-climbing. If you're a beginner, the lower section of Río Verde is an excellent introduction, with shorter rappels and smaller waterfalls for sliding down; our Lentegi trips can be adapted to suit first-timers as well.'

■ **Cristian García**, *river guide with Titan Aventura, Cómpeta, @titanaventura*

27 Costa del Sol's
BEACHES

BEACHES | NATURE | OUTDOORS

Stretching for over 160km from Punta Chullera, south of Estepona, all the way past Nerja to the east, the Costa del Sol is second to none when it comes to beautiful beaches. There are over 125 to choose from – ranging from golden strands of sand packed with beach umbrellas to isolated pebbly coves that you'll have almost to yourself.

BIGDANE/SHUTTERSTOCK ©

🗺 How To

Getting here/around
Many beaches in Málaga, Marbella, Estepona, Torremolinos, Fuengirola and Nerja can be reached by bus. For others, you'll need your own wheels.

When to go Year-round. Beaches are busiest (and hottest) in July and August. In winter, they're largely empty, while spring and autumn means temperate temperatures, with the water warmest in September.

Need to know Beachside parking can be a total nightmare in summer. Get to the beach early.

PACOPTT/SHUTTERSTOCK ©

Left Playa Burriana. **Bottom left** Paddleboarding, Cala de Tarzan.

MÁLAGA EXPERIENCES

Blue Flag Beauties Superb water quality and environmental management have led to 36 of Costa del Sol's beaches to be Blue Flag–certified in 2022. These include Nerja's **Burriana**, **Torrecilla** and **Maro**; **Benajarafe**, **La Caleta** and **Torre del Mar** in Vélez-Málaga; Málaga's **Pedregalejo** and **Malagueta**; Mijas' **La Calahonda**; **Casablanca** and **El Faro** in Marbella; and Fuengirola's **Carvajal** and **Castillo**.

Water Sports Numerous beaches are well set-up for kayaking, snorkelling and SUP. With some, like **Maro** and **Cañuelo** (both near Nerja) and **El Salon** (Nerja), you have to bring your own gear, while **Torreblanca** (Fuengirola), **Malapesquera** (Benalmádena) and **Casablanca** (Marbella) all have gear rentals.

Secluded Strands Take a beach shuttle down to the pebbly **Playa Cañuelo**, or hike down the cliffs to the **Playa de las Arbequillas** or the **Cala Molino del Papel** (all near Nerja). Also near Nerja, the sheltered **Cala de la Doncella** and **Cala de Tarzan** can only be accessed by kayak or SUP. West of Málaga, pretty **Playa de Viborilla** in Benalmádena is a cove surrounded by vegetation-covered cliffs.

Family-Friendly Beaches If you're looking for shallow, calm waters, beachside parks and play areas, and plenty of facilities (sun loungers, nearby restaurants, bathrooms etc), then you're spoiled for choice. **Burriana** (Nerja), **Cabopino** (Marbella), **Carihuela** (Torremolinos), **Playa de la Rada** (Estepona) and **Benajarafe** (Vélez-Málaga) are among many that fit the bill.

Best Beaches for Sunning Your Buns

Playa de Costa Natura (Estepona) Secluded, narrow rock-and-sand beach next to a naturist resort.

Playa de Cabopino (Marbella) Naturist section located at the west end of this long, gold-sand beach, sheltered by sand dunes.

Benalnatura (Benalmádena) Sheltered pebble-and-sand cove, bookended by cliffs.

Guadalmar Beach (Málaga) Wide, sandy beach with no facilities and a naturist section.

Almayate (Vélez-Málaga) Long, dark-sand beach with naturist campsite.

Cala del Pino (Nerja) Intimate cove with crystal-clear waters; steep descent.

Playa Cantarriján (Granada) Pebbly beach with two good *chiringuitos* and clear waters for snorkelling; a rocky headland separates the nude beach from the semi-nude family beach.

28 HIKING THE
Sierra de Tejeda

OUTDOORS | HIKING | ADVENTURE

The barren mountains and deep valleys of *bandolero* (bandit) country, Axarquía, are a fascinating place. Rebublican guerrillas hid in caves here during the Spanish Civil War, while the craggy peaks, plateaus and river gorges offer endless hiking adventures for fresh air fiends.

How To

ITDARBSALAMY STOCK PHOTO ©

Getting here/around Some trailheads are reachable by public transport (if you stay overnight). For maximum flexibility, drive yourself.

When to go March to mid-June and September to mid-November mean balmy weather, but many hikers prefer crisp, sunny winter days. In February, the hillsides are cloaked in almond blossoms.

Did you know? Some hardcore *malagueños* greet the new year by camping on the La Maroma summit on New Year's Eve.

MÁLAGA EXPERIENCES

GEORGE MUNDAY/ALAMY STOCK PHOTO ©

Making a Splash up Río Higuéron

JABLKO02/SHUTTERSTOCK ©

Departing from near the old sugar cane factory in Frigiliana, this moderately demanding river walk (20km, six hours return) is ideal for summer days when it's too hot to hike elsewhere. The mostly level trail follows a beautiful river valley, shaded by pine trees; you have the option of walking in the ankle-deep stream or beside it. When you reach a wide, rock-strewn section of the river bed, the stream disappears underground, but you pick it up again by some ruins. From here, you have no option but to walk in the water, so suitable footwear, a bathing suit and waterproof backpack are boons. You meander through a narrow, vegetation-covered rocky gorge, stopping for dips in clear, turquoise-coloured pools, and scrambling up smallish waterfalls, until you reach a rock face with metal steps

Ancient Trade Routes

Ever wonder why there are so many ruined *cortijos* (farmhouses) along many of the hiking paths through the Sierra de Tejeda y Almijara? It's because these trails were used by ice- and fish-bearing muleteers for centuries as part of an old network of trade routes between the coast and Granada.

Top left Hiking, Río Higuéron.
Top right Abandoned farmhouse, Frigiliana. **Left** El Lucero (p144).

bolted to it. If you climb up, the trail comes to a natural end a short way ahead.

Summiting El Lucero

From Cómpeta, a 50-minute drive along a wide, unpaved mountain road brings you to **Puerto Blanquillo**, a mountain crossroads from where a narrow trail (10.5km return, five hours) climbs up through dense woodland before evening out and passing by an old marble quarry. If you're lucky, you may spot some shy ibex around here. A little way down the valley, a turn-off crosses a stream and takes you along a rocky path up a gentle incline as it meanders through a rock-and-scrubland-dotted landscape between bare-sided hills. Then all vegetation disappears and the climb begins in earnest as the steep, narrow trail zigzags up the mountainside. If it's a windy day, turn back before the exposed section leading to the switchbacks. At the summit (1774m) of this pyramid-shaped peak, there are remnants of

🐾 The 'Lost' Village of Acebuchal

A tiny, picturesque cluster of whitewashed houses clinging to the hillside, Acebuchal is a 'ghost village' come back to life. An overnight stop along one of old trading routes since the 17th century, Acebuchal was targeted by General Franco's forces after the Spanish Civil War, when the village was suspected of providing a group of anti-Franco guerrillas hiding in a nearby cave with food and weapons. The village's 200 inhabitants were forcibly relocated to nearby Cómpeta and Frigiliana in 1948, but in 1998 a trickle of former residents returned and rebuilt their derelict houses. El Acebuchal restaurant is now a prime hiker magnet.

Left Acebuchal. **Below** Hikers, La Moroma.

a hut and stupendous views of the Sierra Nevada, some distance to the northeast.

The Big One: La Maroma

Looming above the Costa del Sol,and occasionally sprinkled with snow, the broad face of La Maroma (2069m) beckons *malagueños*, for whom summiting the province's highest peak is a pilgrimage of sorts. There are several trails up; if you're looking for the toughest challenge on the way up and the most scenic descent (20km, eight hours), take two cars, park one in Robledal, north of the mountain, then begin the ascent from **Sedella**, on the south side. At first, the trail ascends gently along a vegetation-covered hillside before turning sharply near the ruins of **El Fuerte** (a worthwhile detour) and then switchbacking steeply and relentlessly up to the exposed saddle (this section is often fog-shrouded, with Andalucía channelling Wales). It's a fairly gentle uphill along the barren plateau up to the concrete turret marking the peak; the descent along the north side of the mountain, through clearings full of wildflowers and pine forest, is a spectacular finish.

29 AXARQUÍA
Driving Tour

OUTDOORS | ARCHITECTURE | CRAFTS

▬▬▬ Explore timeless *pueblos blancos* (white villages), Moorish relics and winding mountain roads that give you access to olive-planted hillsides of this mountainous pocket of Andalucía. A slow pace of life, artisanal traditions and terrific food add spice to your journey.

EVAN FRANK/SHUTTERSTOCK ©

🗺 Trip Notes

Getting here/around Having your own wheels give you the greatest flexibility. The villages are connected by gorgeous hiking trails. There are also bus links to Málaga or Nerja.

When to go March to mid-June and September to-mid November for balmy weather. In February, white almond blossoms cloak the hills.

Don't miss Axarqíua's steep terrain and Mediterranean climate produce award-winning wines. Tours of the Ordoñez, Bentomiz and Almijara bodegas are a must.

✖ Take a Break

Plaza 45 (Frigiliana) Gourmet burgers, tiny, elaborate boca-dillos and unusual tapas, served alongside gorge views.

Ramon's (Canillas de Albaida) Halfway stop between Cómpeta and Árchez, renowned for its superlative *calamares a la romana* and *patatas bravas*.

Restaurante La Sociedad (Canillas de Aceituno) Feast on goat dishes beneath heavy wooden beams.

05 A short drive west, **Canillas de Aceituno** (pictured opposite), another beautiful Moorish-origin village, played a key role in a failed 16th-century *morisco* (Moorish conversion to Christianity) revolt. Numerous hiking trails start here.

03 Reachable on foot along the picturesque Río Turvilla walk from Cómpeta's sister village, Canillas, **Árchez**'s Moorish roots are evident in its remarkable 14th-century church tower (formerly a minaret).

02 The stunningly beautiful MA-5105 connects Frigiliana to Torrox, from where the A-7207 takes you through valleys of olive groves to **Cómpeta**, a centuries-old trading post between the coast and Granada.

Alcaucín

△ *La Maroma*
(2065m)

Parque Natural
Sierras de Tejeda,
Almijara y Alhama

Caniilas de
Aceituno

Viñuela

Sedella   Salares

Canillas de
Albaida

Árchez

Cómpeta

Arenas

Corumbela

Acebuchal

04 Further northeast, labyrinthine **Salares**, with its flower box–bedecked lanes, is renowned for its olive oil, its own minaret attached to the church of Santa Ana and its centuries-old Moorish-era stone bridge.

Frigiliana

**Torre
del Mar**

Nerja

Torrox
Costa

*Mediterranean
Sea*

01 First up is award-winning **Frigiliana**, its beautiful old Moorish quarter attracting busloads of visitors. Admire the 16th-century Renaissance palace, buy handmade ceramic tiles and hike up Río Higuerón.

Ⓝ 0 ———————— 10 km
   0 ———————— 5 miles

30 Málaga's Roman LEGACY

HISTORY | ARCHITECTURE | OUTDOORS

Few people left a bigger imprint on the Málaga province than the Romans. Everywhere you travel, you find potent reminders of four centuries of a 'Golden Age' of Baetica (roughly modern Andalucía) – Roman-era fragments of walls hidden in cities, remains of baths and extravagant villas along the coast, aqueducts and cobbled roads. Vestiges of an ancient world await your discovery.

JOSE LUIS VEGA GARCIA/GETTY IMAGES ©

🗺 How To

Getting here/around Roman remains in Málaga, Ronda, Marbella and Torrox can be reached on foot, with bus services between the towns. You will require your own wheels to reach remoter ruins.

When to go Anytime, though July and August tend to be hot and crowded and parking in coastal locations can be tricky.

Top tip Pack a bathing suit, since some of the Roman baths are still good for a soak.

CAVAN-IMAGES/SHUTTERSTOCK ©

Left Roman amphitheatre. **Bottom left** Mosaics, Villa Romana Río Verde.

Roman Málaga

A prosperous trading port under the Romans, the present-day city reveals its millennia-old heritage in the form of the largely intact 1st-century BCE **Roman amphitheatre**, beneath the Alcazaba walls. Inside the Universidad de Málaga lobby there are **stone pools** where fish guts were once macerated with vinegar to make *garum* (a salty, punchy condiment highly prized by Romans). Near the river, the Hotel Vincci Posada del Patio has to be contacted in advance for a free tour of the **Roman wall** that's been integrated into the five-star edifice.

Villas with a View

Romans enjoyed residing along prime stretches of the Costa del Sol as much as present-day residents of Marbella or Puerto Banus. Near its namesake Marbella beach, the **Villa Romana Río Verde** features well-preserved mosaics with a culinary motif. Intact Roman mosaics are part of the attraction of the Roman villa of **Clavicum** by the lighthouse in Torrox; there are also remains of baths and amphorae for packaging *garum*.

Bath Time!

Believed to have been used by Julius Caesar's army, the **Hedionda** baths are natural pools in a stunningly pretty riverside location, fed by sulphuric hot springs smelling of rotten eggs. Have a soak there, then stop at the **Roman Thermae of Las Bovedas** in Guadalmina, where the remains of archways and hot and cold pools overlook the aptly named Playa de Linda Vista.

The Lost Town of Acinipo

You're surrounded by rolling countryside; a sheer drop nearby lets you see for miles. Romans resident in the 1st-century BCE town of **Acinipo** (that later drifted into ruin under mysterious circumstances), near Ronda, enjoyed these same views as they went about their business in this prosperous agricultural town, partook in debates at the forum, soaked at the public baths, and traded their fresh produce, marble and fine potters' clay with visiting merchants. The stage backdrop and some seating of the impressive Roman theatre are still intact; to recreate the town from fragments of marble strewn across the hillside, you'll have to use your imagination.

Listings

BEST OF THE REST

 Chiringuitos

Chiringuito de Ayo €

Ignore the menu of grilled fish and meats and go straight for the paella at this Nerja eatery. It's cooked daily in a huge pan on an open wood-burning fire, and you can go back for seconds.

La Escollera €

All plastic tables and paper tablecloths, this portside place serves what's arguably the best and freshest seafood in Estepona. Elbow your way past beer-swigging dock workers and order some clams.

La Cepa Playa €€

Going strong for over 60 years, this Fuengirola institution near the harbour serves a dizzying array of prawns, anchovies, cuttlefish, swordfish, clams, mussels, squid, sardines, hake and more.

Lobito del Mar €€

Helmed by Michelin-starred chef Dani Garcia, this bistro-style Marbella *chiringuito* may be away from the beach, but catch-of-the-day is as fresh as beside the waves. The shellfish and *espetos* (skewers of sardines) are excellent.

Hermanos Muñoz €€

Local crowds pack the tables at the end of Málaga's Marítimo el Pedregal promenade, and wait with great anticipation for the house specialities of grilled dorada, sea bass and *espetos*.

Latin Flavours

La Niña Bonita €

Run by a husband-and-wife team in SOHO, this tiny Mexican joint dishes up fresh tacos *al pastór*, with *cochinita píbil* (slow-cooked pork, Yucatán-style) and other authentic toppings; served with kick-ass homemade salsas.

La Barra Inca €€

Grab some friends and head for this Peruvian restaurant to share a banquet of assorted ceviches and *arroz chaufa de mariscos* (seafood-fried rice), washing it down with superlative pisco sours.

Pampa Grill €€€

Chow down on expertly grilled beef ribs, sirloin and beautiful aged T-bone and Tomahawk rib-eye at this Argentinian restaurant aimed at the carnivorously inclined. Robust Argentinian reds seal the deal.

El Rincón Paisa €

Stop by this Colombian eatery for a heaped plate of *bandeja paisa* (fry-up comprising Colombian sausage, rice, red beans, fried plantain, *arepa*, pork crackling and fried egg).

LaQueFrao €

Speaking of *arepas* (think fluffy tortillas), Málaga's best Venezuelan restaurant excels at them, and serves them with assorted fillings, including cheese and avocado, alongside other Venezuelan staples.

Málaga's Best Tapas

Bodeguita El Gallo

Málaga dessert wines and homemade vermouth provide the perfect accompaniment to braised pork cheeks, superlative oxtail croquettes and tripe casserole at this carnivore-friendly old-school joint.

Cortijo de Pepe

This centrally located rustic 1970s *taberna* is all about the bounty of the sea and the Málaga countryside. Highlights include *porra antequerana* (Antequera's garlicky soup), *salpicón de mariscos* and *gambas al pil pil*.

Mercado Atarazanas

You may have to flit from counter to

counter, but Málaga's wrought-iron market is a superb place to try typical tapas, from *boquerones fritos* and seafood skewers to *berenjenas con miel*.

Las Merchanas

Dine out on homemade croquettes and *montaditos* (small sandwiches) filled with the *pringá del puchero* (slow-cooked pork products with chickpeas), surrounded by hundreds of images of saints and the Virgin Mary.

Mesón Mariano

The artichoke is the star here, prepared many different ways, along with goat and cod dishes from the Málaga region and an extensive list of regional wines from Serrania de Ronda and Axarquía.

Uvedoble Taberna

Expect modern art on walls and a modern spin on classic Málaga ingredients here. The smoked sardines on rosemary-tomato focaccia, and tuna tataki with *porra antequerana* are standouts.

La Farola de Orellana

Dating back to 1938, Málaga's oldest tapas bar serves over 50 tapas, paired with local wines, including *pipirrana, calamaritos fritos* and the house speciality of *bartolos* (similar to empanadas).

 ## Must-Visit Bodegas

Bodegas Ordoñez Málaga

Known for its multiple award-winning Botani Old Vines (DO), a dry white made from a Muscat grape variety originally planted by the Phoenicians in mountainside vineyards. Bodega visits arranged on request; Vélez-Málaga.

Cortijo Los Aguilares

A family-run, high-altitude Ronda winery surrounded by holm-oak woods, where the microclimate allows the cultivation of diverse grape varieties, from pinot noir and garnacha to syrah and cabernet sauvignon. All wines are organic; assorted tours available.

Bodega Antonio Muñoz Cabrera

Almost a century old, this Moclinejo bodega in the shadow of La Maroma produces stellar Axarquía wines. Difficult terrain means that everything is done by hand. Award-winning results speak for themselves.

Bodegas Almijara

A relatively new bodega, located on the premises of an old Cómpeta resin factory. Exclusively muscat and rome tipples, including a fine dry white jarel and a sweet dessert wine.

 ## Málaga Wine Bars

Vineria de Cervantes

A long by-the-glass wine list – including tipples from DO Sierras de Málaga, alongside Rioja and Ribera del Duero wines – is expertly paired with imaginative tapas, such as pickled anchovies, guacamole and mango mousse.

Los Patios de Beatas

Two 18th-century mansions with mosaic-inlaid tables make for a sumptuous space to sample regional wines from one of the city's best-stocked wine cellars. Innovative tapas also on offer.

Antigua Casa de Guardia

Dating back to 1840, this super-traditional tavern is Málaga's oldest bar. Try its own Pajarete 1908, the romantically named *lágrima trasañejo* (very old teardrop), or other Málaga wines served from giant barrels.

Bodegas El Pimpi

This local institution is decorated with historic *feria* posters and photos of visitors past, while the enormous barrels are signed by the likes of Antonio Banderas. Try local dessert wines with cheese.

 Scan to find more things to do in Málaga online

CÓRDOBA

ARCHITECTURE | FOOD | HIKING

Experience
Córdoba
online

Tour **Belalcázar** and other remote villages with dramatic cragtop castles (p168)
🚗 1-2hrs from Córdoba

Be awed by **La Mezquita**, Córdoba's remarkable mosque (p156)

Indulge your taste buds at Córdoba's traditional **tapas bars** (p162)

Taste the province's famous tipples in **Bodegas Alvear**, one of Montilla's historic wineries (p164)
🚗 + 🚌 1hr from Córdoba

Sample the world's best olive oil in **Priego de Córdoba** (p168)
🚗 + 🚶 1½hrs from Córdoba

Summit rugged peaks and tramp through gorges around **Zuheros** in the Sierras Subbéticas (p160)
🚗 + 🚶 1¼hrs from Córdoba

CÓRDOBA
Trip Builder

▬▬ Synonymous with Islamic Spain, sultry Córdoba delights with its wealth of stunning Moorish architecture, as well as traditional tapas bars that dot its medieval street. Elsewhere, you're met with the sight of blufftop castles, remote villages, olive groves, traditional vineyards and terrific hiking trails through gorges and up craggy peaks.

Mediterranean Sea

0 — 40 km
0 — 20 miles

Practicalities

ARRIVING

Aeropuerto de Sevilla Closest airport to Córdoba province. Buses run to/from Sevilla Santa Justa train station (one way/return €4/6, 25 to 30 minutes). Frequent trains to Córdoba (from €8, 42 minutes). Málaga and Granada airports also good options.

FIND YOUR WAY

Park in car parks on the outskirts of villages to avoid breaking into a cold sweat while navigating one-way, narrow medieval lanes.

MONEY

Carry euros on you for dining out and small purchases in remote villages. Accommodation prices shoot up during local holidays.

WHERE TO STAY

City/ Village	Pro/Con
Córdoba	Moorish architecture, terrific gastronomy, flamenco, shopping, galleries, museums, good transport links
Montilla	Award-winning wines, guided bodega visits, small boutique hotels, frequent buses to/from Córdoba
Zuheros	Relaxed vibe, easy trail access in Parque Natural Sierras Subbéticas; infrequent buses
Carca-buey	Rural tourism, proximity to award-winning olive oil cooperatives, good hiking base, regional gastronomy

EATING & DRINKING

Córdoba's buzzy dining scene is one of Andalucía's best, combining traditional tapas and Montilla wines with international fusion cuisine and craft beer.

Salmorejo (pictured top left) Thick, cold tomato soup with breadcrumbs, olive oil, salt, garlic and sherry vinegar, topped with hard-boiled egg and *jamón serrano*.

Rabo de toro (pictured bottom left) Slow-cooked oxtail in a tomato-based stew.

Best olive oil SCA Almazaras de Subbética, Almaliva (p171)

Must-try tapas Garum 2.1, Córdoba (p163)

GETTING AROUND

Train High-speed AVE services connect Córdoba with Cádiz via Seville, and also Málaga. Slower Renfe trains run Granada (change in Antequera for the latter).

Bus Inexpensive bus services cover most towns in the province, though buses in remoter parts tend to be infrequent. The main companies are ALSA (alsa.es) and Autocarres Carrera (autocarrescarrera. es).

Car Having your own wheels gives you maximum flexibility. You can rent a car at Seville, Málaga and Granada airports; Málaga's rates tend to be cheaper, but it's still a good idea to book well in advance.

MAR–MAY
Balmy hiking weather; Feria de Córdoba and Fiesta de Patios in Córdoba

JUL–AUG
Very, very hot; drop in accommodation rates (snag one with a pool!)

SEP–NOV
Fewer crowds, warm weather; grape harvest; excellent hiking

DEC–FEB
Olive harvest, olive oil tours in full swing; cooler weather; affordable accommodation prices

31 Moorish
CÓRDOBA

HISTORY | ARCHITECTURE | CULTURE

▬▬▬ Explore Córdoba's rich Moorish history and heritage first by admiring the splendour of Andalucía's top surviving mosque-turned-cathedral, strolling through the majestic gardens of the Alcazar and peeking inside a 10th-century hammam before indulging in the contemporary version. Then head outside the city to walk the ancient streets of the partially excavated palace-city and peruse its archaeological treasures.

ALEJANDRO ZAMBRANA/SHUTTERSTOCK ©

🗺 How To

Getting here/around
Historic Córdoba is compact and walkable. Buses run from the roundabout stop on Paseo de la Victoria in Córdoba to Medina Azahara (€9 return); book tickets in advance online.

When to go March to May, plus September and October mean balmy weather and fewer crowds.

Need to know Bus services from Córdoba to Medina Azahara run only from April to September. Tickets to La Mezquita must be booked online ahead of time.

DAVID ACOSTA ALLELY/SHUTTERSTOCK ©

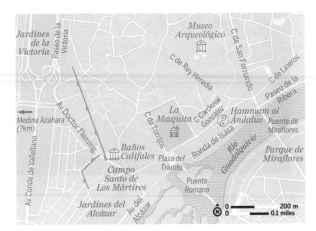

Left La Mezquita. **Bottom left** House of Ya'far, Medina Azahara.

Soaring Arches La Mezquita is one of the most incredible works of Islamic architecture in the world. You'll find yourself staring, slack-jawed, at the forests of marble columns, topped by red-and-white arches, and the seamless amalgamation of cathedral and mosque, with the Gothic chapel sporting carved mahogany choir stalls and a baroque ceiling. The biggest highlight is the stunning 10th-century *mihrab* (prayer niche), its gold mosaics the work of Byzantine craftsmen, and the golden dome of the *maksura* (royal enclosure).

Caliph's City-Palace The partially excavated **Medina Azahara** – the 'Shining City' founded by Caliph Abr ar-Rahman III in 936 CE – is 8km west of Córdoba. A shuttle bus (€2.50) connects the state-of-the-art museum and the ruins. Don't miss the red-striped portico arches, the intricately carved doorway of the House of Ya'far, and views of the imperial garden and the Salon Rico.

Moorish Life The **Museo Arqueológico's** Moorish period (711–1236 CE) collection includes decorative *tawriq* freezes, Almohad ceramics, and an intricately decorated bronze stag, once used as a fountain spout in Medina Azahara, gifted by Byzantine emperor Constantine VII to Abr ar-Rahman III.

Bath Time! Descend into the subterranean depths of the **Baños Califales** – the 10th-century Moorish hammam used by Caliph al-Hakam II for relaxation. Wander through various bathing areas, illuminated by the star-shaped windows in the barrel-vaulted ceilings, or try out the contemporary version – **Hammam al Ándalus** – nearby.

◎ Virtual Medina Azahara Visits

'One of the biggest highlights of the Medina Azahara site – Salon Rico, the royal reception hall – is off-limits to visitors for the foreseeable future while its restoration is ongoing. But there is nothing to stop you from donning a VR (virtual reality) headset and strolling through the iconic building, reconstructed by **Virtual Legacy** using state-of-the-art technology. You can stroll through the surrounding gardens, admire the pavilion's striped arches and the deer sculpture by the pool, and even interact with the objects inside the pavilion using your 'hand'. I suggest a virtual visit before a real visit to Medina Azahara.'

■ **By José Luís Caballero Serrano**, *entrepreneur and creator of Virtual Legacy, Córdoba*
@virtuallegacycordoba

Córdoba: From Augustus to Castilla's Fernando III

JULIAN MALDONADO/SHUTTERSTOCK ©

A STAMPEDE THROUGH CÓRDOBA'S FASCINATING HISTORY

Founded as a Bronze Age Iberian trading settlement, Córdoba rose to prominence under the Romans and particularly flourished under Moorish rule, becoming the Islamic capital of Europe. The city's millennia-long history is a turbulent Game of Thrones–style play in multiple acts, with a cast of Romans, Visigoths, Moors and Christian conquistadors.

Left Visigoth church remains, La Mezquita. **Middle** Statue of the Jewish philosopher Maimonides, Judería. **Right** Bell tower, La Mezquita.

Roman Curduba

The name 'Córdoba' is potentially a corruption of the Phoenican coteba ('oil press'), after the main export that helped the city flourish after Roman Corduba was founded in 152 BCE. During the struggle for political hegemony between Pompey and Caesar, Corduba backed the former, and when Caesar sacked the city in 45 BCE, over 20,000 citizens were executed. Still, under Emperor Augustus, Corduba bounced back and became the prosperous capital of Baetica (present-day Andalucía) in 27 BCE, producing renowned poet Lucan and philosopher Seneca, and expanding trade along the Río Guadalquivir.

Enter the Visigoths

By the 5th century, Roman rule was in terminal decline. The city was overrun by Vandals, but then the Visigoths arrived on the scene, expelling other Germanic tribes from Spain, repelling attacks from the Byzantine Empire and settling in Córdoba for 150 years. Visigoth rule saw the rapid spread of Christianity and the building of Christian basilicas.

The Moorish Golden Era

In 711, Córdoba fell to the Moors from northern Africa. The city became the capital of Moorish Spain in 756, and entered a golden age that lasted for three hundred years. By the 10th century, Córdoba was the world's largest city and rivalled Cairo and Baghdad as a Muslim centre of philosophy, medicine and astronomy, with a world-renowned library in the Alcazar (fortress), over a million residents, hundreds of mosques and bathhouses, and a sophisticated water supply and sewage collection system. La Mezquita was substantially enlarged and the splendid city-palace of Medina Azahara (p156) was built. Yet the decline, when it came, was swift. A series of civil wars in the 11th century saw the dissolution of the caliphate and the splintering of Al-Andalus (Moorish-controlled Spain). Rival

would-be caliphs fought one another for power, and Córdoba was briefly taken by the Berbers, who trashed Medina Azahara at the same time. Though two renowned 12th-century philosophers – Muslim Averroës and Jewish Maimónides – emerged during that turbulent era, the writing was on the wall.

Jews in Córdoba

> By the 10th century, Córdoba was the world's largest city and rivalled Cairo and Baghdad as a Muslim centre of philosophy, medicine and astronomy

When the Romans founded Corduba, the Jews were already there, thought to have arrived aboard Phoenican ships in the 10th century BCE. While under the Romans, Jews were free to practise their own religion and had some degree of autonomous rule, Visigoths brought with them forcible conversion to Christianity, which is why the Moors were welcomed by Jews as liberators. Jews lived in harmony with their Moorish rulers, participating in trade and even occupying important positions in the Ummayad court. But in the 12th century, when the fundamentalist Islamic Almohads supplanted the Ummayads and the re-conquest of Spain by Christian kings gathered pace, the Jews found themselves repressed by both, and confined to what's now known as Córdoba's *judería* (Jewish quarter) from 1236 until their expulsion from Spain in 1492.

Christian Conquest

In 1236, Ferdinand III, king of Castilla and León, laid lengthy siege to Córdoba, expelled the Moors and consecrated La Mezquita as a Catholic church. Even though the professions established under the Moors – silversmiths, parfumiers, leatherworkers – continued under the Christian rulers, the city fell into a long period of neglect and stagnation.

🏛 Building La Mezquita

La Mezquita – the grandest mosque ever built by the Moors, and now a cathedral – was originally built on the site of the 6th-century Visigothic Basilica de San Vicente. Founded in 785, the original mosque was designed by architect Sidi ben Ayub, who used columns salvaged from the Visigothic church and Roman buildings and introduced the distinctive red-and-white, brick-and-stone arches. Enlarged three times between 786 and 994, in 1236 the mosque became a church and was considerably modified over the following 300 years, with the 10th-century minaret becoming a Renaissance-baroque bell tower by 1664. The 2004 petition by Spain's Muslims to worship in the Mezquita once more was denied.

32 Mountain
ESCAPES

HIKING | NATURE | OUTDOORS

▰▰▰▰ A 320-sq-km pocket of green hills, craggy mountain tops, deep valleys, soaring canyons and olive groves, Parque Natural Sierras Subbéticas sits southeast of Córdoba. Dotted with *pueblos blancos* (white villages) and known for some of the world's best olive oil, it offers numerous hiking trails and the chance to sample liquid gold made from the fruit of millennia-old olive trees.

How To

Getting here/around Several daily buses connect Córdoba to Zuheros, Carcabuey and Priego de Córdoba – the most popular access villages. Several hikes start directly in Zuheros; to reach other trailheads, you'll need your own wheels.

When to go May, June, September and October are the best for outdoor pursuits. Weekends and holidays tend to get busy.

Hiking permits Two trails in the park require pre-booked permits (juntadeandalucia.es/medioambiente/cupos-ciudadano). It's worth visiting the Centro de Visitantes Santa Rita off the A-339 for excellent displays on local flora and fauna alone.

Map details:
- 0 — 10 km / 0 — 5 miles
- Baena
- Búnkeres del Alamillio
- Doña Mencía
- Luque
- Zuheros
- Cañón de Bailón Loop
- Cerro del Bramadero
- Lobatejo (1380m)
- El Cañuelo
- Cabra
- Zagrilla
- *Parque Natural Sierras Subbéticas*
- Puente Califal Loop
- Priego de Córdoba
- Caracabuey
- Pico Bermejo (1476m)
- Pico La Tiñosa (1570m)
- Rute
- Algarinejo
- Embalse de Iznájar

Outstanding Hikes

Small but perfectly formed, **Parque Natural Sierras Subbéticas** has hiking opportunities for all abilities. Gentle trails include the **Puente Califal loop** from **Carcabuey** (7.3km, 2¼ hours) that meanders through the countryside and crosses a Moorish bridge, and a 1.3km ramble through olive groves from **Luque** to the Civil War–era **Búnkeres del Alamillio**.

One of the park's most popular hikes is the **Cañón de Bailón loop** (4.4km, two hours) from **Zuheros** that zigzags up from the bridge across Río Bailón before following the dry stream bed though a dramatic canyon. Just before you reach the Fuente de la Moral, you can either take the trail that climbs sharply uphill to the

minor road leading from the **Cueva de los Murciélagos** back to Zuheros, with fantastic bird's-eye views of the village, or circle the **Cerro del Bramadero** hill (13km, 4 ½ hours) before rejoining the original Río Bailón trail.

The park's loftiest point is the **Pico La Tiñosa** (1570m), reached via a strenuous 6.6km ascent from Las Lagunillas. You can retrace your steps or else descend past the Cueva de Morrion to **Priego de Córdoba** (24km in total). Another terrific day trek is the linear hike from **Rute** to Priego de Córdoba (26km, eight hours) – part of the GR7 Route – that passes through pine forest, copses of oaks and olive groves, with wonderful ridgetop views of the countryside.

🥾 Best Climbs

'My favourite climb is the Pico Bermejo (1478m), through a valley full of wildflowers and then a more challenging rocky landscape where you have to blaze your own trail to the top. Your reward is the superb view of the Sierras Súbbeticas, La Tiñosa ('the roof of Córdoba') and the Sierra Nevada.

Olive oil tasting is another terrific reason to come here. Súbbeticas produce some of the best extra virgin olive oil in the world. Fermín of Aceites Vizcántar is extremely knowledgeable and great at communicating his passion for his olive oil to visitors; you'll feel like a real expert after his tour!'

■ **Recommended by Catharina Groot**, *expert hiker and owner of Posada Amena in Carcabuey,* @posada_amena

Above Parque Natural Sierras Subbéticas.

JOSEMA GOMEZ/SHUTTERSTOCK ©

33 A Little Bit M(O)ORISH

FOOD | WINE | CULTURE

■■■■ Córdoba is a master when it comes to the art of *tapear* and the city's dining scene is among the most exciting in Andalucía. Whether you dine in characterful bodegas, sip on celebrated Montilla-Moriles wines or let your taste buds explore edgy contemporary cuisine, you'll never go hungry here.

Best Córdoban Eats

My favourite place in Córdoba is **Jugo**; you can enjoy natural local wines there. **El Bar de Paco** is the tapas bar from the two-Michelin-starred chef, Paco Morales. Then there's **La Bodega**, which has the best Iberian products in town, including the Montilla-Moriles fino. Also, don't miss the *mazmorra cordobesa*.

🗺 Trip Notes

Getting here/around Central Córdoba – from the labyrinthine lanes of Old Town to the newer streets in Centro – is easily explored on foot.

When to go March to May, plus September to November mean warm strolling weather, though late spring is also a hugely popular time to visit. Winter months mean few crowds and cooler temperatures.

Top tours Explore Córdoba's tapas scene with José from **Foodie & Experiences** (foodieandexperiences.com).

 ■ Recommended by José Fabra-Garrido, owner/tour guide at Foodie & Experiences, Córdoba, @josefabragarrido

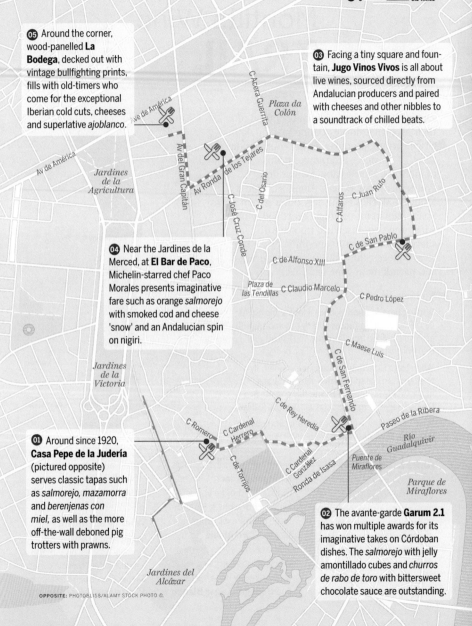

05 Around the corner, wood-panelled **La Bodega**, decked out with vintage bullfighting prints, fills with old-timers who come for the exceptional Iberian cold cuts, cheeses and superlative *ajoblanco*.

03 Facing a tiny square and fountain, **Jugo Vinos Vivos** is all about live wines, sourced directly from Andalucian producers and paired with cheeses and other nibbles to a soundtrack of chilled beats.

04 Near the Jardines de la Merced, at **El Bar de Paco**, Michelin-starred chef Paco Morales presents imaginative fare such as orange *salmorejo* with smoked cod and cheese 'snow' and an Andalucian spin on nigiri.

01 Around since 1920, **Casa Pepe de la Judería** (pictured opposite) serves classic tapas such as *salmorejo*, *mazamorra* and *berenjenas con miel,* as well as the more off-the-wall deboned pig trotters with prawns.

02 The avante-garde **Garum 2.1** has won multiple awards for its imaginative takes on Córdoban dishes. The *salmorejo* with jelly amontillado cubes and *churros de rabo de toro* with bittersweet chocolate sauce are outstanding.

Plaza da Colón

Av de América

Jardines de la Agricultura

C Acera Guerrita

Ave de América

Av del Gran Capitán

Av Ronda de los Tejares

C José Cruz Conde

C del Osario

C Alfaros

C Juan Rufo

C de San Pablo

C de Alfonso XIII

Plaza de las Tendillas

C Claudio Marcelo

C Pedro López

C Maese Luis

C de San Fernando

Jardines de la Victoria

C de Rey Heredia

Paseo de la Ribera

Río Guadalquivir

C Romero

C Cardenal Herrero

C de Torrijos

C Cardenal González

Ronda de Isasa

Puente de Miraflores

Parque de Miraflores

Jardines del Alcázar

0 / 200 m
0 / 0.1 miles

34 Montilla Wine TRAIL

WINE | ARCHITECTURE | OUTDOORS

Córdobans are justifiably proud of their Montilla-Moriles Denominación de Origen wines, produced in the countryside south of Córdoba, around the towns of Montilla, Moriles and Aguilar de la Frontera, among others. Along with Jerez, Montilla-Moriles is the only other region in Spain known for producing fortified wines – just don't confuse local tipples with sherry! Indulge your oenophilia by visiting local bodegas, dining in select restaurants and partaking in wine festivals.

How to

Getting here/around Montilla, Moriles and Aguilar de la Frontera are all accessible by bus and are within an hour's drive from Córdoba. You'll need your own wheels to reach the out-of-town bodegas.

When to go Flowering vineyards are wonderfully photogenic in late spring/early summer. Grape harvests take place between late July and late September. Harvest time coincides with various festivals.

Wine capital Numerous bodegas are conveniently located in Montilla proper.

Tours & Tastings

The heavy, sweet aroma of fortified wine greets you as you venture inside the ageing cellars of local bodegas, stacked with three tiers of enormous oak casks filled with precious liquid cargo. Fifteen are open to visitors and offer introductory tours.

Standouts include Montilla's **Bodegas Alvear** (alvear.es), Spain's third-oldest bodega with award-winning PX and three different wine tastings; Moriles' **Toro Albalá** (toro albala.com), where premium visits include sampling legacy wines directly from barrels; and **Bodegas Lagar Blanco**

(lagarblanco.es), 10km east of Montilla, where you can combine vineyard visits with bodega lunches.

Wining & Dining

Select restaurants in the Montilla-Moriles region and beyond serve Montilla wines. Savour Córdoban classics beneath striped Moorish arches

Map

Córdoba
El Carpio
Sociedad Plateros María Auxiliadora
Río Guadalquivir
Río Guadajoz
Castro del Río
La Carlota
Montemayor
Espejo
La Rambla
Montilla
Taberna Bolero
Santaella
Bodegas Alvear
Bodegas Lagar Blanco
Aguilar de la Frontera
Toro Albalá
Monturque
Cabra
Moriles
Río Genil
Alma Ezequiel
Puente Genil
Lucena
Herrera
Estepa
0 — 10 km
0 — 5 miles
N

🍷 Montilla vs Sherry

'There are similarities between Montilla-Moriles wines and sherry from Jerez, from production methods to categorisation: here you will also encounter delicate, dry and pale fino, golden-coloured, richer-flavoured amontillado, full-bodied oloroso and the dark, syrupy Pedro Jiménez. But Montilla-Moriles wines are made almost exclusively from the pedro jiménez grape, rather than palomino fino; also, our hot summers and relative lack of humidity mean that our grapes have a higher alcohol content. Our fino and amontillado are aged in oak casks in *soleras*, using the *criadera* (nursery) method, under a layer of flor (indigenous yeast) inside the barrels, and we use *tinajas* (clay jars) to mature our PX.'

■ **By Aurora Rodríguez Pino**, *tour guide and wine expert at Bodegas Alvear, Montilla.* @bodegas_alvear

at **Sociedad Plateros María Auxiliadora** (restaurante cordoba.com) in Córdoba, sip a *fino viejes* at **Alma Ezequiel** (almaezequielmontilla.com) in Puente Genil alongside *tagine de cordero* or *arroz meloso*, or enjoy regional dishes with a contemporary twist while sharing a bottle of Dulas Joven at **Taberna Bolero** (taberna bolero.com) in Montilla.

Festival Time!

Every year in April, **Cata del Vino Wine Fest** (cordoba tickets.com/fiestas-de-cordoba/cata-del-vino) is held on Córdoba's Plaza de Colón to celebrate Montilla wine, with stands from over two dozen participating bodegas, as well as select restaurants. In Montilla, September sees the sublime mélange of jazz and fino, aka **Montijazz Vendimia** (montijazz.com), held over the second week of the month at assorted venues around town.

Above Bodegas Alvear.

35 Cordoba's
COURTYARDS

ARCHITECTURE | CULTURE| HISTORY

▬▬▬ Anyone who's been to Córdoba in the summer knows how hot it gets, hence the millennia-old Roman and Moorish tradition of building houses with inner courtyards to facilitate airflow throughout. Córdobans are immensely proud of their photogenic patios and fill them with an abundance of flowers. Some courtyards are open to the public year-round; others, only during a special festival.

🗺 How To

Getting here/around Walking is the best way to experience the labyrinthine maze of Córdoba's medieval lanes and to get from courtyard to courtyard.

When to go Private courtyards are open to the public during the Festival of the Patios during the first half of May, but some patios can be visited year-round.

Best Tour Patios de San Basilio (patiosdesanbasilio.com) offers entertaining tours daily of five private patios year-round.

Map labels: Plaza da Colón; Pálacio de Viana; Jardines de la Agricultura; Av del Gran Capitán; Av Ronda de los Tejares; C Alfaros; C de San Pablo; Jardines de la Victoria; Paseo de la Victoria; Plaza de las Tendillas; C de San Fernando; Av Dr Fleming; Av Conde de Vallellano; Ronda de Isasa; Río Guadalquivir; Parque de Miraflores; Patio de la Muralla; SAN BASILIO; Jardines del Alcázar; Asociación de Amigos de los Patios Cordobeses; Av del Alcázar; N 0 500 m / 0 0.25 miles

La Fiesta de Los Patios Cordobeses

Part of Unesco Intangible Heritage of Humanity, this spirited festival (patios.cordoba.es) celebrates Córdoba's patios over the first two weeks of May every year. The festival dates back to 1921, and it's been growing every year, barring the minor interruption in the form of the Spanish Civil War. Participating courtyard owners along several walking routes in historic Córdoba welcome visitors into their inner sanctums so that you can admire the hanging plant pots, walls clad in creepers, fountains, quirky patio furnishings and particularly exuberant flower arrangements. Cash prizes are awarded for different categories.

Asociación de los Amigos de los Patios Cordobeses

Located on Calle San Basilio 44, this cobbled courtyard

What Makes Courtyards Special

'Córdoba's courtyards are a city feature that's uniquely ours; they lend the city an intimate feel in spite of its size. The best example of this is the Barrio de San Basilio, whose narrow streets and courtyards give you a glimpse of 10th-century Córdoban life.

My favourite patio is without a doubt the Patio de la Muralla. It's the only Córdoban patio where you can see an Almohad wall and an Old City defence tower. The patio has an unusual shape: following the wall instead of being located in the centre of the house, it lowers the temperature by 10 degrees.'

■ **By Meritxell Valle López**, *tour guide with Patios de San Basilio, Córdoba, @meritxell*

is open year-round and features a well wreathed in greenery and different floral displays, depending on the time of year. It's also a great place to shop (p171).

Palacio de Viana

Twelve plant-filled patios are a particular highlight of this antique-filled mansion – the home of the Marqueses of Viana from the 15th century until 1981. You can pay just for courtyard access only and don't need a guide to explore them. Our favourites include **Patio de Las Rejas**, with citrus trees on trellises; **Patio de la Madama**, where a cypress plant structure frames a shaded fountain with nymph statue; and **Patio del Pozo**, with elaborate wrought-iron work decorating an ancient well.

Above Patio de Las Rejas.

36 Córdoba Driving TOUR

OUTDOORS | CASTLES | VILLAGES

▬▬▬ Explore the varied landscapes of Córdoba province by touring far-flung villages from Subbéticas mountains to the Río Guadalquivir valley and remote Los Pedroches farmlands. Craggy castles, hiking, traditional restaurants and Spain's best *jamón iberico bellota* are all on the menu.

CSP/SHUTTERSTOCK ©

📷 Trip Notes

Getting here/around Buses from Córdoba serve some villages, but services are scarce. There's great hiking between two of them; otherwise, you need a car.

When to go Temperate weather in spring (March to June) and autumn (September to mid-November) is ideal. Steer clear of summer heat and crowds during holidays and weekends.

Fun fact Belalcázar was the birthplace of conquistador Sebastián de Belalcázar who founded Quito (Ecuador), Cali and Popayán (Colombia).

🍴 Diverse Village Dining

Gastronómico Gafiq (Belalcázar) *Jamón iberico* and slow-cooked pig's cheeks with dark beer stand out.

Restaurante La Paloma (Santa Eufemia) Superlative paella.

Asador El Campero (Almodóvar del Río) Carnivores' paradise serving expertly grilled lamb chops.

La Pianola Casa Pepe (Priego de Córdoba) No-nonsense, down-home cooking.

Asador Los Polancos (Zuheros) The slow-roasted kid with garlic is superb.

04 Take the back roads to **Belalcázar**, whose main claim to fame is its 15th-century **Castillo de los Sotomayor**, with the tallest keep in Spain (45m). Don't miss the impressively intact **Roman bridge**.

05 Big skies and rolling farmland are your companions as you drive to **Santa Eufemia**, Andalucía's northernmost village, presided over by the formidable **Castillo de Miramontes** – a Moorish ruin with epic views.

02 A short drive north, nestled against steep cliffs in a scenic gorge, the *pueblo blanco* of **Zuheros** is overlooked by the ruins of a **Moorish castle** built onto a spur of reddish rock.

03 A multi-turreted 8th-century **castle** (aka Highgarden in *Game of Thrones*) stands sentinel above **Almodóvar del Río**. Here you may partake in medieval combat training and old-school banquets.

01 Approach **Priego de Córdoba** along the A-333 to appreciate its scattering of white houses along the **Adarve** – the scenic escarpment rising vertically above olive groves (pictured opposite) – and the impressive **Moorish castle**.

LUKASZ JANYST/SHUUTERSTOCK ©

0 50 km
0 25 miles

Cabeza del Buey
Almadén
Santa Eufemia
Belalcázar
Hinojosa del Duque
Alcaracejos
Pozoblanco
Fuencaliente
Peñarroya-Pueblonuevo
Villanueva de Córdoba
Cardeña
Embalse de Puente Nuevo
Villaviciosa de Córdoba
Adamuz
Río Guadiato
Río Guadalquivir
Córdoba
Martos
Jaén
Posadas
Almodóvar del Río
Río Guadajoz
Baena
Alcaudete
Palma del Río
Espejo
Zuheros
Alcalá la Real
Écija
Santaella
Montilla
Cabra
Priego de Córdoba
Aguilar de la Frontera
Monturque
Lucena
La Tiñosa (1570m)
Montefrío
Arahal
Marchena
Río Genil
Herrera
Puente Genil
Rute
Osuna
Estepa
Benamejí
Embalse de Iznájar
Iznájar
Utrera
Morón de la Frontera
Arcos de la Frontera
Ronda

Listings

BEST OF THE REST

 Memorable Stays

Hotel Hacienda Posada de Vallina €€

In a hidden nook near the Mezquita, this centuries-old hotel is decked out with period-style furniture to convey a medieval Córdoba feel. The Mezquita builders stayed here, as did Columbus (in Room 204).

Balcón de Córdoba €€€

A stone's throw from La Mezquita, this restored 17th-century convent combines heavy wooden shutters, brick-arched patios and ancient stone relics with memorable Mezquita views from the rooftop terrace and Córdoban-international fusion cuisine.

Posada Amena €

Run by affable Catharina, this creeper-clad stone house in Carcabuey features beamed ceilings and windows framing Pico La Tiñosa. Linger over superb breakfasts on the terrace.

Hotel Las Casas de la Judería €€€

Spread across 27 traditional houses in Córdoba's *judería,* connected by hidden passages and flowering patios, this hotel blends original features with contemporary perks: a rooftop pool and spa.

Hotel Viento 10 €€

A sensitively updated 17th-century hospital in eastern Córdoba has just eight contemporary, individually styled rooms, juxtaposed with ancient pillars in its courtyard. Terrific La Mezquita vistas from the roof terrace.

Casa Olea €

Run by knowledgeable hosts and set amid olive groves 12km north of Priego de Córdoba, this rustic farmhouse is ideal for hikers and mountain bikers. Home-cooked dinners served on request.

 Creative Gastronomy

Nuur €€€

The tasting menus by Paco Morales at this two-Michelin-star establishment are a playful journey through Córdoba's past. Centuries-old recipes such as *karim de pistachio* (pistachio soup) get the modern treatment.

Restaurante Regadera €€

Grab a table by the river in Córdoba and feast on a mix of traditional dishes (glazed suckling lamb, superlative *salmorejo*) and crossover fusion (oxtail cannelloni, ceviche with gazpacho).

Abrasador Meson Rural de Ronda €

Carcabuey's temple to 'gastronomía Subbética' does wonderful things with free-range Iberian pork and other countryside bounty: asparagus with Romesco sauce and charcoal-grilled artichokes with *jamón* and pistachio stand out.

GastroTaberna La Albahaca €€

A tranquil courtyard behind La Mezquita is the perfect setting for playful reimagining of traditional Córdoban dishes. Expect daring ingredient pairings, such as tuna tartare with bone marrow and *mazamorra* with mango.

Choco €€€

Inside this stylish Córdoba space, local culinary hotshot Kisko García takes you on an edible journey through Andalucía's different regions using his two innovative tasting menus. Beautiful presentation and edible surprises.

Tablao Flamenco El Cardenal

Bodegas & Wine Bars

Bodega Guzmán   €

Ceramic tiling, bullfighting memorabilia and giant wine barrels adorn this cavernous *judería* bar in Córdoba. Sip on a bone-dry Montilla fino, accompanied by the house specials of *salmorejo* and *albóndigas*.

Bodegas Mezquita   €

With four branches scattered around Córdoba's Old Town, this ever-popular tapas bar serves numerous wines from Montilla-Moriles. Start with some viñaverde and finish with the dark and sweet 'fiti-fiti'.

 Olive Oil Tours

Aceites Vizcántar

Near Priego de Córdoba, master olive oil taster Fermín offers tours of the small producer's olive groves (including millennia-old trees) and holds *catas* (tastings). Buy exceptional olive oil and olive products here.

SCA Almazaras de Subbética

Off the A-339, near Carcabuey, this olive-growing cooperative produced the 'World's Best Olive Oil' in 2021. Go for tours of the olive mill (October to March) or buy award-winning oil at the year-round Almaliva shop.

 Art(s) & Crafts

Meryan

Carrying on the centuries-old Moorish tradition of leatherwork, this long-standing shop near Córdoba's La Mezquita sells embossed leather jackets, wallets, leather-covered wooden chests, bags and boxes in a range of colours.

Plata Cordobesa

Find this silversmith in Córdoba's San Basilio neighbourhood, just west of La Mezquita. It's one of the better places in town for fine silver filigree, from rings and pendants to earrings.

Cueros de Córdoba

Located inside a courtyard, this shop specialises in beautiful hand-tooled leather items – from wallets and briefcases to elaborate, framed leather pieces depicting geometric designs.

Ostin Macho

This terrific concept store in Córdoba sells colourful books on contemporary art and design, artworks and prints designed by students at a local art school, as well as quirky ceramics.

Esencia de los Patios

If you love Córdoba's patios so much that you'd like to smell like them, then this parfumerie lets you choose between such scents as white jasmin and orange blossom and tangerine.

Asociación Cordobesa Artesanos ZOCO

Near Córdoba's synagogue, watch artisans at work at this restored Mudéjar building that originally opened as Spain's first designated handicraft market back in the 1950s.

Baraka

Hidden in a tiny lane in Córdoba's *judería,* this shop specialises in caliphal era–style ceramics. It also sells framed leather pieces, ornamental glassware and handmade leather devil masks.

 Flamenco

Tablao Flamenco El Cardenal

A front-line table on the open-air patio inside this 17th-century mansion in the *judería* provides an atmospheric setting for professional, passionate flamenco shows every night bar Sundays.

Taberna La Fuenseca

A much more local scene, this 19th-century taberna near Córdoba's Palacio la Viana plays host to fiery, spontaneous flamenco laments some nights, as well as guitarists and poets.

 Scan to find more things to do in Córdoba online

JAÉN

OUTDOORS | FOOD | ARCHITECTURE

Piedrabuena

Munera

Be awed by the sumptuous interiors of **Úbeda's** historic mansions (p184)

Alcaraz

CASTILLA-LA MANCHA

Elche de la Sierra

Puente de Génave

La Puerta de Segura

Learn all about superlative olive oil at **Oleícola San Francisco** (p176)
🚗 + 🚶 *15 mins from Baeza*

Parque Natural Sierra de Andújar

La Carolina

Orcera
Segura de la Sierra

Villanueva del Arzobispo

Cortijos Nuevos

Parque Natural Sierras de Cazorla, Segura y las Villas

Bailén

Linares

Villacarrillo

Andújar

Río Guadalquivir

Úbeda

Coto Ríos

Hike among the craggy mountains of **Parque Natural Sierras de Cazorla** (p178)
🚗 + 🚶 *1¼hrs from Jaén*

Córdoba

Mengíbar

JAÉN

Baeza

Cazorla

CÓRDOBA

Porcuna

Torre del Campo

Albánchez de Mágina

Empanadas (2107m)

Stroll the narrow medieval lanes of **Jaén** and sample imaginative tapas (p188)
🚶

Martos

Jaén

Quesada

Pozo Alcón

Mancha Real

Mágina (2167m)

Baena

Alcaudete

Parque Natural Sierra Mágina

Guadahortuna

Alcalá la Real

GRANADA

Cúllar

ALMERÍA

Priego de Córdoba

Baza

Iznájar

Granada

Spot **Castillo de Albánchez** on its improbably high crag while road-tripping (p182,
🚗 + 🚶 *1-1½hrs from Jaén*

Archidona

Loja

Almería

JAÉN
Trip Builder

Olive groves carpet the countryside, dotted with remote villages and watched over by crag-top castles. Less touristy than other Andalucian provinces, Jaén beguiles with the superb hiking in its national parks, its olive oil and the Renaissance architecture on its Unesco World Heritage towns.

Mediterranean Sea

PREVIOUS SPREAD: FOTOMICAR/SHUTTERSTOCK ©.
ABOVE: PATJO/SHUTTERSTOCK ©

N
0 — 40 km
0 — 20 miles

Practicalities

ARRIVING

Aeropuerto de Granada Closest airport to the Jaén province. Airport buses run between the airport, main bus station and train station. There are good bus connections between Granada, Jaén, Úbeda, Baeza and Cazorla.

MONEY

In small villages, cash takes precedence over plastic. Some olive oil tours, plus walking tours in Úbeda require a minimum of two people per booking.

FIND YOUR WAY

Jaén's medieval villages and towns are notoriously labyrinthine, with one-way lanes. Find parking elsewhere and walk in.

WHERE TO STAY

Town/ village	Pro/Con
Jaén	Grand hilltop castle, good museums, creative tapas bars, good transport links, limited accommodation
Úbeda	Walkable, Unesco World Heritage architecture, boutique hotels, superb dining, good transport links
Baeza	Compact historic centre, Unesco World Heritage architecture, walkable, good tapas scene, transport links
Cazorla	Great hiking base for Parque Natural Sierras de Cazorla
Cambil	Excellent access to Parque Natural Sierra Mágina; tiny, limited accommodation and dining options, no public transport

EATING & DRINKING

Úbeda has the most creative dining scene, while Jaén excels in the tapas department.

Pipirrana (pictured top left) Salad of finely diced tomatoes, cucumbers, olive oil, salt, garlic and green peppers.

Esparragos esparragados (pictured bottom left) Asparagus stew with *pimiento de chorizo,* garlic, olive oil, vinegar, bread and eggs.

Best olive oil Oleicola San Francisco (p176)

Must-try tasting menu Cibus Renacimiento, Úbeda (p190)

GETTING AROUND

Train Jaén is well connected by train to Córdoba, Sevilla, Huelva, Jerez de la Frontera and Málaga.

Bus Most towns in the Jaén province are well served by buses, though services to more remote villages tend to be infrequent or even non-existent. The main company is Alsa (alsa.es).

Car Driving gives you the greatest flexibility, especially if you have your heart set on touring castles in far-flung parts of the province. Cars are available for rent at Granada airport, Jaén and Úbeda.

JAÉN FIND YOUR FEET

MAR–JUN
Warm hiking weather, spring blooms in the countryside, high prices in Baeza and Úbeda

JUL–AUG
Hot temperatures, Bluescazorla festival rocks Cazorla

SEP–OCT
Fewer crowds, balmy days, excellent hiking

NOV–FEB
Olive harvest, olive oil tours, cool nights, affordable accommodation prices

Jaén's Olive
OIL TRAIL

FOOD | CULTURE | OUTDOORS

Olives rule Jaén: this is a fact. The province is carpeted with over 66 million olive trees, with Jaén responsible for nearly half of Spain's olive harvest. Get up close and personal with Jaén's cherished foodstuffs by tasting exceptional olive oils at numerous restaurants, touring olive farms and mills, and witnessing the fruit being turned into liquid gold.

E. DIEGO/ALAMY STOCK PHOTO ©

🗺 How To

Getting around Visiting olive oil producers in the *campo* requires your own wheels. Oil tasting establishments in Úbeda and Cazorla can be reached on foot.

When to go To witness the olive harvest, visit between October and March. Some producers suspend tours outside olive oil season.

Top tip Hop across the border into the Córdoba province to compare the country's (and the world's!) best olive oils.

JOSE LUCAS/ALAMY STOCK PHOTO ©

Left Olive harvesting, Jaén.
Bottom left Olive oils from Jaén.

JAÉN EXPERIENCES

Tours & Tastings

The best introduction to olive oil is a visit to multiple award-winning small producer **Oleícola San Francisco** during harvest time to participate in *'Acetunero por un día'* – assisting with the harvest, then watching the mechanised process at the factory, followed by a *cata* (tasting). For tastings alone, try the **Centro de Interpretación Olivar y Aceite** in Úbeda that explains the tree-to-table process, or else **Agraria Olearum** in Cazorla.

The Cata

Olive oil is divided into three types: extra virgin, virgin and lampante ('lamp oil', refined to make it fit for consumption). To determine the quality of the oil, during a *cata de aceite* (tasting), the taster focuses on two things: smell and taste. You rub the *copa de cata* to warm up the oil, inhale the aromas, then sip it. Extra virgin olive oils are an olfactory explosion, with spicy, bitter, sweet and grassy tasting notes. By comparison, the scent of lampante is muted, with defects such as mustiness and rancidness, while virgin olive oil displays both attributes and defects.

Labels of Excellence

Jaén's extra virgin olive oil bears the 'IGP Aceite de Jaén', denoting its protected status. 'Oleo Tour Jaén' signs highlight local restaurants that make excellent use of locally produced AOVE/EVOO (extra virgin olive oil), shops selling olive oil and establishments offering *catas*. See jaenparaisointerior.es for a complete list.

Notes from a Small Producer...

'In my father's day, the olive oil process took three days. Now it takes 40 minutes from the moment the olives arrive on the conveyor belt to the decanting. Here, we only sell AOVE. You can certainly use AOVE for frying – it's just best to use oil made from ripe olives or a mix of ripe and green rather than early harvest oil made exclusively from green olives. As for which olives make the best olive oil, it's a matter of personal taste: most of our olive trees are the *picual* variety and I love their bitter aftertaste.'

■ **By José Antonio Jimenez Molina**, *owner/ tour guide at Oleícola San Francisco, Baeza @oleicolasanfrancisco*

38

Sierra de Cazorla
ADVENTURES

HIKING | ADVENTURE | WILDLIFE

 The largest protected area in Spain welcomes fresh-air fiends with 2099 sq km of dramatic gorges, green canyons, rugged mountain ranges, spectacular waterfalls and ample wildlife. Well-marked hiking trails grant easy access to the wilderness, while scenic villages overlooked by ancient castles make excellent bases.

GRETHE ULGJELL/ALAMY STOCK PHOTO ©

🏵 How To

Getting here/around
You need your own wheels to explore the park. For non-drivers, there are 4WD tours, guided hikes and wildlife-spotting trips from Cazorla.

When to go Spring and autumn are best, when the temperatures are

moderate and vegetation flowers/changes colour. Semana Santa and weekends from April to October get very busy; July and August are very hot.

Need to know Some roads inside the park are suitable only for high clearance/4WD vehicles.

OREALES/ALAMY STOCK PHOTO ©

Sierra de Cazorla's Best Hikes

Hiking in Sierra de Cazorla is second to none. Besides short walks up to **castle ruins** in Cazorla, La Iruela and Segura de la Sierra, there are dozens of hiking trails (many of which can also be cycled) that range from the gentle walk from the **Herredías bridge**, which follows the La Mesa ravine before climbing gently through pine forest (two hours return), and the equally undemanding, scenic uphill meander from **Linajeros** to the **Calvares pass** (1½ hours return), with stupendous valley views, to tougher half-day and full-day treks. Challenge yourself with a stiff climb up from the **Virgen de la Cabeza chapel** behind La Iruela to the **Tejo pass** (four hours return), where you'll be rewarded with all-encompassing views of the Guadalquivir valley, or else try a six-hour

JAM WORLD IMAGES/ALAMY STOCK PHOTO ©

△ Flying High in El Yelmo

Over the first weekend in June, the summit of El Yelmo mountain (1808m), off the A6305, hosts the high-flying **Festival Internacional del Aire** (fiaelyelmo.com). Hundreds of paragliders and skydivers ride the air currents, while festivities comprise drone and photography competitions, trail running and aerial acrobatics in small planes.

Top left Hiking, Sierra de Cazorla.
Top right Herredías bridge. **Left** Castle ruins, La Iruela.

exploration of the dramatic **Extremera** and **La Bujea ravines** after hiking up from La Iruela to the **Zamora pass**.

The star walk in the park is the moderately challenging **Río Borosa trail** (22km, seven to eight hours return) that starts from a car park near Torre del Vinagre. It follows the rapids of the crystal-clear river upstream to its source through a densely forested valley. The trail alternates between a wide gravel track and a narrow walkway above inviting swimming holes. The gradient is gentle until you reach the hydroelectric power station, after which the terrain becomes more rugged as you ascend between sheer rock faces, with raptors wheeling on the thermal currents overhead. After passing the **Salto de los Órganos**, where you can swim in the deep, freezing-cold pool beneath the mighty falls, you have to walk through tunnels (pack a flashlight!) to reach the **Valdeazores lagoon** and the source of the river.

Best Village Bases

Sierra de Cazorla is enormous. The big question is: where should you base yourself?

Cazorla is the largest southern gateway, with ample dining, accommodation and companies offering 4WD adventures.

Though **La Iruela's** accommodation and dining is limited, it offers easy access to via ferrata and hiking trails.

The main northern gateway, **Segura de la Sierra** has a dramatic setting, plus accommodation and dining to suit all budgets.

The closest village to the Río Borosa trail is **Coto Ríos**, with ample lodgings and a pleasant river beach.

Left Cazorla.
Below Lammergeier.

Via Ferrata & Canyoning

Based in La Iruela, **Aventura Cazorla** (aventura cazorla.com) operates two via ferrata – obstacle courses consisting of vertical ladders built into the rock face, plus steel cables for balancing on as you cross sheer chasms. **La Mocha** is more challenging, while **La Escaleruela** gives beginners a taste of adrenaline. Alternatively, a half-day canyoning trip will have you rappelling down waterfalls of the **Cañones de la Cerrada del Utrero** section of Río Guadalquivir, getting pummelled by whitewater and swimming in crystal-clear pools.

Return of the Bonebreaker

If you're lucky, and keep your binoculars handy, you may spot the majestic lammergeier or bearded vulture soaring above the Sierra de Cazorla. In 1986, these impressive birds were hunted to extinction in Andalucía, but have now been successfully reintroduced into the wild thanks to the efforts of the **Centro de Cria de Quebrantahuesos** (quebrantahuesos.org). These feathered giants reach a wingspan of 2.7m to 2.9 m and sport distinctive yellow-white leg and neck feathers. They are known as 'bonebreakers' because dropping bones onto rocks from a great height to break them and then eating the marrow constitutes the main part of their diet.

39

Castle-Hopping
AROUND JAÉN

OUTDOORS | ARCHITECTURE | CASTLES

The Jaén province was once a frontier zone where numerous battles took place between Christians and Moors, and its centuries-old castles still stand sentinel above remote villages, ever-ready to repel invaders. Drive the slow, scenic way past ancient fortifications, or perhaps even stay in one.

🗺 Trip Notes

Getting here/around The more remote villages are only reachable by car; Jaén and Cazorla are served by multiple bus services with Alsa (alsa.com).

When to go March to June and September to November for balmy weather and fewer crowds. Olive groves blossom in May and June.

Need to know 'Parador' doesn't always mean 'castle converted to a hotel': sometimes it's a historic hotel in a palace or stately country home.

🏰 Best Paradores

Parador Castillo de Santa Catalina Jaén's luxurious historic hotel with vaulted halls and panoramic views from the terrace.

Parador de Úbeda Slender arches surround the beautiful interior courtyard of this 16th-century Renaissance palace, while rooms boast four-posters.

Parador de Cazorla Panoramic views of the surrounding mountains greet you at this graceful country house.

02 The leaning tower of the 14th-century **Castillo de Albánchez** looks down on its namesake village from its lofty clifftop perch, while the narrow JA3107 zigzags past before swooping up dramatically to the 1250m-high mountain pass.

01 Some 3km from Cazorla, the largely intact walls and keep of the Moorish **Castillo de la Iruela** perch on a craggy outcrop above the La Iruela village.

03 Take the winding road from Jaén to **Castillo de Santa Catalina** (pictured opposite), an impregnable sandstone fortress atop a hill. Stupendous vistas of the city spread out below you at the mirador.

04 A switchbacking detour leads you into the mountains south of Jaén where a lonely watchtower of **Castillo de Otiñar**, dating back to Moorish rule, is precipitously balanced on a cragtop.

05 If you're driving towards Córdoba, you'll see the hilltop fortification long before you reach Alcalá la Real. The mighty walls, keep and church tower of **Fortaleza de la Mota** predate the present-day town below.

Villanueva del Arzobispo

Parque Natural Sierras de Cazorla, Segura y las Villas

Villacarrillo

Linares

Úbeda

Torreperogil

Sierra de Cazorla

Baeza

Parador de Úbeda

Río Guadalquivir

Empanadas (2107m)

Albánchez de Mágina

Bedmar

Peal de Becerro

Cazorla

Parador de Cazorla

Porcuna

Mancha Real

Jódar

Quesada

Torre del Campo

Torres

Jaén

Torredonjimeno

La Guardia de Jaén

Mágina (2167m)
Parque Natural Sierra Mágina

Pozo Alcón

Martos

Parador Castillo de Santa Catalina

Huelma

Río Guadajoz

Alcaudete

Guadahortuna

Priego de Córdoba

Alcalá la Real

Iznalloz

Darro

Montefrío

Guadix

N

0 ___ 20 km
0 ___ 10 miles

40 Úbeda's Jewish LEGACY

ARCHITECTURE | HISTORY | CULTURE

Resident in Úbeda since the late Middle Ages, Jews played an important role in the town's civil life. They were tanners, silversmiths, tax collectors, shoemakers and more; most of the time, they coexisted peacefully with Moors and Christians. Instead of a single *judería* (Jewish barrio), Úbeda has three separate neighbourhoods where Jews lived prior to 1492, with fascinating historic buildings in each.

V. DOROSZ/ALAMY STOCK PHOTO ©

🗺 How To

Getting here/around
There are good transport links between Úbeda, Jaén, Baeza and beyond. Historic Úbeda is extremely walkable and the sights are just a few minutes apart on foot.

When to go Úbeda is ripe for exploration outside

the often extremely hot July and August. Try to avoid the Semana Santa as well, when the town teems with visitors.

Top tip The private house-museums may only be visited by tour with Vandelvira Turismo; book ahead.

RODOLFO CONTRERAS/ALAMY STOCK PHOTO ©

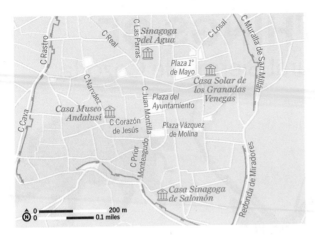

Casa Andalusí A centuries-old door opens into a greenery-clad courtyard with a fountain. This 15th-century house once belonged to the Chirino Narváez family of *conversos* (Jewish converts to Christianity). Spot the painted Mudéjar-style wooden ceilings, a Star of David etched into a 14th-century Gothic-Mudéjar octagonal column, and a 16th-century ivory-inlaid secretaire in an antique-filled room.

Casa Sinagoga de Salomón In the main room of this 14th-century synagogue, a Mudéjar-style archway leads to a small *mikveh* (ritual bath), while the two-storey oratory houses centuries-old Torah scrolls. Upstairs, check out the ornately painted ceilings of the recreated Talmudic school, ivory-inlaid walnut bench and a Sephardic Torah made of gazelle skin.

Casa Solar de los Granadas Venegas The most striking feature of this grand mansion that once belonged to an illustrious family of Islamised Jews (who converted to Christianity) are some remarkably intact 13th-century Mozarabic frescoes. There's also a chapel and two rooms filled with centuries-old Mudéjar and Jewish objects. Don't miss the angular vault in the cellar – one of Úbeda's oldest – or the alchemy workshop with copper still.

Sinagoga del Agua Sensitively restored since 2006, this remarkable 13th-century synagogue is accessible via guided tour. Highlights include the main area of worship, with its stone arches and historic relics, such as a 13th century perfume bottle and the vaulted underground *mikveh* fed by an underground spring.

Left and bottom left Sinagoga del Agua.

Hidden Secrets of Jewish Úbeda

'In Úbeda's three *juderías* you can still make out houses that once belonged to Jews, with whitewash covering ancient Stars of David next to the entrance. Were the *conversos* genuine converts to Christianity? Some were, since conversion was the only way Jews could remain in Spain after 1492, but we also know that some were 'Crypto-Jews' – outwardly Catholic, who continued to practise Judaism in secret. In fact, there may have been a deeper cellar in Casa Andalusí that's been sealed since, potentially used as a Jewish house of worship, while the lower cellar in Los Granadas may have been a *mikveh*.'

■ **By Eva María Castro Martos**, *part-owner of Casa Andalusí/ art historian with Vandelvira Turismo, Úbeda, @vandelviraturismo*

WILD THINGS OF
Parque Natural Sierras de Cazorla

01 Iberian lynx
The world's most endangered feline, endemic to the Iberian Peninsula; numbers around 1000 in the wild due to renewed conservation efforts.

02 Wild boar
Medium-sized wild pig, common throughout the Iberian Peninsula, with poor eyesight, but an excellent sense of smell and acute hearing. Predominantly nocturnal.

03 Red stag
One of the largest deer species, with a reddish-brown coat in summer. They live in same-sex groups for much of the year.

04 Spanish imperial eagle
Large raptor native to the Iberian Peninsula, with a blackish-brown coat and white band on the shoulder. Favourite food: rabbits.

05 Black stork
This red-beaked, white-bellied stork breeds in the marsh-lands of northern Andalucía. Annual migration to West and East Africa between September and April.

06 Eurasian scops owl
Well-camouflaged, golden-eyed, medium-sized owl that lives in woodlands and eats berries, grains, insects and small birds. Nocturnal.

07 Spanish ibex
Shy, sure-footed mountain goat, with long, backward-curving horns, endemic to Andalucía's rocky mountains. Lives in small family groups.

08 Montpellier snake
The largest (up to 2m) and most common snake in Andalucía; mildly venomous; olive green in colour; hisses threateningly when cornered.

09 Mazarine blue butterfly
Very small, iridescent blue butterfly that you're likely to spot in grass fields and meadows between mid-May and mid-July.

41 Jaén Walking
TOUR

ARCHITECTURE | CULTURE | FOOD

The capital of the province, busy Jaén is often overlooked by visitors in favour of its more famous brethren – Úbeda and Baeza. But take the time to explore, and you'll discover a city full of personality, with excellent museums, creative gastronomy and more.

🗺 Trip Notes

Getting here/around Jaén is best explored on foot, or else take advantage of the tram that plies Paseo de la Estación.

When to go March to June, September and October are the balmier months, while winter means few visitors. The agricultural Feria de San Lucas (October) is Jaén's biggest festival.

Top tours Be initiated into Jaén's mysteries with the highly acclaimed Legends and Mysteries tour with **Cláritas Turismo** (claritasturismo.com).

✗ Creative Cuisine

Calle Arroyo is at the heart of Jaén's dining scene.

Bar Bomborombillos Arty space and creative use of local ingredients: don't miss the almond cracker topped with smoked sardine and olive oil 'roe'.

Taberna Pepón Old-school taberna with *jamón* dangling from the ceiling; snails a speciality.

Ajhito Izakaya Jaénponesa Japan meets Jaén at this super-popular contemporary joint.

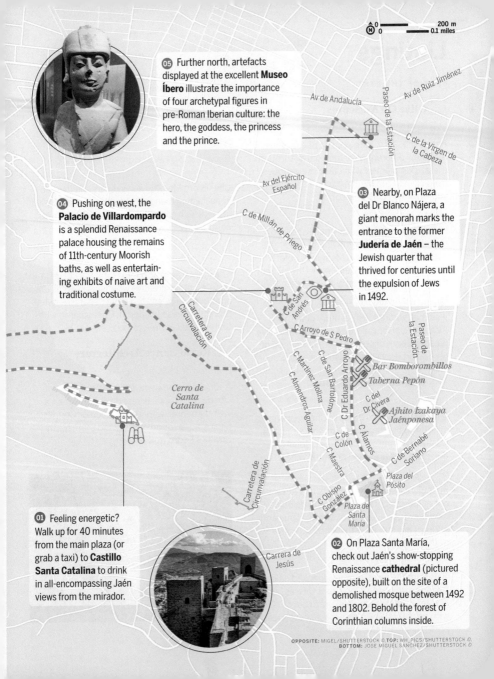

05 Further north, artefacts displayed at the excellent **Museo Íbero** illustrate the importance of four archetypal figures in pre-Roman Iberian culture: the hero, the goddess, the princess and the prince.

04 Pushing on west, the **Palacio de Villardompardo** is a splendid Renaissance palace housing the remains of 11th-century Moorish baths, as well as entertaining exhibits of naive art and traditional costume.

03 Nearby, on Plaza del Dr Blanco Nájera, a giant menorah marks the entrance to the former **Judería de Jaén** – the Jewish quarter that thrived for centuries until the expulsion of Jews in 1492.

01 Feeling energetic? Walk up for 40 minutes from the main plaza (or grab a taxi) to **Castillo Santa Catalina** to drink in all-encompassing Jaén views from the mirador.

02 On Plaza Santa María, check out Jaén's show-stopping Renaissance **cathedral** (pictured opposite), built on the site of a demolished mosque between 1492 and 1802. Behold the forest of Corinthian columns inside.

Av de Ruiz Jiménez
Av de Andalucía
Paseo de la Estación
C de la Virgen de la Cabeza
Av del Ejército Español
C de Millán de Priego
Carretera de Circunvalación
C de San Andrés
C Arroyo de S Pedro
Paseo de la Estación
Cerro de Santa Catalina
C Martínez Molina
C de San Bartolomé
C Dr Eduardo Arroyo
C Almendros Aguilar
Bar Bomborombillos
Taberna Pepón
C del Dr Civera
Ajhito Izakaya Jaénponesa
C Álamos
C de Colón
C de Bernabé Soriano
Carretera de Circunvalación
C de Colón
C Maestra
Plaza del Pósito
C Obispo González
Plaza de Santa María
Carrera de Jesús

Listings

BEST OF THE REST

Olive Oil Museums

Museo de la Cultura del Olivo

At this museum, 8km west of Baeza, you may view different olive mills, stroll through the garden planted with olive tree varieties from all over the Mediterranean and visit the subterranean Cathedral of Oil.

Museo Terra Oleum

Peruse interactive audiovisual displays on sustainability of olive growing at this sleek, contemporary space in Mengíbar, before strolling through the Centenary Olive Forest. Finish your visit with an olive oil *cata*.

Museo del Aceite de Oliva

Visit this restored 19th-century olive mill in Alcalá la Real for a glimpse of old-school olive presses. Learn about the modern method of olive oil production and taste the final product.

Regional Gastronomy

Cibus Renacimiento Culinario €€€

A medieval vaulted cellar in Úbeda provides an intimate setting for multi-course tasting menus that make superb use of local produce, olive oil and Jaén province wines.

Misa de 12 €€

Succulent platters of *presa ibérica* (a tender cut of Iberian pork) and *revuelto de pulpo y gambas* (eggs scrambled with octopus and shrimp) are served with flair by attentive staff at this Úbeda haunt.

Antojitos Mexican Curious €

This thimble-sized, mural-bedecked cellar in Cazorla, run by Mexican expat Ulísses, serves TexMex *antojitos* (snacks), from burritos filled with *cochinita pibíl* (slow-roasted shredded pork) to superlative guacamole.

Macorina €€

Sleek contemporary decor in Cazorla sets the scene for imaginative Andalucian-Asian fusion dishes that bring together regional ingredients and EVOO. Standouts include Korean-style lamb lasagne and leeks with Romesco sauce.

Bagá Espacio Gastronómico €€€

Chef Pedro Morales wows diners with his seasonal tasting menus that feature dishes like kid kidneys with caviar, beef tartare with smoked eel and prawns with marinated partridge.

Bar Pacos €

The intimate cellar bar in Hotel Puerta de la Luna excels at creative whimsies such as *chupachups de queso crujiente* (Spanish-style crunchy cheese lollipops). Drinks come with tasty *cortesías* (free tapas).

Renaissance Architecture

Catedral de la Asunción

Andrés de Vandelvira, the master architect of Úbeda and Baeza, is responsible for Jaén's vast cathedral, with its spectacular Corinthian pillars, huge round arches, and statuary by Seville's Pedro Roldán.

Capilla del Salvador

Catedral de Baeza

Dominating the Plaza de Santa María, this impressive cathedral is a mélange of Gothic-Mudéjar and 16th-century Renaissance design. The nave was designed by Vandelvira while the rejas were painted by Maestro Bartolomé.

Palacio Vela de los Cobos

Sitting on Úbeda's Plaza del Ayuntamiento, this sensitively updated, Vandelvira-designed 16th-century mansion sports a beautiful arcaded gallery. Arrange tours of this private home in advance.

Palacio de Jabalquinto

The 15th-century home of the Benavides clan, Baeza's most flamboyant palace boasts a two-tier Renaissance arcade with marble columns and a spectacular facade in decorative Isabelline Gothic style.

Capilla del Salvador

The flagship of Úbeda Renaissance architecture, this funerary chapel features a plateresque facade, Valdelvira's trademark image of Santiago the Moor slayer, a stately dome and classical sculpture.

Palacio de Vázques de Molina

Built by Vandelvira in 1562, Úbeda's *ayuntamiento* (town hall) is Spain's most beautiful, with an Italian-influenced facade and two storeys of elegant arches in the interior courtyard.

Heritage Hotels

Las Casas del Cónsul €€

Úbeda's 'Consul's Houses' is an appealing Renaissance mansion conversion with elegant rooms, a two-storey pillared patio and a fabulous panoramic pool terrace gazing over olive groves and Cazorla mountains.

Palacio de la Rambla €€

The deliberately old-fashioned rooms at this family-run mansion are clad in precious art and antiques, the ivy-clad patio is suitably romantic and there are two beautiful salons.

Hotel Puerto de la Luna €€

Orange trees surround the pool on the appealing patio of 17th-century mansion turned luxurious Baeza hotel. The spacious rooms are enhanced by classical furnishings and artwork.

Hotel Palacio de Mengíbar €€€

Worth an overnight trip from Jaén, this hotel inside a former 15th-century palace boasts an atmospheric stone-walled, beamed cellar dining room and four-posters in comfortable rooms.

Hotel Palacio de los Salcedo €€

This 16th-century Baeza palace with an original facade comprises a handful of over-the-top Louis-XV–style rooms, some with intricately carved and painted ceilings.

TRH Ciudad de Baeza €€€

A beautiful Renaissance monastery has been converted into a luxurious four-star hotel. Ignore the modern rooms and admire the facade and gorgeous glassed-in patio instead.

Local Crafts

Forja Tiznajo

Wrought ironwork has long been part of Úbeda's craft tradition, and here you can happily drift into insolvency, purchasing lanterns, elaborate wine racks, sculpture and more.

Alfarería.Tito

Also in Úbeda, Juan Tito's distinctive ceramics feature intricate patterns and bright colours, especially blue. His large old-town showroom/workshop displays and sells a big range of wares, from decorative to functional.

GRANADA

HISTORY | ARCHITECTURE | OUTDOORS

Experience
Granada
online

GRANADA
Trip Builder

Architectural jewel box, adventure-activity paradise, low-key beach escape, mountain wonderland, lively academic hub – Granada evokes everything that makes southern Spain so irresistible. From the Mediterranean-washed shores of the Costa Tropical to the Alhambra's Moorish beauty and the Sierra Nevada's sky-reaching peaks, this is one of Andalucía's most bewitching regions.

JAÉN

Join an expert-led **food tour** to learn about Granada's culinary heritage (p198)
🚶 *20min from Granada train station*

Iznalloz

Parque Natural Sierra de Huétor

Alfacar

Pinos
Puente

Embalse de Iznájar ○ Iznájar

Río Genil

Santa Fé

Loja

Granada

Monachil

Savour the after-dark beauty of the **Alhambra's Palacios Nazaríes** with a night visit (p202)
🚶 + 🚌 *15min from central Granada*

Dive into the tapas scene and admire street art in Granada's **Realejo** (p200)
🚶 *20min from Granada train station*

Alhama de Granada

○ Padul

○ Dúrcal

Riogordo

Alcaucín △ Maroma (2065m)

Lanjarón

Parque Natural Sierras de Tejeda, Almijara y Alhama

Velez de Benaudalla

MÁLAGA

○ Cómpeta

Otívar ○

Vélez Málaga

Torrox

Nerja

Torre del Mar

La Herradura

Salobreña

Motril

Almuñécar

Take a dip at secluded swimsuit-optional **Playa de Cantarriján** (p210)
🚐 *1hr from Granada*

Rincón de la Victoria

Torrenueva

Go sunset kayaking past coastal caves in **La Herradura** (p210)
🚌 + 🚐 *1-2hr from Granada*

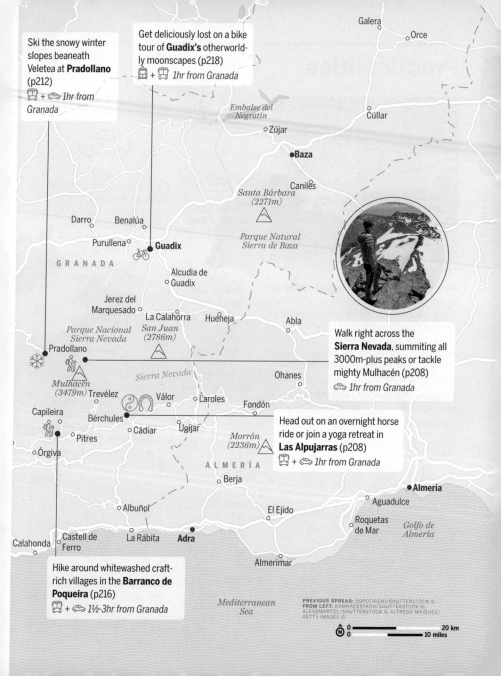

Ski the snowy winter slopes beaneath Veletea at **Pradollano** (p212)

🚌 + 🚗 *1hr from Granada*

Get deliciously lost on a bike tour of **Guadix's** otherworldly moonscapes (p218)

🚌 + 🚆 *1hr from Granada*

Galera

○ Orce

Embalse del Negratín

○ Zújar

●**Baza**

Cúllar

Canilés

Santa Bárbara (2271m) △

Darro ○   Benalúa ○

Purullena ○   ●**Guadix** 🚲

Parque Natural Sierra de Baza

G R A N A D A

Alcudia de Guadix ○

Jerez del Marquesado ○

La Calahorra ○   Hueneja ○   Abla ○

Parque Nacional Sierra Nevada   *San Juan (2786m)* △

❋ Pradollano ○ 🚶🧍

Walk right across the **Sierra Nevada**, summiting all 3000m-plus peaks or tackle mighty Mulhacén (p208)

🚗 *1hr from Granada*

Mulhacén (3479m) △ Trevélez ○   ☯   Válor ○   ○ Laroles

Sierra Nevada   Ohanes ○

Fondón ○

Capileira ○ 🚶🧍

Bérchules ○ ♞

○ Cádiar   Ugíjar ○

○ Pitres

Morrón (2236m) △

Head out on an overnight horse ride or join a yoga retreat in **Las Alpujarras** (p208)

🚌 + 🚗 *1hr from Granada*

○ Órgiva

A L M E R Í A

○ Berja

●**Almería**

Albuñol ○

El Ejido ○

Aguadulce ○

Roquetas de Mar ○

Golfo de Almería

Calahonda ○   Castell de Ferro ○   La Rábita ○   **Adra**

Almerimar ○

Hike around whitewashed craft-rich villages in the **Barranco de Poqueira** (p216)

🚌 + 🚗 *1½-3hr from Granada*

Mediterranean Sea

Ⓝ 0 _____ 20 km
   0 _____ 10 miles

Practicalities

JOSERA/SHUTTERSTOCK ©

ARRIVING

Aeropuerto Federico García Lorca Granada–Jaén
The province's only airport (pictured) is 17km west of Granada, with domestic and international flights; frequent Alsa buses (alsa.com) connect the airport with Granada (€3, 20 to 40 minutes), and taxis cost around €30. It's also easy to reach Granada by train or bus, and most destinations across the province have good bus connections.

Aeropuerto Málaga–Costa del Sol With excellent train and bus links to Granada city, as well as the Costa Tropical, Málaga is a handy alternative gateway.

HOW MUCH FOR A

Jamón tapa
Free with a drink!

Walking tour from €15 per person

Alhambra tickets €14

GETTING AROUND

Car The ideal way to get around the province is with a hire car, though it's best to pick one up after you've finished exploring Granada city, as parking there is a nightmare. Car-hire outlets congregate at Granada train station, 1.5km northwest of the centre.

Bus If you don't have your own wheels, much of Granada province is accessible by bus (alsa. com); most villages have bus services, though schedules can be limited. In Granada city, there's a handy urban bus network (movilidadgranada.com).

Walking The provincial capital is best explored on foot and there are wonderful hiking routes linking the villages in Las Alpujarras.

WHEN TO GO

APR–JUN
Easter festivities; warm spring weather; perfect Alpujarras hiking

JUL–AUG
Peak beach-holiday time; walking season in the high Sierra Nevada

SEP–OCT
Calmer but still warm on the coast and in Granada city; good walking weather

NOV–MAR
Sierra Nevada ski season; a quieter time to explore Granada city

EATING & DRINKING

While life might seem to revolve around the provincial capital, much of Granada's fresh produce is grown along the Costa Tropical, where the sun-soaked climate is perfect for fruits such as mangos, avocados and custard apples (pictured top right). Meanwhile, Mediterranean-hugging Motril brings in the fresh seafood catch, and Trevélez in Las Alpujarras is famed across Spain for its mountain-aged *jamón serrano* (pictured bottom right). A key part of the Granada food scene, of course, is the age-old tradition of offering a free tapa with every drink, which gives rise to a raft of bite-sized local specialities (p198). Locally made wines from the DOP Vinos de Granada, produced in the Contraviesa–Alpujarras and Guadix/El Altiplanos areas, are on the up too.

Best fine dining Damasqueros, Granada (p220)

Must-try traditional tapas Bar Provincias, Granada (p199)

CONNECT & FIND YOUR WAY

Wi-fi Pretty much everywhere has free wi-fi, including cafes, restaurants and hotels, though the signal can be weak in historical buildings or remote mountain spots.

Navigation Anyone heading out hiking in the Sierra Nevada mountains should be adequately prepared with navigation tools, as well as supplies for fast-changing weather.

WHERE TO STAY

Granada city has accommodation to suit all budgets, with most options centrally located. There are excellent-value escapes in the mountains.

Area	Pros/Cons
Albayzín (Granada)	Beautiful views; historical hotels; steep streets; tricky to access by car
Realejo (Granada)	Great tapas scene; boutique hotels; central; can be noisy; close to the Alhambra
Centro (Granada)	Buzzy urban atmosphere; noisy at night; lots of hotel choice; convenient for everything
Pradollano (Sierra Nevada)	Winter ski hub; pricey in winter; most businesses close in summer
Las Alpujarras	Charming rural hotels/retreats; mountain views; great for hikers; remote
Costa Tropical	Beach scene and accommodation; water sports; busy/pricey in summer; *very* quiet in winter

GRANADA CARD

The **Granada Card** offers a range of multiday monument-and-transport combinations, all including some kind of Alhambra visit (granadatur.com/granada-card).

MONEY

Economise on a Granada trip by visiting outside high season and taking full advantage of the free-tapas scene. Most (not all) businesses accept card payments, though it's best to carry some cash for remote mountain areas.

42 On Granada's TAPAS TRAIL

FOOD | WINE | CULTURE

████ Granada is one of Andalucía's greatest destinations for food lovers, with an endlessly thrilling gastronomic scene that revolves around the freshest local produce, traditional regional recipes (often with a creative twist) and the fabulous, ancient tradition of serving a free tapa with every drink. Arrive hungry, rustle up a *tinto de verano* (red wine with lemonade) and dig in!

🗺 How To

Getting here/around Granada airport, 15km west of the city centre, has international and domestic connections, and there are good bus and train links across Spain. Granada is a very walkable city, though urban buses (movilidadgranada.com) are handy.

When to go Spring and autumn are the loveliest seasons; avoid sweltering July and August. Or sidestep the crowds with a winter visit (November to February).

Top tip Spanish dining hours: 1pm to 4pm for lunch and from 8pm (ideally later) for dinner.

The Free Tapa

From slivers of Montefrío cheese to mini-portions of paella, the art of a free tapa magically appearing alongside every drink you order is a Granada special-ity. Classic *granadino* tapas include *jamón asado* (roast ham), velvety croquettes, *migas* (fried breadcrumbs), *arroces* (rice dishes), fried fish and *berenjenas con miel* (eggplant with cane honey), all best enjoyed with one of the province's up-and-coming wines from the Guadix or Contraviesa–Alpujarras areas. Among the best places to dive into Granada's tapas delights are the **Realejo** neighbourhood and the streets to the south and west of the cathedral.

Market Time

The scent of fresh spices wafts through the air as you stroll around Granada's buzzy streets – no surprise given the city's strong Moorish heritage and the many fresh-produce

🍴 Top Tapas Bars

Las Titas Tapas, sharing plates and outdoor seating on the Genil riverbank; the Spanish omelette is delicious.

Bar Provincias A traditional bar at the heart of the old town since 1945, for fried fish and seafood tapas.

Bar de Fede A friendly, relaxed spot serving tasty tapas and good-value midweek menús; just off Gran Vía.

Bar Patio Braserito In the busy Realejo quarter, Braserito is a local favourite. Try the *huevos rotos* (broken eggs) or the salad made with Costa Tropical avocados.

Ávila Popular for its *jamón asado* (roast ham), this busy tapas bar off San Antón has been in business since 1967.

■ Recommended by **Molly Sears-Piccavey**, *Granada-based travel blogger and food-tour guide*, @piccavey

stalls that still line its alleys. At the **Mercado San Agustín**, near the cathedral, you'll find a clutch of lively tapas bars serving just-sliced *jamón,* homemade tortilla and other bites, while stands overflow with fruit from the Costa Tropical, buckets of Andalucian olives, locally made cheeses, Motril-caught seafood and more.

Fabulous Food Tours

For an expert-led gastronomic jaunt around Granada, join **Spain Food Sherpas** (spainfoodsherpas.com) on a culture-focused food tour or a wine-tasting session showcasing local drops. Well-established **Granada Tapas Tours** (granadatapastours. com) also runs excellent gastronomic itineraries around town, including a classic tapas trail and a 'local life' route highlighting small-scale family businesses.

Above Mercado San Agustín.

Tales of
GRANADA

NEIGHBOURHOODS | CULTURE | HISTORY

▬▬▬ Savour Granada's historical heritage and contemporary urban vibe on a culture-loaded roam around its key neighbourhoods, each of which has its own character and backstory – from the view-laden, Moorish-era Albayzín to the sloping streets of the buzzy Realejo.

LUIS OVERLANDER/SHUTTERSTOCK ©

🗺 Trip Notes

Getting around Granada is best explored by walking. Take bus C31 for the Albayzín, C34 for the Sacromonte or C30 for the Realejo.

When to go April to June, September and October bring festivals and warm weather. Winter (November to February) is cold, but has Christmas lights and fewer tourists.

Take a break Palm-shaded, pedestrianised Plaza de la Romanilla, next to the cathedral, is a locally loved spot for drinks and tapas.

◎ Cármenes

In the Albayzín and Realejo, keep your eyes peeled for beautiful *cármenes* – these secluded homes with exquisite gardens hidden behind walls have their roots in Moorish times. Explore a floral oasis at the **Carmen de los Mártires** (pictured) and a *carmen*-turned-gallery at the **Fundación Rodríguez Acosta**, or stay a few nights at charming **Carmen de la Alcubilla del Caracol**.

05 Northwest from the centre, the residential **La Chana** neighbourhood is typically off the tourist trail and has some excellent tapas bars, with tables spilling out onto streetside terraces.

02 Delve into the **Sacromonte**, Granada's traditional Roma neighbourhood on the northeast edge of town, on a guided walking tour to discover its ancient cave-houses, important flamenco legacy and multicultural identity.

01 Most Granada wanders begin with the magical **Albayzín**, the old Muslim quarter perched on the hillside opposite the Alhambra, where cobbled alleys weave between lively plazas, centuries-old churches and exquisite city panoramas.

03 A cascade of colourful homes and jumbled streets on the slopes of the Alhambra, the **Realejo** was medieval Granada's Jewish quarter. Today it's known for its tapas-bar scene and vibrant street art, including thought-provoking murals by local artist El Niño de las Pinturas.

04 Feel modern Granada's urban buzz as you weave between spice shops, fashion boutiques, tapas hangouts and speciality coffee spots in the **Centro** area, which sprawls around the cathedral.

La Chana (2.2km)

Av de la Constitución
Jardines del Triunfo
Plaza del Triunfo
Cuesta de la Alhacaba
C Panaderos
Cuesta del Chapiz

Gran Vía de Colón
C de Elvira
C San Juan de los Reyes
Carrera del Darro
Río Darro

C San Jerónimo
C Cárcel Baja
Plaza de la Trinidad
C Reyes Católicos
C Pavaneras
Cuesta de Gomérez
Alhambra

Fundación Rodríguez-Acosta
Carmen de la Alcubilla del Caracol

C Ángel Ganivet
C San Matías
Cuesta del Realejo
C Santiago

Carmen de los Mártires

Plaza Campillo
C de las Recogidas
C Acera del Darro

N 0 ———— 200 m
   0 ———— 0.1 miles

44 Moorish GRANADA

ARCHITECTURE | HISTORY | GARDENS

Once the opulent retreat of Granada's Nasrid rulers, the magical Alhambra looms against the snow-dusted Sierra Nevada. Uncover a new side to this millennia-old beauty, delve deep into Granada's Moorish heritage and explore lesser-known corners on an after-dark visit to the unparalleled, Unesco-listed palace-fortress.

How To

Getting around Pedestrian streets lead to the Alhambra, including Cuesta de Gomérez. Urban bus C30 runs between Plaza Isabel II and the Alhambra, via the Realejo.

When to go There are night visits to the Palacios Nazaríes year-round; for the gardens and Generalife, it's April, May, September and October only.

Tips Book tickets well ahead (alhambra-patronato.es). Thanks to the Espacio del Mes project, each month a different off-limits Alhambra space is opened up.

The Alhambra by Night

Thought to have first originated in the 9th century (though there have been buildings here since Roman times), the Alhambra morphed into its current lavish palatial form in the 13th and 14th centuries, with Granada under Nasrid rule. Today, it's one of Spain's most-visited monuments, with almost 2.5 million arrivals each year.

Wandering through the show-stopping **Palacios Nazaríes** (Nasrid Palaces) outside daylight hours, the intricate carvings and tile-work take on crisp new hues, while the towers, columns and wood-beamed ceilings cast a moonlit glow across the water-fed patios. Rippling *acequias* (irrigation channels) and gurgling fountains tinkle in the quiet, crowd-free night and as you emerge into lovingly tended cypress-scented gardens, you'll be engulfed in

Nature Walks

The Alhambra's natural beauty extends well beyond the complex's walls. For a fresh perspective, explore the leafy Cuesta de los Chinos, the Nasrid-era Acequia Real and the olive-tree-filled Dehesa del Generalife. Long-established **Cicerone** (ciceronegranada.com) runs excellent tours tapping into these lesser-known pockets of the Alhambra's story.

Top left Alhambra. **Top right** Acequia Real.
Left Detail, Palacios Nazaríes.

a feast of floral fragrances. It's also possible to (separately) visit the 14th-century **Generalife** after dark; the Alhambra's 'summer palace' reveals a series of elegant, flower-filled courtyards washed by rushing-water channels.

Sleep in the Alhambra

Few Granada moments rival waking up within the Alhambra grounds, hearing the birds chirping away and sipping your morning *café con leche* overlooking the Generalife, before the crowds begin to arrive. Book in (well ahead!) at the luxurious **Parador de Granada**, a 14th-century Nasrid palace that later became the Catholic Convento de San Francisco (parador.es). Surrounded by the 20th-century Jardines del Partal, this is one of Spain's most beloved hotels, with soothingly styled rooms, herb-filled gardens, Moorish-design patios and an elegant Granada-inspired restaurant.

After-Hours Albayzín

As the sun sets over the city, the Alhambra is illuminated in dazzling gold, and it's the

🏛 Special Alhambra Corners

Escalera del agua Among the Alhambra's oldest documented sites; protected by a laurel vault with water flowing down its handrail, the 'water staircase' is one of the most magical places inside the complex.

Mirador de Lindaraja Its interior contains the most exquisite decorations in the whole palace, with geometric and epigraphic compositions and very delicate plasterwork.

Baño del Polinario Arab baths once used by a family. It later became a tavern, where Granada's greatest flamenco evenings happened in the early 1920s, overseen by Federico García Lorca. Now it hosts a museum devoted to the great classical guitarist Ángel Barrios, whose family owned the tavern.

■ **Recommended by María A. Valdecasas**, *CEO of Cicerone Granada*, @ciceronegranada

Far left *Escalera del agua.*
Near left Mirador de Lindaraja.
Below Generalife,

Albayzín (Granada's original Muslim quarter) that has the most soul-stirring views. Several operators run evening tours of this labyrinthine *barrio*, where the sound of flamenco guitars tinkles across spectacularly perched *miradores* (lookouts). Alternatively, catch the sunrise glow over Granada from a hotel in the upper Albayzín, such as **Santa Isabel La Real**, a lovingly converted 16th-century home (hotelsantaisabellareal.com).

Other Moorish Jewels

Beyond the Alhambra, Granada's Moorish legacy is felt in the twisting-and-turning streets and a clutch of intriguing monuments. The upper Albayzín's 16th-century **Colegiata de San Salvador** retains the original horseshoe arches, *aljibe* (cistern) and patio of the mosque that once stood on this same spot. A few streets away, the curious **Puerta de Hernán Román** was one of the Albayzín's original gates, while the 15th-century **Palacio de Dar-al-Horra** was once the home of sultana Aixa, whose son Boabdil famously became Granada's final Muslim ruler. Dotted all over the Albayzín are gurgling *aljibes* (cisterns), built in distinctive red brick during Granada's time under Moorish rule. Down by the Río Darro, wander into the beautifully preserved **El Bañuelo bathhouse**, from the 11th or 12th century.

Moorish Architecture

ANDALUCÍA'S LONG, CONVOLUTED BACKSTORY UNFOLDS THROUGH ITS INTRICATE MOORISH-ERA ARCHITECTURE.

Beautiful scented gardens, tinkling water features, intimate courtyards, medina-like historic centres – Andalucía's most dazzling architectural creations are infused with Moorish heritage, courtesy of Spain's seven centuries under Islamic rule. Queen among these is the extraordinarily beautiful Alhambra, the elaborately adorned Nasrid fortress-palace that still stands guard over Granada, which became the final stronghold of Islamic Al-Andalus until its fall in 1492.

Left La Mezquita, Córdoba.
Middle Giralda. **Right** White houses, Alpujarras.

Repurposing Buildings

Following the Christian conquest of Al-Andalus, the Catholics often repurposed existing Islamic buildings, from converting mosques into chapels to reusing palaces and fortresses, which means many of Andalucía's most fabled buildings are today a fusion of Christian and Moorish elements. Patterned plasterwork, colourful tiling, geometrical shapes and floral motifs are among the classic, eye-catching features of this region's Moorish architecture.

Córdoba & the Umayyads

One of the world's greatest examples of Islamic architecture rests on the banks of the Río Guadalquivir in Córdoba, though since the mid-16th century there has been an elaborate Christian cathedral at its core, added under King Carlos I. Built in the late 8th century on the site of a Visigothic church and much-expanded over subsequent centuries, the **Mezquita-Catedral** represents the high point of Córdoba's time as one of Europe's most cultured cities, which began with the arrival of Abd ar-Rahman I, who launched the Umayyad dynasty here. With its rows of red-and-white-striped arches leading to a *mihrab* (prayer niche) decorated with gold-mosaic floral motifs, it combined the influence of earlier Umayyad architectural masterpieces (including the Great Mosque of Damascus) with new ideas.

The ruined city of **Medina Azahara**, just outside Córdoba, is another jewel of early-Moorish Al-Andalus, constructed in the mid-10th century by Caliph Abd ar-Rahman III.

Seville & the Almohads

Seville's brick-panelled **Giralda** and riverside **Torre del Oro**, along with the elegant **Alcázar** of Jerez de la Frontera, are

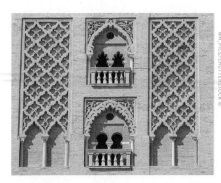

among the most notable relics left behind by the Almohad dynasty, who took over Al-Andalus in the late 12th century and erected a swath of defensive buildings and mosques. It was their capital Seville that was most embellished; today, the city's cathedral still retains the original Puerta del Perdón gate and Patio de los Naranjos of the Alhomad-built mosque that once stood here, as well as a 104m-tall brick tower, the Giralda, which began life as a minaret.

Nasrid Granada

The elegantly landscaped **Alhambra** is Andalucía's unparalleled jewel of Moorish architecture: a dazzling palace-fortress encircled by defensive walls, where the art of richly adorned arches and other decorative features, as well as the importance of flowing water, were elevated more than ever before. It was here, under the Islamic Nasrid emirate (in particular the 14th-century emirs Yusuf I and Mohammed V), that Moorish architecture on the Iberian Peninsula reached both its peak and its final flourish. Paradisiacal gardens and a (comparatively) unassuming exterior give way to gurgling waterways, shaded patios and domed halls, with stuccowork that is mesmerising in its detail.

> Many of Andalucía's most fabled buildings are today a fusion of Christian and Moorish elements.

After the fall of Granada, many Moorish architectural principles continued to be used across Spain, often by Muslim craftworkers creating buildings under Christian direction, resulting in what is today called the Mudéjar style.

Alpujarras Architecture

The white villages of Granada's mountainous Alpujarras feel instantly distinct from Andalucía's other *pueblos blancos*, thanks to their Berber-style architecture – another Moorish legacy. *Alpujarreño* homes are typically built into the hillside, using local stone, wood and clay, and have flat roofs, chunky chimneys and thick, weather-withstanding walls. Classic village features include *terraos* (interconnecting terraces), *bancales* (terraced orchards) and *tinaos* (beam-covered parts of a street), and although homes are now whitewashed, they were originally camouflaged against the mountains. The **Barranco del Poqueira** villages – Pampaneira, Bubión and Capileira – are the most famous examples of *alpujarreño* architecture, but it shines all over these hills.

45 SKY-HIGH HIKES:
Alpujarras & Sierra Nevada

HIKING | MOUNTAINS | WILDLIFE

■■■■ Welcome to Andalucía's most inspiring walkers' wonderland, where mainland Spain's formidable tallest peak, Mulhacén, towers high above ancient mule paths, and gurgling *acequias* (water channels) rush between Las Alpujarras's Moorish-origin villages. Adding to the Sierra Nevada's magic is the chance to spot ibex, birds of prey and unique plant species among the jaw-droppingly spectacular mountain scenery.

🗺️ How To

Getting here Alsa (alsa.com) buses from Granada serve Alpujarras villages, and Autocares Tocina (autotransportetocina.es) serves Hoya de la Mora (2512m) above the Pradollano ski resort. The Parque Nacional Sierra Nevada runs summer (June–October) shuttle buses from Capileira and Hoya de la Mora to more elevated starting points for summiting Mulhacén; book ahead (reservatuvisita.es).

When to go The best months for Las Alpujarras are April to June, September and October. Tackle the high Sierra Nevada in summer (July to mid-September).

Into the Sky

The 862-sq-km Parque Nacional Sierra Nevada revolves around 3479m-high **Mulhacén**, the most-elevated point in mainland Spain. It's possible to summit Mulhacén in a day, though do check weather conditions. On the north side, begin from Hoya de la Mora or Posiciones del Veleta at 3100m; from the latter, it's 14km (four to five hours) to the top of Mulhacén. From the south, trails lead up from above Capileira; from the Mirador de Trevélez (2710m), the 5km walk takes three hours one way. You can also hike up Mulhacén from Trevélez (24km, 10 to 12 hours return).

Poqueira Villages & La Tahá

There are plenty of rewarding routes around **Pampaneira**,

IMAGEBROKER/ALAMY STOCK PHOTO ©

Off the Beaten Track

Eastern Alpujarras A less-rugged contrast to the western Alpujarras; you'll encounter few others here. The 2000m-high Puerta de la Ragua pass provides access to hills over 2500m.

Integral de los Tres Miles A five-day crossing of the Sierra Nevada taking in all the main 3000m-plus peaks, from Jerez del Marquesado to Lanjarón.

Northern Sierra Nevada North of Alcazaba, the peaks are rough and quiet, with access from Güéjar Sierra, Jerez del Marquesado or the long valleys up from Trevélez.

Vereda de Estrella A 'classic' path within the local community, with wooded chestnut trees and many beautiful waterfalls, starting near Güéjar Sierra.

■ **Recommended by Emma Hartley**, *walking guide at Spanish Highs in the Sierra Nevada,* @spanishhighsmountainguides

Bubión and, especially, **Capileira** in the western Alpujarras. The 17km Acequias del Poqueira walk from Capileira (six to seven hours) climbs to 2100m before looping back past a series of *acequias*. For blissfully quiet hikes along paths that have stood strong since Moorish times, dip into **La Tahá valley** around Pitres.

Across the Sierra Nevada

The long-distance GR7 trail tracks across Spain from Tarifa in Cádiz to Andorra, with one branch traversing Las Alpujarras – perfect for linking villages or multiday hikes. The 270km-long GR240 (Sulayr) encircles the Sierra Nevada, doable in two weeks.

Guided Walks

Local adventure operators such as **Nevadensis** (nevadensis.com) and **Spanish Highs** (spanishhighs.com) offer expert-led walks, from a few hours' hiking to multiweek treks.

Above Mulhacén peak.

46 Kayak & Snorkel the COSTA TROPICAL

BEACHES | ADVENTURE | NATURE

▬▬▬ Extending along 90km of dramatic cliff-edged coastline, Granada's mellow Costa Tropical is a little-developed, activity-filled paradise. Easy-going bougainvillea-clad towns sit between rugged headlands that frame dreamy silver-sand beaches, several of them with a laid-back naturist vibe. These calm, gin-clear Mediterranean waters are best enjoyed from aboard a kayak or paddleboard, while beneath the rippling waves there are vibrant corals and fluttering fish to discover.

ROD JONES/ALAMY STOCK PHOTO ©

🗺 How To

Getting here/around The main Costa Tropical beach towns of Almuñécar, La Herradura and Salobreña have bus connections to/from Granada, Málaga and beyond. For off-the-beaten-track beaches, you'll need a car.

When to go July/August is peak beach-holiday season; May/June and September/October are quieter and cheaper but still warm.

Beach restaurants Serving fresh seafood and sizzling paellas, the Costa Tropical's beachfront *chiringuitos* are a delight; book ahead, particularly in summer.

SUZYANNELIE/SHUTTERSTOCK ©

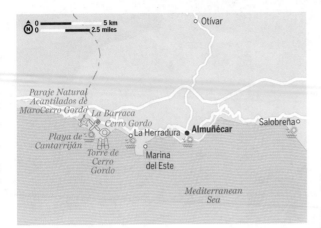

Left La Barraca.
Bottom left Kayaking. Granada,

Playa de Cantarriján The first Granada beach east from Málaga province is knockout-pretty nudist spot Cantarriján, where the Mediterranean washes onto a silver-pebble cove hemmed between craggy headlands; **La Barraca** (labarracacantarrijan. com) here serves delicious *arroces* (rice dishes) and fresh fish, and you can rent kayaks and paddleboards.

Water Sports in La Herradura East from Cantarriján, this 2km-long horseshoe bay and low-key beach town has grown into an easy-going water sports hub. From Easter to October, stands along the sand hire out kayaks and paddleboards, including **Windsurf La Herradura** (windsurflaherradura.com), which also runs expert-guided kayaking trips past sea caves and summer stand-up paddleboarding yoga sessions. This is a great spot for snorkelling too, especially around the **Cerro Gordo** cliffs at the northwest end of the main beach (part of a protected marine reserve) and, to the southeast, off Playa Berengueles. La Herradura's Marina del Este harbour has a clutch of diving schools, offering everything from try-dives for beginners to advanced training, including well-established **Buceo La Herradura** (buceolaherradura.com).

Almuñécar & Salobreña A clutch of silvery pebble beaches sits below the sloping, castle-topped old town in **Almuñécar**, which offers a scenic backdrop for a sunset paddleboard or swim. A little further east, **Salobreña** has a twisting-and-turning historic core set behind two locally loved beaches, where the **Guardian Sea Club** (theguardianseaclub.es) runs paddleboarding and kayaking excursions.

Acantilados de Maro–Cerro Gordo

The 19-sq-km **Paraje Natural Acantilados de Maro–Cerro Gordo** protects a string of sheer sea cliffs and tucked-away coves between Maro (in Málaga province) and La Herradura on Granada's Costa Tropical. This is one of just a few spots in the Mediterranean where you'll find the oxygen-producing *posidonia* seagrass, which gives the water its ultra-clear, turquoise beauty. Birds of prey circle high above, ibex leap around the rocks and you might spot dolphins playing in the waves. Up on the cliffs above La Herradura, a short trail leads to the **Torre de Cerro Gordo**, a 16th-century watchtower with spectacular coastal views.

47

Outdoors Sierra
NEVADA

ADVENTURE | NATURE | OUTDOORS

Endless adventure activities, inspired creative retreats, outstanding hiking and the continent's southernmost ski resort collide in the wonderfully wild Sierra Nevada, one of Spain's most spectacular mountain escapes, where gleaming-white villages cling to craggy slopes beneath snow-topped peaks.

Above Pradollano. **Far right** Mountain goat. **Near right** Golden eagle.

📝 How To

Getting here/around
The easiest way to access the Sierra Nevada is with your own wheels. There are also buses to most Alpujarras villages with Alsa (alsa.com) and to Pradollano with Autocares Tocina (auto transportetocina.es).

When to go The ski season runs from November to April. For other activities, go for March–June, September or October, when the weather is warm but not sweltering.

City to pistes If you're staying in Granada city, it's perfectly possible to day-trip to Pradollano for skiing.

Southern Pistes

Here in Granada's Sierra Nevada lies Europe's most southerly ski resort, centred on 2100m-high **Pradollano** village (which has a touch of alpine charm). Around 110km of adrenaline-filled pistes stretch down from almost the top of Veleta (3395m), Spain's fourth-highest peak. This is a great place for beginners, with 19 green runs and a string of well-established ski schools offering everything from group sessions to one-on-one training. But there are also plenty of challenging red and black runs to thrill advanced skiers and snowboarders. Ski-season weekends can get packed with day trippers from Granada, meaning midweek visits are most peaceful (sierranevada.es).

🐦 Flora & Fauna

The wonderfully biodiverse **Parque Nacional Sierra Nevada** sprawls across 862 sq km, surrounded by a 864-sq-km *parque natural*. The most emblematic local inhabitant is the Iberian ibex – around 15,000 of these astonishingly agile creatures jump around the craggy landscapes. Other stars include wild boars, foxes, wild cats, griffon vultures and golden eagles, along with over 2000 plant species.

GRANADA EXPERIENCES

Active Retreats

Over the years, a raft of highly original rural hotels hosting exciting active escapes has sprung up across the Alpujarras, many with a creative atmosphere. Stretch into the day with sun salutations on a wisteria-clad terrace overlooking La Tahá's rugged valley on a yoga retreat at **Casa Ana** (casa-ana.com); set in the pretty white village of Ferreirola, this is a beautifully converted 400-year-old house with just 10 rooms, plus walking, writing and painting holidays. There are more excellent yoga retreats over in secluded Mairena at **Las Chimeneas** (laschimeneas.com), which has its own studio as well as a *shala* among the olive groves; guests stay in an 800-year-old town house and dine in the fabulous organic-fired restaurant, all powered by renewable energy, while cycling, cooking, hiking and birdwatching escapes add to the appeal.

☆ Unique Experience

Equi-libre Equestrian Clara and local vaquero Antonio run this astonishing Laroles venture (equi-libre.es): part farm, part zoo and part trekking centre, with a strong sustainable ethos. Join them for half-day or multi-night hacks across the Sierra Nevada.

Be Natural An outdoor adventure set-up (bnaturalsport.com) in Bayárcal for canyoning, archery, a slackline, e-bikes and Andalucía's longest zipwire, an adrenalised 600m flight above a scarily deep gorge.

El Paraje del Chef Juan Carlos Espejo has created an elegant dining room (elparajedelchef.com) in the middle of a field just outside Júbar in the eastern Alpujarras, where the gourmet seven-course tasting menu shines for its originality and freshness.

■ **Recommended by Emma Illsley**, *owner of Las Chimeneas hotel-restaurant in Mairena, @laschimeneas*

Far left Horse-riding, Sierra Nevada. **Near left** Snowshoeing, Sierra Nevada. **Below** Yoga, Alpujarras.

Horse-Riding Heaven

With its reliably sunny weather, wide-open views and strong equestrian heritage, the Sierra Nevada is one of the most rewarding parts of Andalucía to explore on horseback. Many of the old mule trails here have existed since Moorish times and the ever-changing landscapes never fail to inspire, whether you're wandering through fields of almond blossom, trotting through the sun-soaked olive groves or arriving into one of the Alpujarra's white-walled villages. Local equestrian centres run everything from half-day rides to overnight horseback treks through the silent hills, meaning it's easy to get off the beaten track. **Caballo Blanco** (*caballo blancotrekking.com*) near Lanjarón and Órgiva, in the western Alpujarras, is a well-established ranch offering trips, and also doubles as a rescue and rehabilitation centre for mistreated horses.

Adrenaline Thrills

From via ferrate routes and canyoning down gorges to 4WD national park expeditions and high-altitude snowshoeing, there's little this spectacular outdoor-adventure playground doesn't offer, with something going on at all times of year. Respected Pampaneira-based operator **Nevadensis** (*nevadensis.com*) has been organising all the main activities since 1989 and is also recommended for guided hikes.

Alpujarras **ROAD TRIP**

ARCHITECTURE | OUTDOORS | CRAFTS

Escape into the *granadino* hills in the timeworn Alpujarras, where flat-roofed, whitewashed villages simmer with Moorish history, ancient artisanal crafts live on and days move to a decidedly rural rhythm. On a go-slow Alpujarras adventure, rugged mountain landscapes set the scene for thrilling hikes, traditional meals, local festivals and more.

🍽 Best Restaurants

El Corral del Castaño (Capileira) *Alpujarreño* favourites with a creative touch.

L'Atelier (Mecina Fondales) Exquisite vegetarian meals fuelled by local produce.

La Fragua (Trevélez) Rustic setting for mountain cooking.

Alquería de Morayma (Cádiar) Organic-focused wine estate with excellent local-style cuisine.

Las Chimeneas (Mairena) Home-grown produce meets Andalucian-international flair.

🗺 Trip Notes

Getting here/around A car gives you most freedom, though most villages have decent bus links with **Alsa** (alsa.com) and there are lovely hiking routes between them.

When to go April to mid-June and September to-mid November for the best weather and, in spring, flower-covered hills.

Tip Some of Granada's best wines are made at visitor-welcoming bodegas in the Contraviesa–Alpujarras area between the Sierra Nevada and the coast – well worth a detour (see p221).

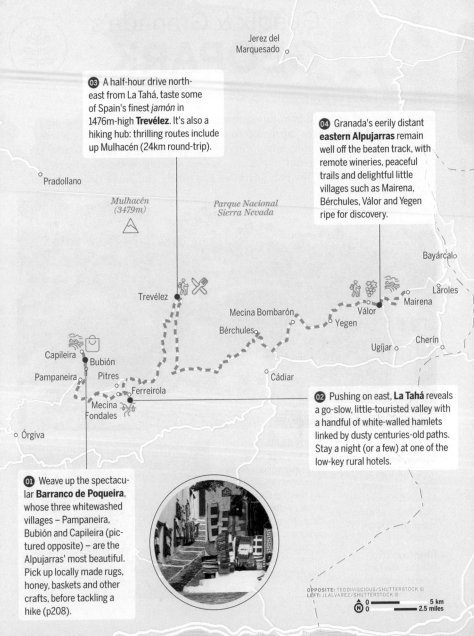

03 A half-hour drive north-east from La Tahá, taste some of Spain's finest *jamón* in 1476m-high **Trevélez**. It's also a hiking hub: thrilling routes include up Mulhacén (24km round-trip).

04 Granada's eerily distant **eastern Alpujarras** remain well off the beaten track, with remote wineries, peaceful trails and delightful little villages such as Mairena, Bérchules, Válor and Yegen ripe for discovery.

Jerez del Marquesado

Pradollano

Mulhacén (3479m)

Parque Nacional Sierra Nevada

Bayárcal

Lároles

Trevélez

Mecina Bombarón

Bérchules

Válor

Mairena

Yegen

Capileira

Bubión

Pitres

Pampaneira

Ferreirola

Cádiar

Ugíjar

Cherín

Mecina Fondales

Órgiva

02 Pushing on east, **La Tahá** reveals a go-slow, little-touristed valley with a handful of white-walled hamlets linked by dusty centuries-old paths. Stay a night (or a few) at one of the low-key rural hotels.

01 Weave up the spectacular **Barranco de Poqueira**, whose three whitewashed villages – Pampaneira, Bubión and Capileira (pictured opposite) – are the Alpujarras' most beautiful. Pick up locally made rugs, honey, baskets and other crafts, before tackling a hike (p208).

N
0   5 km
0   2.5 miles

49

Guadix & Granada's
GEOPARK

OUTDOORS | CAVES | WINE

━━━ Crammed with otherworldly landscapes, the Unesco-listed Geoparque de Granada sprawls across northeastern Granada province. Here in the remote, semi-desert Altiplano region, a haunting off-the-beaten-track natural beauty lays the stage for exploring centuries-old cave-houses, visiting on-the-up wineries, roaming around ruined Moorish fortresses and hiking and horse-riding through endless lunar-like hills.

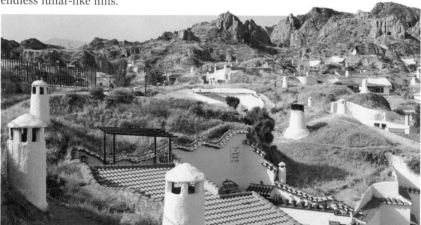

JOTAQUI/SHUTTERSTOCK ©

🗺 How To

Getting here/around
Guadix has train and bus links to Granada, Almería and beyond, but you'll need a car, a bike or a guide to explore the geopark.

When to go Spring (March to May) and autumn (September to November) are the best weather-wise.

Starry nights The blissfully unpolluted skies above this sparsely populated region offer outstanding star-gazing; there's a choice of Starlight-certified accommodation, and Granada's Sierra Nevada is in the process of becoming a Starlight Destination.

TOKAR/SHUTTERSTOCK ©

Left Cave houses, Guadix.
Bottom left Castillo de la Calahorra.

 Must-do Geopark

Cave stays The number-one experience you can't miss is staying a night or two in a real-life cave-house; every dwelling is naturally climatised.

Human history The Geopark has over 1500 archaeological sites, excellent interpretation centres and relics ranging from a million years ago to the present day.

Lunar landscapes To fully appreciate the scenery, hop in a hot-air balloon for a bird's-eye view or explore the **Desierto de los Coloraos**, **Miradores Fin del Mundo** and **Desierto Blanco** by 4WD.

Embalse del Negratín Between Guadix and Orce, take in an autumn sunset or sunrise over the emerald waters of Andalucía's 'interior sea', with its flocks of flamingos.

 ■ Recommended by **Goyo Garrido**, *adventure tour guide in Guadix*, @goyogarridoadventures

Unesco Global Geopark Sculpted by fluvial erosion over the last half a million years, the 4772-sq-km **Geoparque de Granada** protects a third of the province, yet remains little-explored by visitors. Arid ochre-hued badlands disappear into rock-hewn valleys, with the Sierra Nevada's snowy peaks glinting on the horizon. It's a paradise for hiking, biking, horse-riding and adventure sports.

Into the Caves This part of Granada is dotted with curious cave dwellings, most of which date from the 15th or 16th centuries (some even have Moorish origins) and are still home for countless local families. The best place to jump in is **Guadix**, a buzzy town with a spectacular cathedral, a down-to-earth tapas scene and its own Barrio de las Cuevas, where 2000 cave-houses await. Don't miss a stay in a cave converted into a cosy rural hotel, such as **Casas Cueva Tío Tobas** (cuevastiotobas.com).

World of Wines The Guadix/El Altiplano area is a star on Granada's flourishing wine scene, known for its rich reds grown at up to 1500m and for grape varieties found nowhere else. Get a taste at **Bodega Anchurón** (anchuron.es), where the Romero García family has been making wines using renewable energy since the 1980s.

Moorish Echoes In the Sierra Nevada's northern foothills, a rewarding detour leads to the imposing Renaissance-style **Castillo de La Calahorra** (lacalahorra.es), built in the 16th century on the site of a ruined Moorish fortress.

Listings

BEST OF THE REST

 ## Tapas Havens & Creative Cuisine

Picoteca 3 Maneras €€

Granada-sourced ingredients meet globe-trotting flavours at this creative restaurant in the Realejo. Elegant Spanish wines are paired with fresh-mango salad, date-dressed eggplant and pork-and-mushroom rice.

Más Que Vinos €€

A few steps from Granada cathedral and Plaza Bib-Rambla, this is a down-to-earth spot for local-produce tapas and wines from across the province. Try the Güejar Sierra potatoes with *jamón* and *huevos rotos* (fried eggs).

R Bar €€

A vibey, all-day restaurant-bar with a sunny terrace on central Granada's palm-studded Plaza de la Romanilla, for local vermouths and creative *granadino*-style tapas.

Hicuri €

The Realejo's go-to vegan restaurant is plastered with original murals by local street artist El Niño de las Pinturas and serves tempting bites such as seitan stir-fries and *salmorejo* with avocado.

Damasqueros €€€

Hidden away in the Realejo and with respected local chef Lola Marín at the helm, Damasqueros is locally loved for its weekly-changing market-fresh menus inspired by Granada's culinary heritage.

Rosario Varela €€

Another Realejo favourite, where vintage-inspired design sets the tone for tapas and *raciones* fusing flavours from all over the world – Canaries-style *papas arrugadas*, mix-your-own guacamole, and oven-fired sardines.

Bodegas Castañeda €

Quite possibly Granada's most famous tapas spot, with *jamón* legs dangling in the tile-walled interior. Arrive early to perch at the bar for bite-sized tortilla, charcuterie platters and *raciones* of Andalucian cheeses.

Vino y Rosas €€

An imaginative, local-fired kitchen opposite Granada's Mercado de San Agustín, with standout dishes including wild-mushroom scrambles and prize-winning croquettes.

Casa Torcuato €

A classic family-owned tapas bar in the upper Albayzín, running since the 1930s and famous for its *arroz* tapa and traditional bites.

Historical Hotels

Hotel Casa 1800 Granada €€€

Among Granada's most memorable experiences is the chance to stay in a centuries-old mansion in the ancient Albayzín. Original tiling, exposed brick, intricate woodwork, gold-toned rooms and a traditional fountain-bathed patio recall the building's 16th-century origins.

Cortijo del Marqués €€€

Like visiting an ancient Andalucian village: in the thick of the olive-growing region north of Granada, this sensitively converted 16th-century farmstead retains its original chapel, cobblestone patio and citrus-scented terraces.

Coffee Culture

Noat €

In the capital's Realejo quarter, Noat collaborates with prize-winning Barcelona coffee roaster Right Side and serves home-baked pastries to enjoy on the steps outside.

La Finca €

Get your caffeine kick just steps from Granada's cathedral at this third-wave micro-roaster with a sustainable, fairtrade ethos, which sources beans from small-scale producers.

Lorca & Literature

Centro Federico García Lorca

Spain's greatest playwright, the *granadino* Federico García Lorca (1898–1936), is celebrated through exhibitions, readings and performances at his namesake foundation, next to Granada's cathedral.

Huerta de San Vicente

On the western edge of central Granada city, the Lorca family's summer house is where the young Federico penned such fabled pieces as *Blood Wedding* and *Yerma;* now it's open for pre-booked guided tours.

Local Crafts & Gourmet Foods

Al Sur de Granada

Hand-painted pottery, speciality coffee, natural *granadino* wines, artisanal olive oils and other local-focused treats await in a stylish deli-boutique on Granada's Calle de Elvira.

Fajalauza

Albayzín family business crafting classic *granadino* pottery in *fajalauza* style since the 17th century, with hand-painted bowls, plates, mugs, pots and more in an ocean of blues.

Artesanías González

Granada's world of *taracea* (marquetry), a dwindling art with its roots in the 14th century, is on show at this long-established craft shop on the slopes of the Alhambra.

Jamones Cano González

Pick your very own *jamón* in the lofty *alpujarreño* village of Trevélez or stock up on olive oils, Alpujarras wines and Granada cheeses.

Flamenco

Peña La Platería

Cádiz and Seville might steal Andalucía's flamenco show, but Granada has its own rich flamenco heritage. Catch a glimpse at the Albayzín's respected *peña,* founded in 1949.

 Bodegas & Wine Bars

Dominio Buenavista

In the Contraviesa–Alpujarras region, near Ugíjar, this respected winery founded in 1990 is behind some of province's most irresistible labels, with vines grown at 2500m and grapes harvested by hand. There are tastings and tours with prior booking.

Taberna La Tana €

A legend of Andalucía's wine-bar scene, La Tana stocks over 500 Spanish wines and serves them alongside elegant tapas, from zingy tomato salads to cheese and *jamón* platters, in the Realejo quarter.

Casa de Vinos La Brujidera €

Dive into the world of Spanish wines at this popular haunt just off Plaza Nueva in central Granada, where tortilla *pinchos* accompany drops from all over the country, whether you fancy a local red or a Galician *albariño*.

Granada History

Capilla Real

The marble-sculpted tombs of Spain's Reyes Católicos (Catholic monarchs), Isabel I de Castilla (1451–1504) and Fernando II de Aragón (1452–1516), await in Granada's Royal Chapel, attached to the cathedral.

Museo Arqueológico

A 16th-century Renaissance-style mansion is the setting for the city's intimate and intriguing archaeological collection, which includes a human tooth unearthed in the Orce area and thought to be 1.4 million years old.

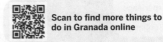 Scan to find more things to do in Granada online

ALMERÍA

NATURE | BEACHES | ARCHITECTURE

Experience
Almería
online

Bailén Linares

Baeza

Jaén

JAÉN

Caravaca de la Cruz

MURCIA

Catch a Wild West shootout in the Desierto de Tabernas (p226)

🚗 *30 mins from Almería*

Be awed by the sparkling crystals of La Geoda de Pulpí (p000)

🚗 *1¼hrs from Almería*

Vélez Rubio

Puerto Lumbreras

Águilas

GRANADA Cúllar

Baza

Huércal-Overa

Albox

San Juan de los

Guadix

ALMERÍA

Vera Terreros

La Calahorra

Mojácar Garrucha

Buitre (2465m)

Tabernas

Sorbas

Parque Natural Sierra Nevada

Níjar Carboneras

Berja

Almería

Parque Natural de Cabo de Gata-Níjar

San José

Adra

Almerimar

Mediterranean Sea

Descend into the subterranean world of the Cuevas de Sorbas (p236)

🚗 + 🚶 *50 mins from Almería*

Chill out on pristine beaches while hiking in Parque Natural Cabo de Gata (p232)

🚗 + 🚶 *1hr from Almería*

Admire Almería's mighty Alcazaba and other vestiges of Moorish legacy (p230)

Treat your taste buds to tapas, tipples and tagine in Almería (p228)

ALMERÍA
Trip Builder

Unspoiled white-sand coves, clifftop hiking trails, tranquil seaside villages, spaghetti-western badlands, spectacular caves – Almería province has all that in spades! Add a mighty fortress and other remnants of Moorish legacy in the handsome city of Almería, and you have plenty of reasons to linger.

N 0 ——— 40 km
    0 ——— 20 miles

Practicalities

Aeropuerto de Almería Small airport 9km east of the city; connected to central Almería by public bus (€1.05, 30 minutes) and taxi (around €15).

MONEY

Avoid Cabo del Gata in the height of summer, when accommodation prices go through the roof. Carry euros on you for dining out and small purchases.

FIND YOUR WAY

Take your time driving along minor roads in Parque Nacional Cabo de Gata; some of them have potholes large enough to swallow a car.

WHERE TO STAY

Town/village	Pro/con
Almería	Moorish architecture, excellent dining scene, museums, bars, ample accommodation, good transport links
Agua Amarga	Great beach, varied dining, proximity to coastal hiking, shopping, limited public transport
Las Negras	Relaxed vibe; easy trail access in Parque Natural Cabo del Gata, limited accommodation and dining, infrequent buses
San José	Good access to Cabo del Gata trails, beachside accommodation, numerous dining options, overly touristy, bus connections to Almería

EATING & DRINKING

Named Spain's culinary capital in 2019, Almería takes its credentials seriously, and its tapas and wine scene is superb. Beyond the city's reaches, the seaside villages in Cabo de Gata treat you to stellar seafood and rice dishes.

Gurullos con conejo (pictured top left) Elongated, rice-shaped pasta cooked with rabbit and saffron.

Ajo colorao (pictured bottom left) Chilled soup made from potatoes, salted cod, dried choricero peppers, garlic, tomato and cumin. Typically served with cornbread.

Best Moroccan-style tagine Teteria Almedina (p229)

Must-try tapas El Quinto Toro, Almería (p238)

GETTING AROUND

Train Several daily services connect Almería with Granada, Seville and Córdoba.

Bus Services cover most towns in the province, though village services are sporadic. The main bus company is ALSA (alsa.es); Autocares Bernardo (autocarresbernardo.com) connects to San José while Autocarres Frahermar (frahermar.com) connects to Agua Amarga in July and August.

Car The maximum flexibility option when it comes to reaching remote attractions. Car hire available at Almería's airport.

ALMERÍA FIND YOUR FEET

MAR–MAY
Warm hiking weather, desert in full bloom

JUN–AUG
Very hot in the arid interior, beach crowds and accommodation prices surge in July and August

SEP–NOV
Fewer crowds, warm sea, excellent time for hiking

DEC–FEB
Ample sunshine, cool nights, few visitors, bargain hotel prices

50 ALMERÍA'S
Wild West

FILM | CULTURE | NATURE

▬▬▬ It's high noon. You're standing by the saloon when a horse-drawn cart pulls up in the dusty main square in front of the sheriff's office. An outlaw arrives on horseback. Fisticuffs commence; a gunfight breaks out... Since the mid-1960s partnership between Sergio Leone and Clint Eastwood, Spain's only desert, Desierto de Tabernas, has been used to shoot numerous spaghetti westerns and you can visit the film sets.

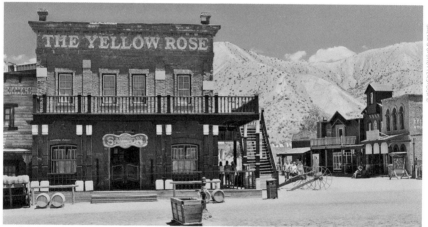

SALVA G C/SHUTTERSTOCK ©

📍 How To

Getting here/around
Driving is the easiest way to reach Oasys MiniHollywood and Fort Bravo.

When to go While the two amusement parks/spaghetti western sets are open year-round, avoid July and August heat and busy weekends.

The desert is in flower in spring.

Best tour Based in Tabernas, **Malcaminos** (malcaminos.com) offers engaging 4WD tours of the various movie locations in the Desierto de Tabernas, as well as horseback riding and guided hikes.

SONIA BONET/SHUTTERSTOCK ©

Oasys MiniHollywood

A huge hit with families, this amusement park is particularly famous as the set for *A Fistful of Dollars* and *The Good, The Bad and The Ugly* (remember the water tower?), though Doctor Who fans will get a sense of déjà vu as well. In summer, there are twice-daily **shootouts** between the sheriff's men and Jesse James, while dancing girls show off their petticoats during cancan dancing at the saloon. You can also escape the Wild West by visiting the well-curated **cactus garden**, with all things thorny and prickly from across five continents; commune with rhinoceros iguanas in the **reptile house**; or take your kids around the well-kept **zoo**.

Fort Bravo

Fans of *Once Upon a Time in the West* won't want to miss this **movie set** – still in use – slightly further along the N-340A from Almería than Oasys. Wander through the US cavalry frontier fort, a Mexican border town and among the Indian teepees, set against a dramatic backdrop of gulches and ochre-coloured scrubland, or quench your thirst at the saloon while watching the cancan dancing, gunslinging demonstrations and the entertainingly choreographed cowboy and outlaw fights in the main square. You also have the opportunity to explore Europe's only desert landscape more intimately on two-hour **horseback rides**, or opt for a genteel horse-drawn **buggy ride** through the film set.

Almería's Filming Locations

If you're a movie or TV show buff, you'll be thrilled to learn that it's not just the harsh, rugged desert landscape that's been used as a film set in Almería. Famous locations include:

Alcazaba, Almería Appeared as Sunspear in Dorne in *Game of Thrones*.

Playa de Mónsul Indiana Jones brought down a plane with a flock of birds here in *The Last Crusade*.

Playa Algarróbico A replica of the Jordanian city of Áqaba was built here for *Lawrence of Arabia*.

Desierto de Tabernas Michael Blomkvist and Harriet Vagner met in the Australian Outback in *Girl With the Dragon Tattoo*.

51 Tapas, Tagine
& TIPPLES

FOOD | WINE | CULTURE

████ Almería's north African flavours reflect the city's Moorish heyday. Taking its food seriously, Andalucía's millennia-old port is justifiably proud of the region's fresh produce and its unique wines, both of which dominate its menus. Whether you're here to partake in extensive *tapear* sessions, indulge in a superlative tagine or acquaint yourself with local tipples, there's plenty to tempt you here.

ANTONIO LASO/SHUTTERSTOCK ©

🗺 How To

Getting around Doing a tapas bar crawl is a wonderful way to experience Almería's dining scene. Tapas bars are close together and reachable on foot.

When to go Anytime, though the city is packed during the summer beach season. Almería's Ruta de Tapa festival is in late March/early April.

Gastronomy capital Almería was named Spain's Capital of Gastronomy in 2019.

EUSEBIO TORRES/SHUTTERSTOCK ©

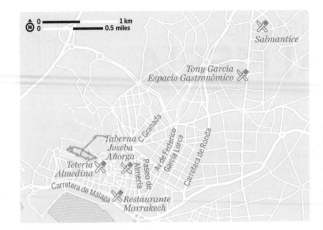

Left Octopus tapa. **Bottom left** Red prawns from Garrucha.

Tapas

Almería's tapas scene is defined by the province's raw ingredients – red prawns from Garrucha, octopus and other sea bounty. Look out also for *gurullos* with cuttlefish and fried hake cheeks. Many tapas bars are concentrated along Calles Jovellanos and Alfonso Torres.

Tipples

Of Andalucía's 16 geographical locations granted the Vinos de la Tierra quality wine classification, five are in Almería province. These wines are defined by the climatic conditions of where they are produced, be it the desert or the mountains. All these wineries plant their vines at altitudes of 500m to 1200m, so the grapes benefit from both the Andalucian sun and the highlands' cool nights. Few Almería wines are exported so the city's bars are among the best places to try them. Don't miss Brut Blue from the desert Bodegas Perfer, the smoky, full-bodied Tetas de la Sacristiana from mountainous Laujar and the intensely fruity, golden yellow Flor de Indalia from Padules.

Tagine

The main port in Al-Andalus under the Moors, today's Almería welcomes ferries from Morocco, which has reinforced the cross-cultural pollination of its dining scene. With stellar views of the Alcazaba from its roof terrace, family-run **Tetería Almedina** is best-known for its superb lamb tagines. Near the waterfront, unassuming decor at **Restaurante Marrakech** belies the fact that its beef tagine and couscous is second to none.

Michelin-Recommended Dining

Tony García Espacio Gastronómico Red prawn carpaccio with swordfish roe and mélange of red tuna tartare and steak tartare are just some of examples of traditional-meets-contemporary Almerían cuisine served here.

Salmantice Simple, flawless presentation and quality of ingredients define the dishes at this family-run restaurant, whether it's aged steak from Avileña-Black Iberian cattle or Asian-style mussels with salmon roe.

Taberna Joseba Añorga The menu at this centrally located taberna shines a spotlight on the best of modern Basque flavours. Nibble on tapas such as glazed pig trotters and robalo ceviche, or go for a full *sidrería* (cider bar) experience and order a tasting menu.

Historic
ALMERÍA

HISTORY | ARCHITECTURE | CULTURE

Founded by the Moors, this sultry, palm-studded port city feels different from other Andalucian cities. You can almost smell Africa from here. Explore Almería's multi-faceted heritage on a stroll through its historical *barrios*, from the labyrinthine Moorish Almedina to medieval Old Town.

🗺 Trip Notes

Getting around Almería is best explored on foot. Alternatively, take the L1 bus that loops around Almedina, connecting Old Town to the Alcazaba.

When to go March to May, and September and October mean mild and warm weather. Almería's biggest festivals happen during sweltering July and August.

Take a break Pause your perambulations and refuel at the tapas bars dotting Calle Jovellanos, a halfway stop between the city's main attractions.

🏛 Almería's Offbeat Heritage

Museo de La Guitarra Española (pictured) Nineteenth-century Almerían guitar-maker Antonio de Torres is the father of the modern acoustic guitar; explore guitar-making through the ages here.

Casa del Cine Delve into Almería's cinematographic past inside this mansion, which hosted Clint Eastwood, Brigitte Bardot and John Lennon during Almería's heyday as 'European Hollywood'.

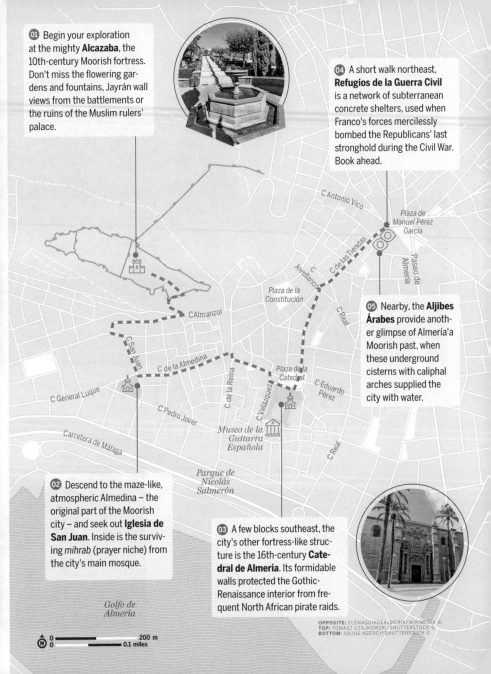

01 Begin your exploration at the mighty **Alcazaba**, the 10th-century Moorish fortress. Don't miss the flowering gardens and fountains, Jayrán wall views from the battlements or the ruins of the Muslim rulers' palace.

04 A short walk northeast, **Refugios de la Guerra Civil** is a network of subterranean concrete shelters, used when Franco's forces mercilessly bombed the Republicans' last stronghold during the Civil War. Book ahead.

05 Nearby, the **Aljibes Árabes** provide another glimpse of Almería'a Moorish past, when these underground cisterns with caliphal arches supplied the city with water.

02 Descend to the maze-like, atmospheric Almedina – the original part of the Moorish city – and seek out **Iglesia de San Juan**. Inside is the surviving *mihrab* (prayer niche) from the city's main mosque.

03 A few blocks southeast, the city's other fortress-like structure is the 16th-century **Catedral de Almería**. Its formidable walls protected the Gothic-Renaissance interior from frequent North African pirate raids.

Plaza de Manuel Pérez García

C Antonio Vico

Paseo de Almería

C de las Tiendas

C Joyellanos

Plaza de la Constitución

C Real

C San Juan

C Almanzor

C de la Almedina

C de la Reina

Plaza de la Catedral

C Velázquez

C Eduardo Pérez

C General Luque

C Pedro Jover

Carretera de Málaga

Museo de la Guitarra Española

C Real

Parque de Nicolás Salmerón

Golfo de Almería

N 0 — 200 m
0 — 0.1 miles

53 HIKE & BATHE
in a National Park

BEACHES | HIKING | VIEWPOINTS

Dramatic cliffs, deserted white-sand beaches and strange rock formations define this semi-arid, 340-sq-km protected area that encompasses a sizeable slice of Almería coast. Base yourself in one of the coastal villages and indulge in outdoor adventure above and below the waves.

🗺 How To

Getting here/around Bus services connect Almería and San José. You'll need your own wheels to access other villages and trailheads.

When to go Cabo de Gata is spectacular year-round. Most diving and water-sports operators are active from June to September. Avoid the beach season crowds and high accommodation prices (July and August).

Best birdwatching spot A hide at the north end of Las Salinas, near the village of Cabo de Gata.

Cabo's Best Beaches

Cabo de Gata's unspoiled beaches range from long sandy stretches to secluded sugary-white coves. Highlights include:

Playa de Los Muertos Long, wide stretch of sand, bookended by cliffs.

Playa de Agua Amarga Gorgeous white-sand village beach, overlooked by tapas bars.

Cala de Enmedio Sheltered cove 2km south of Agua Amarga with rock slabs for sunbathing.

Playa San Pedro Scenic cove framed by dramatic headlands; pedestrian access only.

Calas de Barronal Four stunning, isolated coves reached on foot from Playa de Mónsul. Striking rock formations.

Playa de Mónsul Unpaved 5km road from San José leads to this wide beach, dominated by a large, freestanding rock.

🐦 Cabo de Gata Bird Life

At **Las Salinas** – one of Spain's most important wetlands – you can glimpse migrating pink flamingos, drawn to the salt flats in great numbers in July and August, as well as egrets, storks, avocet and over 100 other species of waterfowl. Bonelli's eagle, eagle owl and Andouin's gull are spotted around the cliffs.

Top left Playa de Los Muertos.
Top right Pink flamingo, Cabo de Gata.
Left Calas de Barronal.

Playa de los Genoveses Broad, super-popular beach 3km south of San José; accessed via a dirt road.

Stupendous Hikes

Cabo de Gata features a dramatic coastline that stretches some 65km from San Miguel de Cabo to Playa Algarróbico, and what better way to explore it than on foot?

The **Faro del Cabo de Gata–San José** (14km) hike takes four to five hours. From the lighthouse, a strenuous uphill slog along a

3km-long, hideously potholed road gets you to **Torre de Vela Blanca**. From here, it's a gentle descent along a wide dirt trail, with vistas of scrubland-covered hills descending steeply towards teal-coloured waters. You pass a couple secluded coves before reaching the wave-battered **Playa Mónsul**. Follow the blue-and-white trail markers uphill to reach the naturist **Playa Barronal**. If it's low tide, proceed along the base of the black volcanic cliffs, past the four **Calas Barronal**, before ascending the

Cabo's Best Dive Sites

'La Chocolita' A fun, shallow (10m) wreck dive to a sunken steamboat, where you hang out with octopus, damselfish and other marine squatters.

Cueva del Francés Take a torch to illuminate the morays, octopus, scorpion fish and other denizens of this small cave.

Playa La Isleta Beginner beach dive, with conger eels, morays, seahorses and shoals of small fish darting around La Punta.

Piedra de los Meros This 26m-deep rock is home to conger eels, morays, haddock and sea bass. Advanced divers only.

Cala Los Amarillos Expert dive due to strong currents. Watch out for territorial triggerfish and spot cuttlefish, octopus and morays among the rocks.

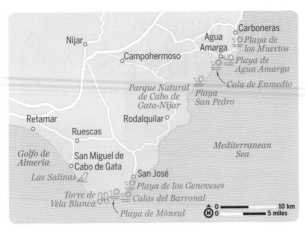

Far left Snorkeling, Cabo de Gata
Below Dunes, Playa de Los Genoveses.

Morrón de Los Genoveses and descending to the **Playa de los Genoveses**. At high tide, climb the steep path from cove to cove.

The park's most scenic day walk is the 13km stretch (four to five hours) between **Las Negras** and **Agua Amarga**. The wide dirt trail skirts the coast before narrowing to a precipitous coastal path and winding its way down to the **ruined 16th-century castle** and **Playa San Pedro** – a white-sand cove with turquoise waters. A hippy community resides here in rehabilitated ruins hidden in the greenery; there's even a rustic beach bar. An almost vertical half-hour switchback climb takes you up the opposite side of the valley, before the trail levels off. After a steady descent to the sandy **Cala del Plomo**, skirt the hill and make your way to **Cala de Enmedio**. A gentle climb over another hill brings you to Agua Amarga.

Lofty Viewpoints

For the best views of Cabo del Gata's coastline, head for the following:

Torre de Vela Blanca All-encompassing views of the south coast from a centuries-old watchtower.

Miradór de Los Muertos Splendid bird's-eye view of an arrow-straight, remote beach.

Torre de Mesa Roldán Fifteenth-century fortification looks out over the Agua Amarga coastline.

54 Subterranean
TREASURES

DAY TRIP | ADVENTURE | CAVES

There's a whole world beneath the ground in Almería. A rich, labyrinthine underworld of shimmering caverns filled with stalactites and stalagmites, dark tunnels leading to giant glittering crystals and places where you can experience complete darkness or explore an underground river. Above ground, ancient caves showcase millennia-old paintings. Delve deeper via a straightforward stroll or a full-on spelunking adventure.

How To

Getting here/around It's easiest to reach all the caves by car.

When to go Year-round.

Need to know All access is via guided tour. Book your slot online for Geoda de Pulpí at least a week ahead. Sorbas must be booked at least a day ahead; two-person minimum. Tours of Letreros run at 7pm Wednesday, Saturday, Sunday and holidays (June to August); 4.30pm Wednesday, Saturday and holidays, and noon on Sunday (rest of year).

Geoda de Pulpí

In 2019, geologists from Madrid made a startling discovery in an abandoned silver, iron and lead mine in the Sierra de Aguilón: the world's second-largest geode – 8m long and 2m tall. Guided tours take you through a series of tunnels glistening with mineral deposits, teach you about the history of mining in the area and show off a cathedral-like cavern with a massive spiral staircase. The tour de force is the descent some 50m below the surface, where you get to climb inside the geode, akin to a sparkling cave lined with translucent gypsum crystals.

Cuevas de Sorbas

This vast network of caves in the Karst en Yesos de Sorbas protected area is utterly spectacular. Some bristle with stalagmites, others with spiky stalactite ceilings

reflected in subterranean ponds. The basic tour (two hours) has you admiring the galleries of a gypsum cave, while the tougher combined route (four hours) has you scrambling and crawling through some tight gaps to reach a second cave with impressive calcium formations.

Cueva de Los Letreros

You follow a path through the arid landscape for 1.5km until you reach the *abrigo* (overhang). Here, the rock face is decorated with *indalos* (matchstick figures with arms outstretched, holding arcs) – symbols drawn to ward off evil – as well as astronomical signs, birds and assorted animals. The red paint looks remarkably fresh, considering that the drawings, done by the first settlers of Vélez, date back to around 4000 BCE!

Extreme Challenges of the Cuevas de Sorbas

If you're a serious spelunker, then the **Cueva del Agua** (Water Cave), part of the Sorbas karst network of caves, is a must. Round up three friends (four-person minimum), and join your guide in the detailed exploration of this remarkable cave's nooks and crannies, alternating between watching the light of your head torch dance on the gypsum crystals, climbing and wading through startlingly cold, chest-deep pools of water. Sorbas' most active challenge (and the biggest gypsum crystals!) is found inside the **Cueva de Tesoro** (Treasure Cave), where you'll be dangling in a harness above the abyss and rappelling down sheer walls.

Above Karst en Yesos de Sorbas.

Listings

 Nature Reserves

Parque Natural Sierra María-Los Vélez

Fringed with holm-oak and pine forest, the craggy peaks and barren plains of this 226-sq-km wilderness in the north of the province offers fantastic hiking and also ancient cave paintings.

Paraje Natural Karst en Yesos

Dominated by the cubist architecture of the village of Sorbas and a spectacular network of underground caves, this 24-sq-km protected area is an eroded Martian landscape of dramatic karst.

Parque Natural Sierra de Alhamilla

Near Almería, this rugged and largely barren 85-sq-km mountain range is known for the 10km ascent of the Pico de Colativí (1387m), for amazing views of the desert and coast.

Paraje Natural Desierto de Tabernas

Surrounded by the Gador, Filabres, Alhamilla and Sierra Nevada mountains, the lunar landscape of Europe's only desert is home to assorted succulents, kestrels, eagle owls, ladder snakes and Algerian hedgehogs.

 Special Stays

Murallas de Jayrán   €€€

In the heart of historic Almería, this intimate six-room boutique hotel is the ultimate in eclectic design. Choose between Moorish arches, industrial chic, exposed brick walls and circular soaking tubs.

La Almendra y El Gitano   €€

This countryside oasis near Agua Amarga comprises eight Moroccan-style beamed rooms connected by pergolas (plant-covered walkways). Enjoy desert views from the hot tub or savour the subtly lit pool at night.

Cortijo La Alberca   €

Sample country life at this 250-year-old farmhouse in the Ribera de Huebro valley, where home-cooked paella and rabbit dinners and soaks in the Moorish-style ancient pool are among the highlights.

MC San José   €€

Clean lines and slate-grey and cool white decor with driftwood and pebble accents define this boho-chic San José hotel. Relax over a glass of local wine at the in-house wine cellar.

AIRE Hotel & Ancient Baths   €€€

This elegant Almería hotel is all airy, contemporary rooms and rooftop pool views of the Alcazaba. Its most atmospheric feature is the subterranean hammam with six pools (including a salt water bath).

Almería's Tapa Trail

El Quinto Toro   €

A traditional atmosphere and a stuffed bull's head reign at this old-school tapas bar with its classic menu of Andalucian tapas and *raciones*. Standouts include *albóndigas* (meatballs) and *callos* (tripe).

Casa Puga   €

Shelves of decades-old wine bottles and walls plastered with ancient maps set the scene at this 1870s institution that serves classics such as *bacalao frito* and tiny morcilla sandwiches.

Taberna Nuestra Tierra   €€

Arrive early, grab a table outside, order from the menu of Almería wines, nibble on your courtesy tapa and feast on lamb with caramelised peppers, *ajoblanco* (cold almond and garlic soup) and assorted regional cheeses.

Tortillería La Mala   €

Chilled beats, crimson walls and a youthful ambience define this corner bar. Speciality

of the house is the tortillas (omelettes), with everything from onions and garlic to prawns and chilli.

Jovellanos 16 €

With a prime people-watching location, this popular joint on Almería's 'tapas row' serves petite red tuna 'hamburgers' and *secreto con ajo verde* (pork with garlicky sauce) alongside a respectable list of local wines.

La Consentida €€

Chargrilled meat tapas named after celebrities draw the carnivorously inclined to this bright, contemporary spot. How about a 'Lola Flores' (beef-cheek meatballs) or a 'Miley Cyrus' (gourmet hot dog)?

Crafty Almería

La Tienda de Los Milagros

This is the Níjar workshop of ceramicist Matthew Weir and artisan Isabel Hernández, who produces artistic *jarapa* (cotton-rag) rugs. Matthew also makes woodblock prints and works with stoneware and porcelain.

La Jarapa

Also in Níjar, this friendly shop sells colourful *jarapa* rugs, woven on looms in locals' homes. The tradition dates back to Moorish times and utilises leftover fabric scraps.

Artesanía Muro

Marblework is another centuries-old Almería craft. This artisanal workshop in Macael specialises in kitchen mortars and pestles, made of local marble, as well as goblets and elaborate sculpture.

Almería Water sports

Diving Center Isub

This professional PADI-certified diving outfit in San José runs dives for beginners (€75) and qualified divers (from €32, or €50 with equipment hire); snorkelling outings (€25 to €30) too.

Parque Natural Sierra Alhamilla

Atlantis Xtrem Jet-ski & Flyboard

Speed across the waves on a jet ski (€60 for 20 minutes), engage in extreme water sports on a flyboard (€80 for 20 minutes) or chillax on a paddleboard in Garrucha.

Buceo en Cabo de Gata

Let this highly regarded diving operator in La Isleta introduce you to Cabo's underwater world via a PADI diving course (€399) or a beginner's tasting session (€70) with semi-private instruction.

MedialunAventura

Get out on the water and explore Cabo's coast on a guided kayaking trip (from €28). This San José outfit also offers mountain-bike hire, SUP rental and boat trips (€34).

Cabo de Gata Activo

Paddle your way along the coast (€39) on a guided outing or view Cabo's underwater topography through a snorkelling mask with the help of this friendly outfit south of Las Negras.

 Scan to find more things to do in Almería online

Practicalities

ARRIVING

242

GETTING AROUND

244

SAFE TRAVEL

246

MONEY

247

RESPONSIBLE TRAVEL

248

ACCOMMODATION

250

ESSENTIALS

252

LANGUAGE

254

Right Frigiliana, Málaga (p143)

EASY STEPS FROM THE AIRPORT TO THE CITY CENTRE

The fifth-busiest airport in Spain by passenger volume (19.8 million in 2019), and known as the gateway to Andalucía, Málaga-Costa del Sol airport is 8km west of the city centre. Of its three terminals, only T2 (EasyJet, EasyJet Switzerland and Ryanair) and T3 (all other airlines) are currently in use. It has plenty of shops and facilities for those arriving by air.

AT THE AIRPORT

A G BAXTER/SHUTTERSTOCK ©

WI-FI
You can rent a mini 4G wi-fi hotspot from €3.89/day at the Travelwifi counter in arrivals, opposite Duty Free. Euro SIM is €39.95 (20GB of data plus calls) and the Euro+USA SIM from €38 (2GB). Relay shop in arrivals sells SIMs from €10 (add credit) to €40 (55MB).

CURRENCY EXCHANGE
The airport's currency exchange offices (including in the baggage reclaim and arrivals halls) were closed due to the pandemic, but may well have reopened by the time you read this.

FREE WI-FI
You can use airport_free_wifi_aena for up to four hours (max 6GB); the VIP lounge connection is faster.

ATMS
There are Unicaja and Euronet (beware high fees) ATMs around the airport, with Euronet in the baggage hall and arrivals.

CHARGING STATIONS
You can find 69 charging points in the airport, plus more in restaurants too. This includes 20 in the arrivals area.

IMMIGRATION AND ACCESSIBILITY

Those arriving from Schengen area countries only need ID cards; others must show a passport. From May 2023 non-Schengen visitors to Spain who do not currently need a visa have to register with ETIAS (European Travel Information and Authorisation System). New requirements for Brits arriving in Spain may require them to show proof of onward travel and accommodation; see gov.uk/foreign-travel-advice/spain/entry-requirements.

Visitors with reduced mobility should book assistance at least 48 hours prior to their journey; look for the yellow Sin Barreras meeting points for special-needs passengers.

GETTING TO THE CITY CENTRE

HOW MUCH FOR A...

Taxi
€25
10 mins

Bus
€4
30 mins

Train
€1.80
8-12 mins

TRAIN
The local train service (*cercanías* C1) to the centre leaves Terminal 3 every 20 minutes between 6.44am and 12.54am, arriving at María Zambrano station (eight minutes) and Centro Alameda bus stop (12 minutes). Tickets cost €1.80. Fast, cheap and reliable.

BUS
The A bus (EMT Línea Express Aeropuerto) runs to the city centre (Plaza del General Torrijos) from Terminal 3 every 25 to 30 minutes 7am to 10.15pm, then at 11pm and midnight. It takes 15 to 25 minutes (depending on the traffic, with possible delays during rush hour) and costs €4.

TAXI
A taxi from the airport (near Terminal 3 arrivals) will cost around €25, depending on the time and day. Supplements are charged from midnight to 6am, and for luggage larger than 60cm.

TAXI APPS
Taxi apps like Uber and Cabify operate from the airport; rates are usually cheaper than taxis, depending on availability of vehicles.

OTHER POINTS OF ENTRY
Other airports in Andalucía are Seville (handy for Huelva and Córdoba), Jerez (well placed for Cádiz city, the coast and white villages), Granada-Jaén (north to Jaén; south to the Sierra Nevada and Alpujarra) and Almería (the unspoiled Cabo de Gata coast).

International cruise ships dock at Málaga cruise port's terminals A, B and El Palmeral, in the heart of the city, with free wi-fi, plus ATM, foreign exchange and banking services.

International ferries to Morocco leave from Algeciras, Almería, Motril and Tarifa. The shortest crossing point across the Straits of Gibraltar to Africa is from Tarifa to Tangier (14km, 35 minutes), which makes a good day trip. Be careful to distinguish between the two ports: Tangier Med, which is 40km outside the city, and Tangier Town. These routes get busier in summer, especially in late June/early July, as Moroccans working in Spain return home for their holidays.

International AVE high-speed trains leave Paris for Barcelona (twice daily, six hours 40 minutes), from where AVEs depart for Córdoba and Seville.

International land border crossing to/from the British territory of Gibraltar from La Linea de la Concepción (Cádiz) by car can take several hours, especially on weekends.

TRANSPORT TIPS TO HELP YOU GET AROUND

Andalucía has a good public transport network, from buses that serve remote mountain areas to fast, reliable trains. Connections between major cities are frequent by both bus and train, although the former is usually cheaper and slower. Hiring a car is more expensive, but gives you greater flexibility and the freedom to explore more remote areas.

BUS While most city surburbs are served by *cercanías* (local trains), rural areas rely on buses, especially between smaller towns in the hills not served by trains (or where the train station is rurally located), and are usually well priced. Use websites like omnio.com or busbud.com to find schedules.

TREN AL ANDALUS Be swept along in luxury on the Tren Al Andalus (eltrenal andalus.com), the 'Palace on Wheels'. This sumptuous train's Andalucian Route has an enviable six-night itinerary, with prices as you'd expect. Sevilla–Jerez–Sanlúcar de Barrameda–Cádiz–Ronda–Granada–Úbeda–Baeza–Córdoba–Sevilla. Worth it for a one-off.

TRAINS

Trains in Andalucía are operated by RENFE. High-speed links between provincial capitals Seville, Córdoba, Granada, Málaga and also intermediary towns like Antequera, Loja and Puente Genil/Herrera should become more economical in 2023, with the advent of Renfe's AVLO and SNCF's Ouigo low-cost fast train services.

FLIGHTS

The only regional flight route within Andalucía is Seville (SVQ) to Almería (LEI) on Iberia. Flights operate three times a week to the eastern port city, with four weekly flights from Almería to Seville. It takes one hour 20 minutes (410km by road).

CAR RENTAL PER DAY

€20 per day

Cost of diesel €1.96/litre

Cost of petrol €1.99/litre

DRIVING ESSENTIALS

In Spain, you drive on the right.

Speed limits vary from 20km on urban roads to 120km on motorways and dual carriageways.

The legal driving age is 18.

.05 Blood alcohol limit is 0.5mg/litre.

You must carry two warning triangles (or a V16 emergency light) and a reflective jacket.

Train fares vary hugely, with the AVE obviously the most expensive. Offers are usually available on renfe.es, especially on advance bookings (advisable on weekends and around pubilc holidays, to avoid queues at ticket offices and full trains). Return fares are usually around 10% to 20% cheaper than singles. Holders of student/youth cards get up to 30% off, while travellers with disabilities and children aged four to 13 enjoy reductions of up to 40%.

CYCLING Bike touring in Andalucía offers some spectacular routes, as seen in the Vuelta a Andalucía (or Ruta del Sol) regional bike race in February every year. It is a mountainous region, so there are some challenging climbs. Note that cyclists must always ride on the right-hand side, and also always be sure to lock your bike, especially in a city, as theft is extremely common.

CAR POOLING BlaBlaCar car-pooling service (App Store and Google Play) is a popular option, with excellent prices (Seville to Málaga €15; Granada to Almería €12). You can usually find a ride between major cities, especially at weekends when students head home. Women can use the 'Ladies Only' option.

LEFT LUGGAGE Services are becoming more widely available, especially in cities, in centrally located shops and hotels as well as train and bus stations – handy if you have to vacate your accommodation early. Try Radical Storage and Bounce (App Store and Google Play), especially in Seville and Málaga, for around €5 per day.

KNOW YOUR CARBON FOOTPRINT A car-share ride with a driver and three passengers from Málaga to Seville (210km) would emit 75kg of carbon dioxide per person. In terms of public transport, a bus would emit 4.5kg for the same distance, per passenger, while a high-speed train would emit about 0.3kg.

There are a number of carbon calculators online. We use calculator.carbonfootprint.com.

ROAD DISTANCE CHART (KMS)

ANDALUCÍA

	Cádiz	Málaga	Granada	Ronda	Jaén	Gibraltar	Almería	Seville
Málaga	295							
Granada	295	130						
Ronda	295	130	1573					
Jaén	325	190	95	220				
Gibraltar	120	135	260	115	320			
Almería	435	205	170	305	220	340		
Seville	125	205	250	135	245	200	415	
Córdoba	235	160	165	165	110	290	360	140

SAFE TRAVEL

Andalucía is a safe area to travel, whether as a family, group or alone. In the cities and on the beaches, the same applies as for anywhere – always keep your belongings safe and respect the local environment.

PERSONAL SAFETY

Like most cities, those in Andalucía experience street crime in busy areas, such as the main tourist sights, and bus and train stations, with pick-pockets and teams using distraction techniques. Use common sense and ensure you are carrying copies of important documents.

CATERPILLARS

If you're hiking in winter or spring, beware of processionary caterpillars, which make nests in pine trees but also move along the ground. They can cause a painful rash and are especially dangerous for dogs and children.

FOREST FIRES

Forest fires are a high risk in Andalucía during the long, hot, dry summer, especially when fanned by winds. Barbecues and fires are prohibited in most forested areas during the summer months, apart from in designated zones.

MEDICATION

In Spain, commonly used medicines such as paracetamol are not available in beauty stores or supermarkets – you need to ask for them in a pharmacy. Generally, it's best to bring any medication.

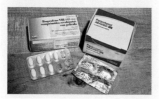

ROCKET STOCK/SHUTTERSTOCK ©

MLLE SONYAH/SHUTTERSTOCK ©

CANNABIS

Possession of cannabis for personal use is legal, but it cannot be smoked in a public area.

JELLYFISH

Look out for jellyfish on the beach in summer, especially on the Málaga coast; they have a painful sting. InfoMedusa website and app has up-to-date information about jellyfish risk on beaches.

INSURANCE

Persons from the European Economic Area (EEA) must bring their EHIC card to be entitled to healthcare. Persons from outside the EEA must pay for medical assistance in full and can seek reimbursement afterwards.

QUICK TIPS TO HELP YOU MANAGE YOUR MONEY

CREDIT CARDS

(Visa and Mastercard) are widely accepted at most hotels and restaurants, all supermarket chains, and some bars and cafes, as well as car parks, train and bus stations. Always carry some cash to use in smaller local shops and bars, as well as market stalls (especially flea markets), which may not accept cards, or may prefer cash to avoid paying transaction fees.

CAR HIRE

When hiring a car, the company will usually ask for a credit card to block a certain amount as a deposit. Some will accept debit cards; be sure to check in advance.

CURRENCY EXCHANGE

You will find *oficinas de cambio* (currency exchange offices) in tourist areas, well as counters in larger hotels and department stores, train and bus stations, and airports.

CURRENCY

Euro

HOW MUCH FOR A...

Large plate of *jamón ibérico de bellota (100g)*
€20

Espresso
€1.30

Glass of sherry
€3

ATMs are widely available in all towns, cities and most villages, as well as transport hubs. Beware EuroNet's high fees.

PAYMENT APPS

(Google Pay, Apple Pay) used on mobile devices such as phones and watches are becoming more widely accepted, especially in cities. Always have a bank card available too.

TRAVEL CARDS

Pre-pay travel cards, where you load a set amount of euros on a bank card to spend while abroad, are a good way to avoid fluctuating exchange rates. Check at money savingexpert.com.

NON-EU VISITORS

Visitors from non-EU countries (such as the UK and USA) can claim refunds of IVA (VAT or sales tax; mostly 21%) on certain goods – look for the 'Tax-free shopping' signs in stores. Fill in the electronic DER form at the shop when you purchase, and then get your electronic tax-free documents validated (you'll need the relevant goods and receipts) at a DIVA terminal (Málaga airport) or by a customs officer. The refund money can be claimed from the retailer or through the Tax Free office (fee applies).

ANDALUCÍA MONEY

RESPONSIBLE TRAVEL

Tips to leave a lighter footprint, support local and have a positive impact on local communities.

ON THE ROAD

Look for eco-certified businesses including the EU Ecolabel for accommodation (energy-efficient heating, air-conditioning and lighting, and reduced food waste, among others); and the Biosphere Sustainability Certificate for hotels, museums and activity companies, which recognises the UN's 17 sustainable development goals, such as using clean energy, water and energy efficiency, accessibility, gender equality and employing local staff.

Hire an electric car for shorter journeys – there are more than 2000 charging points around Andalucía, largely in cities, and often in hotel, supermarket and underground car parks, although increasingly in towns too. Plan ahead according to where the next point is (map.electromaps. com).

Ask for tap water (*agua del grifo*) in bars and restaurants – it's perfectly safe to drink. They will fill up your water bottle too. However, on the coast you may need to drink bottled water.

VF/AA/GETTY IMAGES ©

GIVE BACK

Workaway is a great way to experience Andalucía. You get free board and lodging from your host in return for helping on cultural exchanges, such as teaching English, or working on sustainable projects like an organic farm, looking after rescue animals or working on a permaculture garden. You can sign up as a single person, couple or family. Note that you will need a visa to work, volunteer or study if travelling from outside the EU (workaway.info).

Volunteer with a Spain-based social enterprise. Check current projects at Impactrip.com.

Food banks often organise donation campaigns at supermarkets – you add a little extra to your shopping bill, which goes to feed the disadvantaged (afandaluzas.org/federacion-de-bancos-de-alimentos-de-andalucia-ceuta-y-melilla).

LEAVE A SMALL FOOTPRINT

When visiting small villages with narrow streets that are tricky to negotiate, with little space to park, leave your vehicle in the car park or parking spaces at the village entrance.

Use a fan rather than air-conditioning, if possible.

Recycle. It may seem obvious, but not everyone does it – use the separate recycling bins: green for glass (all types), yellow for plastic and food cartons, and blue for paper and cardboard. Cities will have recycling points for batteries and light bulbs too.

LOCAL ETIQUETTE It isn't recommended to walk around a town wearing only a bikini, swimsuit or swimming shorts/trunks. Some local councils will impose fines if you're caught wearing swimwear on the seafront promenade or the adjacent streets. If in doubt, ask in your hotel or apartment; alternatively, the tourist office can inform you.

SUPPORT LOCAL

Andalucía has a bountiful supply of fresh fruit, vegetables, seafood and *jamón ibérico*. Shop locally – most towns and cities have a *mercado* (indoor fresh produce market), plus a weekly or fortnightly organic street market (*mercadillo*).

Look out for regular outdoor craft markets too. Gift ideas for traditional, locally made artisanal goods: olive oil, wine, honey, ceramics, *esparto* grass woven baskets, *jarapa* rugs (Alpujarras), embroidered scarves and leatherwork.

CLIMATE CHANGE & TRAVEL

It's impossible to ignore the impact we have when travelling, and the importance of making changes where we can. Lonely Planet urges all travellers to engage with their travel carbon footprint. There are many carbon calculators online that allow travellers to estimate the carbon emissions generated by their journey; try resurgence.org/resources/carbon-calculator.html. Many airlines and booking sites offer travellers the option of offsetting the impact of greenhouse gas emissions by contributing to climate-friendly initiatives around the world. We continue to offset the carbon footprint of all Lonely Planet staff travel, while recognising this is a mitigation more than a solution.

RESOURCES

workaway.info
biospheresustainable.com (sustainable businesses, including hotels)
andalucia.org/en/andalusian-crafts
ecoagricultor.com/mercados-productos-ecologicos-andalucia (organic food markets)

UNIQUE AND LOCAL WAYS TO STAY

The standard and choice of accommodation in Andalucía has improved massively over recent years, from chic boutique hotels and stylish self-catering apartments to characterful B&Bs, cute country cottages and well-appointed villas with all mod cons and infinity pools. Throw in caves, yurts and converted historic palaces, and you have an exceptional range to suit all tastes and budgets.

HOW MUCH FOR A...

Casa rural
€60

Beach apartment
€80

Hostel bed in city centre
€20

JAVI_INDY/SHUTTERSTOCK ©

HOTELS

Hotels in Andalucía are becoming more accessible, especially in main cities and large coastal resorts. Rooms adapted for guests with reduced mobility feature wet-room showers, shower seats, and hand-rails in the shower and toilet, as well as basic necessities like wheelchair ramps; some swimming pools have lifts.

WELLNESS RETREATS

In line with the trend for wellness breaks, Andalucía offers an excellent selection of spas, yoga retreats and fitness resorts. Whether you want to balance your chakras or follow an intensive Pilates program, practise mindfulness or restore your gut health, the choice is ever-expanding.

Traditional spas with healing mineral waters in Granada, Jaén and Almería range from basic accommodation to the pampering deluxe. Unsurprisingly, the coast is well supplied with five-star thalassotherapy resorts, especially the Costa del Sol and Costa de la Luz.

CAVE STAYS One of the most unique places to stay in Andalucía is a cave. Located in Guadix and the Altiplano of Granada around Baza, these rustic troglodyte houses and hotels maintain the same temperature all year round.

J.L. LAGO/SHUTTERSTOCK ©

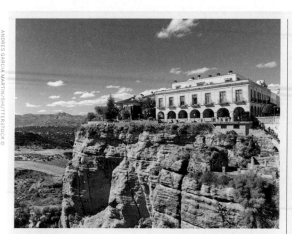

ANDRES GARCIA MARTIN/SHUTTERSTOCK ©

PARADORS

Paradors are a chain of hotels started in 1928 by King Alfonso XIII (*parar* means to stop) to preserve important historic buildings and to promote tourism, so that travellers could stay in hotels of reliable quality. Today, many are still housed in majestic edifices – palaces, convents, monasteries and castles – and often in exceptional locations, with outstanding views. Modern paradors have also been built, complementing their surroundings. Recently the paradors have upped their game in the food stakes, with excellent, creative dishes on the menu, as well as local and regional speciality dishes, and wines too.

There are 16 paradors in Andalucía: seven on the coast (in Huelva, Cádiz, Málaga and Almería provinces), eight in inland towns and cities (Arcos de la Frontera, Ronda, Carmona, Córdoba, Granada, Antequera, Úbeda and Jaén) and one in a national park (Cazorla). Carmona's parador is a mighty fortress overlooking the Río Corbones, while in Jaén, a parador on Santa Catalina hill watches over the city from its mountain perch. Staying overnight in the Alhambra complex, in the San Francisco Convent parador, once all the visitors have left, allows you a privileged view of the monument. In Cazorla, you can enjoy the unspoiled mountain landscapes of the Parque Nacional de La Sierra de Cazorla, while Cádiz city's stunning contemporary building right on the seafront has pools overlooking the ocean.

BOOKING

Mid-June to mid-September (school holidays) is peak season, so booking is essential, as it is Semana Santa (Holy Week). You should also check not only local/regional/national holidays, but also the days around them, especially if they fall on a Thursday or Tuesday, as the intervening Friday or Monday will be added on to make a *puente* (long weekend).

Lonely Planet (lonelyplanet.com/spain/hotels) Independent reviews of hotels all over Andalucía.

Rustic Blue (rusticblue.com) Alpujarra-based company offering stylish rental villas, cottages and *fincas* (farmhouses) in Andalucía, from one to six-plus bedrooms, most with swimming pools.

Paradores de España (parador.es) Chain of 97 state-owned hotels in tastefully restored and converted historic buildings, and contemporary ones too. Around €150 per night; look out for special offers.

Glamping Hub *(glampinghub.com)* Camping and unusual outdoor accommodation, from gypsy caravans and tipis to straw huts and pods. Search results are shown on a map.

Rusticae (rusticae.es) Charming hotels, rural houses, apartments – *fincas* and pretty cottages in the countryside and towns.

ESSENTIAL NUTS-&-BOLTS

QUEUES

When joining a queue, ask *'Quien es el último?'* (Who is the last person?) The next person arrives, asks the same question, and you reply *'Soy yo.'* (I am.)

ETIAS

From May 2023, non-Schengen and non-EU passengers who don't currently need a visa will need an ETIAS authorisation (European Travel Information and Authorisation System).

TOILETS

Public toilets in shopping centres are your best bet. Restaurants and bars will often let you use theirs.

FAST FACTS

Time Zone
GMT+2

Country Code
+34

Electricity
230V 50Hz

GOOD TO KNOW

The legal drinking age in Spain is 18. Drinking in public spaces (*botellón*) is prohibited in Andalucía.

Tax-free shopping is available for non-EU visitors using an electronic DER form.

Andalucía has 12 public holidays, plus there are many more local ones.

EU nationals have medical cover through their EHIC, but others should get health insurance.

Air quality, measured from good to very bad, is shown on screens in major towns and cities.

ACCESSIBLE TRAVEL

PMR – Personas con Movilidad Reducida (people with reduced mobility) – is the Spanish expression for people with mobility challenges.

More hotels are offering accessible rooms, while restaurants are increasingly offering disabled toilets. New and refurbished buildings must be fully wheelchair accessible.

Historic city centres are not very accessible, due to cobbled streets, narrow pavements and ancient monuments with steps and level changes. Cádiz has an accessible tourist route, with map.

Pubic transport is problematic, with many trains and buses largely inaccessible to wheelchair users, except AVE high-speed trains. More modern city bus and metro services (Málaga, Seville and Granada) and Málaga cruise port, are accessible. Car parks have plenty of disabled spaces. Eurotaxis are adapted for wheelchairs.

Facilities for visual- and hearing-impaired people are not great, although some museums and monuments have Braille guides (Guadix Caves Visitor Centre) and videos with subtitles; many have audio guides.

Reduced entry prices are available for people with disabilities at most monuments and museums.

Useful resources include tur4all.com/es, accessible spaintravel.com, playeros.es/es/playas-discapacitados/andalucia.

TOURIST INFO

Visit local tourist offices for maps, brochures and up-to-date information on monuments and activities. Some will only provide QR codes.

APPS

Most provinces and popular tourist destinations have tourism apps, divided into themes like gastronomy, fiestas, heritage/monuments and nature.

HEALTH REQUIREMENTS

Check the latest entry requirements, in terms of health and vaccines, at Spain Travel Health: spth.gob.es (in English).

FAMILY TRAVEL

Discounted entry to sites and tickets on public transport help the budget.

Children's meals are available in tourist resorts, but otherwise croquetas and tortilla go down a treat; Spanish children stay out and about till late at night.

Larger hotels will offer kids' clubs or activities in high season.

Order a child seat in advance if you're hiring a car.

High chairs are available in most restaurants.

Bring any necessary medication, but pharmacists are helpful and knowledgeable.

OPENING HOURS for shops are generally 10am to 2pm and 5pm to 8pm, with up to an hour's variation either way, plus Saturday morning. Bigger chain and department stores do not close for lunch and stay open all day Saturday. Banking hours are 8.30am to 2pm Monday to Friday.

SMOKING IS FORBIDDEN in all indoor public places, including bars and restaurants and on public transport. You can smoke on outdoor restaurant terraces. Vaping is allowed inside bars and restaurants at the owner's discretion.

LGBTIQ+ TRAVELLERS

Same-sex marriage has been legal in Spain since 2005 – the country has a progressive record on LGBTIQ+ rights.

Transgender Law, allowing people to change the name and gender on their ID document, was passed in Spain in 2007. Andalucía passed its own law against discrimination on gender identity grounds and recognising transexual rights in 2014.

Seville, Cádiz and Torremolinos have the biggest ambientes gay (gay scenes) in Andalucía.

Useful contacts include andalucialgbt.com, federacionarcoiris.com and defrente.org.

LANGUAGE

Spanish (*español*) – often referred to as *castellano* (Castilian) to distinguish it from other languages spoken in Spain – is the language of Andalucía.

Travellers who learn a little Spanish will be amply rewarded as Spaniards appreciate the effort, no matter how basic your understanding of the language.

Just read our pronunciation guides as if they were English and you'll be understood. Note that (m/f) indicates masculine and feminine forms.

To enhance your trip with a phrasebook, visit **lonelyplanet.com**.

BASICS

Hello.	*Hola*	o·la
Goodbye.	*Adiós*	a·dyos
Yes./No.	*Sí./No.*	see/no
Please.	*Por favor.*	por fa·vor
Thank you.	*Gracias.*	gra·thyas
Excuse me.	*Perdón.*	per·don
Sorry.	*Lo siento.*	lo syen·t

Do you speak English?
¿Habla (inglés)? — a·bla (een·gles)

I don't understand.
Yo (no) entiendo. — yo (no) en·tyen·do

I'm a vegetarian. (m/f)
Soy vegetariano/a — soy ve·khe·ta·rya·no/a

I'd like ...
Quisiera ... — kee·sye·ra ...

TIME & NUMBERS

What time is it?	*¿Qué hora es?*	ke o·ra es
It's (10) o'clock.	*Son (las diez).*	son (las dyeth)
morning	*mañana*	ma·nya·na
afternoon	*tarde*	tar·de
evening	*noche*	no·che
yesterday	*ayer*	a·yer
today	*hoy*	oy
tomorrow	*mañana*	ma·nya·na

1	*uno*	oo·no	**6**	*seis*	seys
2	*dos*	dos	**7**	*siete*	sye·te
3	*tres*	tres	**8**	*ocho*	o·cho
4	*cuatro*	kwa·tro	**9**	*nueve*	nwe·ve
5	*cinco*	theen·ko	**10**	*diez*	dyeth

EMERGENCIES

Help!	*¡Socorro!*	so·ko·ro

Call a doctor!
¡Llame a un médico! — lya·me a oon me·dee·ko

Call the police!
¡Llame a la policía! — lya·me a la po·lee·thee·a

I'm lost. (m/f)
Estoy perdido/a. — es·toy per·dee·do/

Where are the toilets?
¿Dónde están los baños? — don·de es·tan los ba·nyos

Index

000 Map pages

00 Map pages

'The countless times I've wandered across Tarifa's Punta Paloma dune at sunset, with Morocco glinting on the horizon across the Atlantic.'
ISABELLA NOBLE

'Stumbling upon a religious procession in Seville one evening, the sight of the Virgin on her paso (float) in the golden evening light, sun glinting off her embroidered mantle, took my breath away.'
FIONA FLORES WATSON

'How I've introduced all my friend's to Granada's Alhambra, and still visit every year — absolutely worth the 6am start from Cómpeta last time!'
ISABELLA NOBLE

'On my very first visit to the Top of the Rock in Gibraltar as a backpacker, I was contemplated with disapproval by one of their resident tailless macaques, who came up to me and pinched me hard on the arm.'
ANNA KAMINSKI

'Watching a violin recital in the Alcazar palace gardens, by the corner of the grutesco wall, on a balmy summer night under the gently swaying palm trees. Best concert location ever.'
FIONA FLORES WATSON

DESIGN PICS INC/ALAMY STOCK PHOTO ©, LIQUID STUDIOS/SHUTTERSTOCK ©

THIS BOOK

Design development
Lauren Egan, Tina García, Fergal Condon

Content development
Anne Mason

Cartography development
Wayne Murphy, Katerina Pavkova

Production development
Mario D'Arco, Dan Moore, Sandie Kestell, Virginia Moreno, Juan Winata

Series development leadership
Liz Heynes, Darren O'Connell, Piers Pickard, Chris Zeiher

Commissioning editor
Amy Lynch

Production editor
Alison Killilea

Cartographer
Anthony Phelan

Book designer
Fergal Condon

Assisting book designer
Gwen Cotter

Assisting editors
Carly Hall

Cover researcher
Hannah Blackie

Thanks James Appleton, Gwen Cotter, Pete Cruttenden, John Taufa

■■■■ Lace up your boots and hike between ancient villages. Spy on endangered Iberian lynx in natural parks. Get lost in the winding streets of historic neighbourhoods. Join the fun at a local *feria*. Sample spicy extra virgin olive oil on a farm. Absorb the musty, grapey scent at a sherry bodega. Amire ceramic tiles in a Mudéjar palace. Explore spectacular natural scenery on two wheels. Soak up the year-round sunshine on a sandy beach. Chuckle at the wit of satirical singing groups.

This is Andalucía.

**TURN THE PAGE AND START PLANNING
YOUR NEXT BEST TRIP →**